INTERRACIAL MARRIAGE:
Expectations and Realities

Also available:

CHILDREN OF SEPARATION AND DIVORCE
Edited by Irving R. Stuart and Lawrence Edwin Abt

THE CREATIVE EXPERIENCE
Edited by Stanley Rosner and Lawrence Edwin Abt

EDITED AND WITH NOTES AND INTRODUCTIONS

BY IRVING R. STUART, PH.D.

AND LAWRENCE EDWIN ABT, PH.D.

.

GROSSMAN PUBLISHERS, NEW YORK, 1973

Interracial Marriage: Expectations and Realities

First published in 1973 by Grossman Publishers
625 Madison Avenue, New York, N.Y. 10022
Published simultaneously in Canada by
Fitzhenry and Whiteside, Ltd.
SBN 670–40014–9
Library of Congress Catalogue Card Number: 72–77705
Printed in U.S.A.

ACKNOWLEDGMENT
In chapter 6, Psychiatry: Tables 1, 3, 4, 5, and 6 from *The Black Family: Myth and Reality,* ("Psychiatry" (1970) 33:145–173.) Reprinted by special permission of the William Alanson White Psychiatric Foundation.

To the memory of Jonathan David Abt
who loved life so much

CONTENTS

Contents

PREFACE

The outlook of any person concerned with human affairs in the end rests on his conception of what man is and what he can be. A person's thoughts and feelings are better understood by grasping his core notion or view—which may be implicit, but determines his picture of the world—than by listening to the most forceful overt arguments with which he defends his views and refutes actual and possible objections.

This book is predicated on the notion that we need to know what people think, particularly about matters of interracial marriage, and what are the grounds for their beliefs. In order to know such grounds, we need to know something of the person's origin, of his development, of his value orientation—something that will tell us why he holds on to and proclaims his point of view. Also, since thought is rarely, if ever, without emotional coloration, in order to understand we need to know how people *feel*.

It is to this complex of matters—thought and feeling, implicit as well as explicit, about the sensitive issue of interracial marriage—that this work addresses itself. It seeks to do so without either overt or concealed ideological bias toward interracial marriage and the many social issues and consideratons that are involved. Of course, the editors do not fully excuse themselves from bias; but they certainly have attempted to remain impartial. The book aims to please or succor no group: rather, it is an effort to examine, now in one way, now in anothor, the central issues of an important social phenomenon of our time and their background.

Although this work aims for a kind of completeness, it offers no apology for being incomplete; we realize that our concern is large, and that we can only approximate a broad canvas containing the historical, cultural, and social factors related to interracial marriage.

We have started with the premise that marriage is not made in heaven, that it is the ultimate test of one's capacity for intimate human relationships, and that every marriage, although like all others, is quite different from all others. We have started with yet another premise, which grows out of both study and experience. It is that because of the racial discrimination which exists in large segments of American society, interracial marriages and the children of such unions are confronted with a broader range of difficulties than those normally encountered by spouses of similar racial backgrounds and by their children.

We believe that both these assumptions are tenable. Other assumptions are of course possible, but this work is based on these two premises and, we believe, generally consistent with them.

It is common scientific procedure to set up one or more hypotheses and then direct an investigation to ascertain their validity or invalidity. In a rough way, this is the procedure we have followed, with results that the reader himself must judge. This work certainly does not purport to be a scientific inquiry in the sense that its objectivity is unquestionable, since experiments in the behavioral sciences produce results dependent on human variability. Its subject is man and his relationships, and its scientific status must therefore be related to the present development of the social and behavioral sciences.

Few would question the fact that the United States has undergone in the past quarter century or so a significant change of public attitudes toward minority groups. While asserting this, we are faced with a related question: Have there been corresponding changes in thinking and feeling, particularly with regard to the intimate relations of marriage? This book seeks an answer to this question among others.

There have, moreover, been changes in interpersonal contacts, especially among young people, across race lines in the United States. These contacts have become even broader and deeper as young people have involved themselves in political causes, share educational and job opportunities, and move in the generally "liberated" social climate. These social changes offer far greater latitude for young people to meet on an equal level and learn to know each other better.

However, in another trend, there seems to be increasing separatism advocated by members of the black community. What are its possible effects upon interracial relationships, and upon black-white marriages in particular? Perhaps it is much too early to know.

This book consists of the contributions of a number of social and behavioral scientists, both from the United States and from foreign countries, who have had either professional or personal experiences, or both, with racial relationships. Each contributor has been asked to describe the situation or area of his competence as he knows it to exist. On the basis of the material in this collection, we hope that the reader will be able to arrive at a reasonably comprehensive picture of the effects of racial discrimination upon the partners of interracial marriages—in the full range of their social, cultural, and emotional dimensions.

These are some of the questions that we hope this work will help to answer.

1. Are interracial marriages, particularly those contracted between a white and a black partner, statistically significant in relation to all marriages in the United States?

2. Are biracial marriages on the rise in the face of what we know to be significant changes in American attitudes toward such unions?

3. In comparison with the experiences of biracial couples in other cultures, do interracial couples in the United States experience greater or lesser stress in their daily lives?

4. What adjustment problems, other than those usually anticipated in a marriage relationship, have the contributors found to exist within the areas of their specialties?

5. Can personal adjustment difficulties be traced to attitudes of the races to which biracial marriage partners belong?

6. What can we learn from the practices of other cultures which may be of assistance in effecting change in attitudes toward interracial marriages in this country?

7. What experiences can be anticipated for the children of biracial unions? And to which extend will such experiences influence their adult personalities?

Finally, this book seeks to bring together the personal and the social, the human and the cultural, in an effort to reach a broader perspective and a deeper understanding of interracial marriage.

I. R. S. and L. E. A.

Psychodynamics: Emotional, Social, and Economic Aspects of Interracial Marriage in the United States

Part One

INTRODUCTION

Beyond doubt, interracial marriages are in many respects like non-interracial marriages: they involve the same expectations, are subject to the same vicissitudes, involve the same problems of living together, and face the same stresses and the same opportunities of any intimate relationships. But beyond these similarities, there are differences—differences rooted in historical/social and emotional/economic considerations. Part I of this book seeks to make explicit for the reader the range of these considerations, and tries to set forth, now in one way, now in another, the assets and the liabilities of biracial unions in terms of the many personal and social factors involved.

Chapter 1, by Algernon D. Black, looks at the expectations of biracial unions against the background of the realities of everyday living. It is a sincerely human approach that invites our deepest consideration.

What are the needs that two people seek to satisfy in their choice of each other as marital partners? How can the intangibles of "falling in love" be structured in a conceptual framework that the psychologist can use to draw meaningful conclusions? And what are the special elements that enter the picture when the marriage partners are of different races? Chapter 2 seeks answers to these questions through an investigation of the psychodynamic—that is to say, the emotional and psychological—factors underlying marital choice.

In Chapter 3 we are introduced to a series of assumptions, based on what we know about black-white marriages of the recent past, that the author uses as sources of predictions about potential role conflicts in biracial marriages. Mrs. Rose's lucid discussion allows the reader a new and deeper awareness of the social forces—historical, legal, attitudinal—that find their specific expression in interracial unions.

A central problem of many biracial couples—the fate of their children—is addressed and given full and thoughtful consideration in Chapter 4. As we review this material, we confront new problems, new solutions, new opportunities, and the expression of deeper human feelings.

Chapter 5 is perhaps the only "regional" chapter in *Interracial Marriage*, but it is appropriately "regional." There are special problems in biracial unions in the American South, and Dr. Paul Adams, with wise care, guides us to a better understanding of what it means —for black and white—to grow up in the South and contend with its cultural imperatives.

With Chapter 6 we are at the heart of much thinking, and much agonizing, about the power structure of the black family and the practices of the black family seen within—and inevitably compared with—the larger white community. The material set forth here should help to clarify our thinking, and to correct our errors of fact and belief concerning the actual situation within the typical black family.

An important experience for a limited few couples is that of adoption. Are there special problems when the child to be adopted is of different racial stock, and just what are these problems? Chapter 7 offers some helpful and humane answers.

Chapter 8, in a time of rapid change in mores and youthful practices, looks at interracial dating—the whys, wherefores, and outcomes. This study brings to this "emotionally charged" subject a controlled and yet deeply compassionate dimension.

Chapter 9, a review and evaluation of the empirical data available on American black-white unions, should provide a useful compendium of what is known from actual research studies about interracial marriage frequency, features, and trends, all within the matrix of changing social patterns so characteristic of the current scene. Both attitudes and practices change, but this chapter should offer information useful in forecasting trends in the 1970's.

Of a somewhat different sort is Chapter 10, in which the author addresses himself to the more immediately personal and intimate aspects of biracial unions. Seen within both a historical and a psychiatric context, such marriages may be perceived as involving a series of interpersonal interchanges peculiarly susceptible to both inner and outer stresses. These stresses are cultural and social, historical and legal, as well as personal and familial. The social psychiatric point of view that underlies the chapter's presentation helps us witness, with direct immediacy, the real struggles of real persons in their everyday transactions with each other. Finally, Chapter 11 consists of several interviews with young people concerning their own views of interracial relationships and marriages. It is refreshing to learn about their attitudes, their feelings, and their relative freedom from prejudices so characteristic of earlier generations.

1

ALGERNON D. BLACK, B.A.

Expectations and Realities of Interracial Marriage

A prominent clergyman and educator, who for many years has been identified with the movement toward healthy race relations, reviews the history of black-white, face-to-face contacts in the United States. Much of his discussion concerns the effects of increasing black militancy which, he believes, poses a new threat to the interracial marriages that have survived the many years of social, economic, and political discrimination. Mr. A.D. Black, who, in his capacity as Leader of the Society for Ethical Culture in the City of New York, has married and counseled significant numbers of interracial couples, expects that the pressure for racial separatism in the black community will prove to be a passing phase.

With increasing economic, and consequently social, equality between the races, he predicts that interracial marriages will increase. In his account of his intimate and revealing contacts with biracial couples, he discusses, among other things, the significance of the parents' attitude toward interracial marriage—a discussion which should be of particular value to those contemplating such a union.

IN THE Western world, freedom of choice and the romantic idea of marrying for love have won in modern times increasing acceptance. The changes in attitudes and practices have not come easily or without serious resistance. Traditional patterns of regulation and limitation on choice of partner have deep historic and cultural roots. Psychological needs and the preservation of familial and economic institutions have played a part in setting limits to individual freedom of choice. In the United States, despite its freedom and individualism, marriage between persons of different faiths and interracial marriage have for the most part been socially resisted, forbidden, and condemned by families and the larger community. The intensity of the resistance and condemnation has varied according to the period of time, the geographic area, and religious and other cultural factors.

The "race problem" in the United States usually refers to the relations of whites and blacks. White Americans, whether early settlers or later immigrant groups from many national, religious, and cultural backgrounds, all tended to condemn interracial marriage with black people. But the condemnation was not limited to marriage with blacks. It included marriages with American Indians and with Orientals, such as the Chinese, Japanese, and Filipinos, whether born in the United States or abroad. Much of the prejudice against the stereotyping of these groups was due to the influence of racism. The majority of white Americans were conditioned to believe that human beings could be classified into racial groups according to certain physical characteristics, and that these physical characteristics were hereditary and fixed. That these physical characteristics were related to personality type, levels of intelligence, talent, capacities, and moral character was taken for granted, and so was the idea that some racial groups were superior to others. It was assumed that God and Nature meant that the races be kept separate. Thus, "race purity" should be protected and preserved; interracial mixing of the sexes and intermarriage should be forbidden and prevented.

Because of the background of slavery of the Negro in America, with its concomitant exploitation and denial of freedom, human rights, and opportunities, relationships between whites and blacks have presented the most severe race problems. Gunnar Myrdal's *The American Dilemma* found fear of intermarriage the first of all concerns in the attitudes of the whites toward the blacks. Many would say that the racial discrimination, segregation, and persecution that have pervaded American life in all parts of the nation had one prime purpose: to prevent the mingling of the sexes and interracial marriage. Violations of this social tabu have incurred resistance, condemnation, ostracism, brutal violence, and even death.

Despite this, there has always been some miscegenation between blacks and whites. And this has taken place even in the Deep South, for many white slave owners had liaisons and took advantage of the black women who were their property and their chattel. Many of the white men who called for race purity and lynched black men for the act or the rumored act of social or sexual relations with a white woman, and sometimes for even looking at one, were not above patronizing black brothels or having children by black women. As a result, much of the Negro population in the United States is of mixed blood, like the mulatto and the Creole.

A number of factors have changed the picture in the United States in recent years and have brought together young people of diverse racial, national, and religious backgrounds. The struggle for civil rights has broken down many of the barriers which in the past had kept the races separate. More and more people, including black people, have migrated to the North and to the cities. More and more young people are in contact with one another across racial lines in schools and colleges, jobs, public places, integrated housing, recreational and cultural activities, and in cooperation and fellowship in churches, political parties, and social movements. The involvement in wars and military occupation in other countries, the sharing of

common tasks and goals in the Peace Corps and Vista, the opportunities for exchange fellowships and travel abroad—all these have
brought about contacts and relationships that have often lead to
attachments and deep friendships.

These changes are taking place at the very time that the authority of the family has lost some of its control and influence on the
young. Furthermore, they occur in a social climate of increasing
acceptance of interracial marriage by the whites. In 1965, a Gallup
Poll indicated that 48 percent—almost half of those questioned—
approved of legal prohibition of marriage between whites and
blacks. By 1970, that number had fallen to 35 percent, and 56 percent disapproved of laws prohibiting interracial marriage—a surprising change within a period of five years.

On June 12, 1967, the Supreme Court of the United States
stated, "Under our Constitution, the freedom to marry a person of
another race resides with the individual and canot be infringed by
the State." The court based its ruling on the ground that restricting
the freedom to marry violates the equal protection clause of the
Fourteenth Amendment of the United States Constitution/ The
court's decision specifically voided the entire statutory scheme
adopted by the State of Virginia to prevent marriage between persons on the basis of racial classification. The language of the ruling
was broad enough to void similar antimiscegenation statutes in
fifteen other states—statutes which banned marriage between
whites and American Indians, Chinese, Filipinos, etc. A number of
states had already repealed their laws, including Indiana, Wyoming,
and Maryland. (The latter had repealed a 306-year-old statute ban-
ning marriages between whites and nonwhites.)

While the Myrdal study had shown that the white community
put first its fear of white-black intermarriage, the black community
rated intermarriage as the last thing they were concerned about and
the last right they would demand. Then, in the 1960's, growing black
militancy in the United States began to stress "separatism," black
identity, "black is beautiful," Afro styles of clothing and hairdos, and
"soul" in all aspects of life and the arts. Separatism has now come to
mean *separate* and *equal,* a true equality not as a handout and *not*
on white terms. One of the outcomes of this emphasis on "black
consciousness" has been that some of the black men and women who
have married whites have felt and feel the pressure to terminate

their relationships. Among the extreme black militants, the program of separatism may be as strong against relationships with whites as it was in the past when advocated so fiercely by the whites.

This tendency toward separatism is understandable. But as black people achieve true equality and as America achieves increasing integration, black separatism may prove to have been a phase of the civil-rights movement. If this is true, the trend toward more and more interracial marriages will continue. If so, it may be evidence of the increasing opportunity for democratic relationships and of the eventual easing of the race issue in all aspects of American life.

It is one thing to theorize from the point of view of social science, anthropology, and intergroup relations; it is quite another matter to deal with interracial marriage on the personal and family levels. Parents who are racists are uncompromising in their condemnation of interracial dating and socializing in ways which might lead to marriage. Indeed, their persistent racism accounts for much of the resistance to integration in education and housing. A fair-sized section of the parent population feels that their own standards and beliefs are so threatened that they will utterly reject a son or daughter who enters an interracial marriage. They will use every possible means—the church, the law, money—to prevent such a marriage. In some cases, they have resorted to destructive pressures on the black person, using whatever influence they had to impair his or her opportunity for schooling, employment, and social advancement.

Other parents may not be racist, but may have a genuine concern for what they believe to be the best interests of a son or daughter. They consider it their duty to resist interracial dating and socializing because they assume that it may lead to interracial marriage. If the son or daughter declares such intention, they will ask the couple to take time to think it over, to "stop seeing one another" for a while. They may urge them to mix with other people, attend school or college, take a job "somewhere else," or travel abroad. They will ask them to seek counseling.

They are concerned that the young people know the realities they will have to face and deal with. In many cases mixed couples have had to find their social and cultural life in a community away from their own families and away from the neighborhoods in which they grew up.

Mixed couples have had to live in secret and in isolation without normal social contacts. They have been thrown in on one another. Very often they have decided not to have children because they feared the impact of social ostracism and rejection for their young.

 Such parents may also point out that a black man who marries a white girl will have trouble getting a job, a job he might well deserve by merit. They might stress the difficulties the couple will encounter in getting housing, and the difficulties the children will have since they will belong neither to the "white nor the black world." If it is a son planning to marry a black woman, they will tell him that the marriage will limit his chances for advancement. They will also warn their child that he or she will lose contact with relatives and that many neighbors will not accept them.

Most such parents may want their son or daughter to know the tough realities of race attitudes and practices in American life. But after they have tried to dissuade them; after they have offered every resistance and opposition, and after they have resorted to delaying tactics, if the young people persist in their desire to marry, the parents will often give them support. Some parents will come around very slowly; others right away, and will attend the wedding and give presents and financial help. Some will be won over only when a baby is born or when there is a serious illness, and the family is reunited because of the tragedy.

Some will be genuinely concerned and counsel wisely for the sake of the young couple. Many persons, including clergy, will quote statistics on the divorce rate among interracial marriages. Many of those who quote the high divorce rate argument do not do so because they are afraid of intermarriage, but because they are afraid it will not work because the differences are too great. Other parents are concerned less about the young couple than about the effect the marriage will have on their own relationships and status with their relatives and neighbors.

Some are conscious of the fact that often an interracial marriage is also an interfaith marriage that will take a young person away from his or her particular church or synagogue. Professional marriage counselors will stress the psychological factors. With sound basis and justification, they may point out that people sometimes marry without really knowing each other, without seeing the real person in the other one. They may marry because of a particular need at a particular time in their lives. And some may enter an interracial marriage because they are rebelling against their parents or against society. Or they may marry because they feel sorry for the other person, out of compassion or out of guilt for what society has done to the member of the other racial group.

People may use one another without even being aware of what they are doing, any more than they may be aware of their own rebellions, of their own decisions based on guilt. A neurotic person chooses a partner who will sustain his neuroticism; if a person's neuroticism leads him to withdraw from society and from the give and take of normal relationships, marrying outside his group and taking refuge in a person with whom he can be rejected by society may feed his need to withdraw from the realities of life.

If some people marry for the wrong reasons and with the wrong person, others marry for good reasons and with the elements that generally make a good marriage; but the pressures of life and the course of events can make it too difficult for them also. Other men or women entering interracial marriage do so because they may need the sense of security that they believe marriage will bring, or they may be materialistic enough to see an opportunity for comfort and status which otherwise would not be open to them.

The real question, apart from such external factors as parent attitudes and social customs and practices, is: What are the elements in a man and a woman and in their relationship which are essential to a good marriage? If these elements are lacking, the married couple will have difficulty whether they are white to white, black to black, Catholic to Catholic, Jew to Jew, rich to rich, or poor to poor. Indeed, they will have difficulty no matter how much their marriage may be accepted and supported by the family and the community. No matter how strong they may be and how strong their love may be, their marriage is very fragile.

We can generally agree on the elements that make a good marriage. First, there must be love between the partners—physical attraction, sexual desire, but beyond this, a desire for the whole person with concern and affection, and a willingness to take responsibility and care for the other's life as one's own. In other words, there must be strength and the will and the maturity to make a true commitment beyond the immediate desire of a particular moment, of a particular period of one's life.

Second, there should be shared interests, a capacity to enjoy things together, as well as separate interests so that each enriches and enlarges the life of the other.

Third, each partner should be mentally and emotionally secure and stable and capable of adjusting to the reality of living together and of dealing with the pressures, difficulties, and crises of life. Illness, financial troubles, conflicts within the family, pressures from the community, all these have to be dealt with and dealt with together. Each then can depend on the support of the other. As the years go by and the partners age, the marriage goes through various phases. People have to be able to make the transition.

Finally, it is of utmost importance that the husband and wife share the same sense of priorities, the same sense of values. If there is basic agreement concerning children, family, friends, sources of enjoyment, money, status, material comforts, popularity, outward appearance, there is less likelihood that the marriage will be torn apart by fundamental conflict. When they agree on priorities and values, the partners have a better chance of solving whatever problems they may have. They can say, "Well, we may not always be in the same mood or always agree about ideas, but when it comes to what is important, there is no question between us. We have common goals, we understand what we mean by happiness, and we can make decisions together."

With these essential elements a marriage should work; it can stand bad days and severe strains and even social crisis in the larger community.

Interracial marriages can be the source of a richer life for both partners, of a truly happy and creative husband-and-wife relationship, of unusual and gifted children. Such marriages can do a great deal for the members of the two families of origin and also for the education and enrichment of the community. But they also can fail, and when they do, there is a great deal of misery, possibly more than in the ordinary separation or divorce between two people from the same background because there may be a tendency to blame the inadequacies on the racial factor and to fall back on stereotypes in criticizing the other party.

Where frictions develop and one or both parties suffer in the relationship, counseling may be of help. Therapy, on the other hand, may bring to the surface hidden aspects of the personality and reveal that the marriage was a mistake. The placid, gentle, compassionate person may become aggressive and openly resentful and critical, and demand adjustments rather than make them.

Much of the difficulty of interracial marriages would be obviated, and the benefits of interracial marriages enjoyed, if more children and youth were taught to respect all people and all differences, to reach out for their fellow men, and to strive for understanding of other human beings. The more we rid ourselves of prejudices, stereotypes, and scapegoats, the more we can help create a climate in which people can communicate, trust, know, and enjoy one another. Out of the rich mixture and interplay of differences can come a better and richer life for all of us.

If we succeed, the concept of "half-breed" as a mark of inferiority will fade out of the human mind and heart. Mixed marriages will enjoy acceptance and support from the community. Men and women of different racial backgrounds will be able to work out their marriages under material, psychological, social, and spiritual conditions that give support to all that is best in marriage and family life as part of a truly democratic culture.

2

BERNARD I. MURSTEIN Ph.D.

A Theory of Marital Choice Applied to Interracial Marriage

Within the context of a theory of marital choice on which he has been doing research for a number of years, Dr. B. I. Murstein in the following contribution directs our attention to an understanding of the wide range of factors—social, cultural, economic, racial, etc.—that underlie choice in biracial unions.

Many of the conclusions that Dr. Murstein draws are based on a theory of reciprocal satisfaction of needs in marriage. He shows how these may become known to prospective partners, and how social and racial factors operate to facilitate or discourage contacts among races of different races.

Murstein's interesting discussion offers us a kind of self-administering inventory of interests, values, and intentions that partners in interracial marriages, or those contemplating such unions, may find useful in the evaluation of their roles.

mutual
affection

ACCORDING TO what I jocularly refer to as Murstein's Law, "the amount of research devoted to a topic in human behavior is inversely proportional to its importance and interest" (14). Although at first glance this law may seem a bit eccentric, to say the least, I believe it is not only plausible but true. Once an individual has surmounted the basic problems of economic subsistence, some of the chief problems he concerns himself with are the meaning of his life in the face of death, his erotic ranking, and the quality of his interpersonal relationships. These are areas that have been less experimentally investigated by social scientists than other topics which, if less interesting, are also less threatening since they touch so little on personal concerns.

In this chapter, I shall focus on a concern that touches well over 90 percent of the population in the United States at some time in their lives: the choice of a marital partner. I shall attempt to utilize a general theory of marital choice developed earlier to derive some predictions for a theory of interracial marriage.

Because of limitation of space, among other reasons, I shall focus on black-white marriage in the United States. Oriental-white and oriental-black marriage and the intermarriage situation in Hawaii are surely of interest, but the smaller number of these marriages make data more difficult to come by. In addition, the long-standing favorable intermarriage climate in Hawaii and the resultant mixed

I am indebted to Nelly K. Murstein and Regina Roth for reading and commenting on this chapter.

status of so many of the races make the situation infinitely more complex than the case of black-white marriage in the continental United States. Even when we confine ourselves to the factors that influence black-white marriage, however, we shall see that the situation is complex enough.

Before turning specifically to black-white intermarriage, however, it may be of interest to note the conclusions of some earlier theories of marital choice and their implications for interracial marriage.

THEORIES OF MARITAL CHOICE

PRINCIPLE OF HOMOGAMY

The most popular approach to marital choice is the idea that "birds of a feather flock together." In other words, individuals are drawn together by the similarities of their characteristics. These simularities have been verified for race, education, socioeconomic status, age, previous marital status, and religion, to name just a few variables. Attempts to extend this finding of homogamy to personality traits however, have not been very successful.

NEED COMPLEMENTARITY

Aware of the shortcomings of a totally homogamous approach, Winch has proposed what in essence is a two-stage theory (23). He has acknowledged the importance of the aforementioned homogeneous cultural variables, but has denied that they are ultimately selective. Rather, they define a field of eligibles from which the choice is made on the basis of unfulfilled personality needs classified as Type I and Type II. If a couple is indicated by the letters A and B, the two types of need complementarity are as follows:

Type I. The same need is gratified in both A and B, but at very different levels of intensity. A negative interspousal relationship is hypothesized.

Type II. Different needs are gratified in A and B. The interspousal relationship may by hypothesized either to be positive or negative, contingent upon the pair of needs involved (23, pp. 94–95).

An example of Type I need complementarity would be if the husband were high on dominance and the wife were low on it. An example of a satisfactory Type II relationship would be a wife who is high on the need for nurturance and a husband who is high in a need for succorance and would therefore appreciate a nurturing wife.

Neither the homogamy nor the need-complementarity theory has a very good record in accurately forecasting marital choice (8, 11, 12, 19). More germane to our immediate concern, neither really accounts for racial intermarriage. Indeed, race has been the most homogamously selective variable in marital choice. It is, therefore, scarcely surprising that the small number of exceptions to racially homogamous marriage have not been treated in either theory.

Before turning to a theory which aspires to account for racial intermarriage within the tenets of a general theory of marital choice, we should consider at some length an earlier "mini-theory" which does deal specifically with racial intermarriage.

MERTON'S THEORY OF INTERRACIAL MARRIAGE

Robert Merton, borrowing heavily from an earlier study by Kinglsey Davis (4), emphasizes the reasons why endogamous rules (the tendency to marry within a particular group, caste, or class) are so firmly entrenched in all societies.

Endogamy expects that, because of common socialization, the marriage partners have a roughly similar cultural background. Because of this, there is likely to be less intrafamilial conflict growing out of different values of the spouses. The family instability that might result when children tend to identify with the upper-status parent and comdemn the lower-status parent is usually absent because of the endogamous nature of the marriage (10, pp. 368–369).

Merton goes on to explain that deviations from the norm involving upper- and lower-caste groups elicit a kind of exchange in which the lower-caste person gives something extra to the relationship to compensate for the higher status of the "upper" person. He deals with color (white) as one example of status, and socioeconomic class as another, and then makes three hypotheses:

1. The marriage of a white lower-class female to a black lower-class male should occur no more frequently than that of a black lower-class female to a white lower-class male. The dimensions of status would be equally distributed in such an arrangement.

2. The most frequent combination should be that of a white

lower-class female marrying a black upper-class male. Presumably, the "whiteness" of the lower-class female would balance off the upper-classness of her consort.* Many other combinations would not provide for a balancing of caste and class. Marriage where both the white and black were either of the lower or the upper class would be imbalanced to the detriment of the white, and white upper-class black lower-class marriage would be even more imbalanced.

3. The least frequent type of marriage should be one that combines race and class hypogamy—i.e., one in which a white upper-class female marries a black lower-class male.

The evidence bearing on these hypotheses is rather sparse, but the data of Wirth and Goldhamer on black-white marriage in Boston between 1914 and 1938 do not support any of the hypotheses. Regarding hypothesis 1, marriages of lower-class white females to lower-class black males, occurred, contrary to prediction, three times as frequently as those of lower-class black females and white males (24).

The second hypothesis, which says that the most frequent combination is that of a white lower-class female and a black upper-class male, was also not supported. Marriage was far more prevalent when the black groom and white bride were in identical or nearly identical occupational levels. That the tendency toward homogamy in socioeconomic status is prevalent in interracial marriages was also reported in a study of Los Angeles County in the 1950's and 1960's (2).

Merton's third hypothesis has not yet been tested. In sum, neither the general theories of marital choice nor the specific theory of interracial marriage reviewed so far shed much light on an understanding of why people marry a partner of another race. We shall take another approach, therefore, and ask whether or not a theory of interracial marriage is necessary in the first place.

IS A THEORY OF INTERRACIAL MARRIAGE NECESSARY?

It might be argued by some that, under the skin, blacks and whites are just people and, if they interact, they may fall in love and marry for the same reasons that two whites or two blacks marry. But we

---

*It might be thought that a lower-class white male and an upper-class black female should be equally balanced in rewarding power; however, Merton does not deal with this possibility.

know that race is the most endogamously selective variable of marriage. Even an adherent of the romantic school, therefore, would have to acknowledge that before a black person and a white one can be struck by Cupid's arrow, they must come within range of his bow. The likelihood of a black and a white marrying, therefore, may be seen as resulting from two distinct sets of probabilities: first, the probability that they will ever meet in a relationship in which marriage is at least conceivable;* second, the probability that they will marry, given that they meet in a potentially marriageable situation.

A study by David Heer bears on the first set of probabilities (7). Studying the State of California, he found a strong correlation between the actual and the expected intermarriage rates for whites, based on the proportion of blacks in each of twenty-six areal units. In other words, the greater the proportion of blacks in an area, the greater the probability of racial intermarriage in the area. Using a measure of residential segregation, he found that this index was negatively related to the ratio between actual and expected intermarriage. In short, the greater the tendency of the residences of blacks to be clustered together, the smaller the rate of intermarriage. Last, the ratio of white-collar whites to white-collar blacks was negatively related to the ratio of actual to expected intermarriage. Thus the smaller the proportion of blacks who were white-collar workers, the smaller the rate of intermarriage. In sum, the number of blacks in a county, their degree of residential segregation, and the kinds of jobs they hold influence the rate of interracial marriage by affecting the probability that white and black will meet as eligibles for marriage.

We are now at the second set of probabilities, one in which we need a workable theory to predict which individuals will marry within a pool of eligibles. With the aid of this theory—that we shall call the SVR theory—we hope to be able to account for intermarriage as a specific subsystem.

The two principles which form the scaffold of the theory are that (1) marital choice involves a series of sequential stages (at least three) that are labeled *stimulus, value,* and *role,* and that (2) at any given

*Certain contacts are relatively inconducive to marriage possibilities (e.g. janitor-secretary, stock clerk-buyer, shoe shiner-employer); hence the necessity of stipulating reasonable status equivalence which makes the possibility of marriage conceivable.

point of the relationship, its viability can be determined as a function of the equality of exchange subjectively experienced by its participants.

SEQUENTIAL STAGES

Stimulus stage. In an "open field" where interaction is not forced, an individual may be drawn to another because of his perception of the other's physical, social, mental, or reputational attributes. Because attraction is based largely on noninteractional cues, this stage refers to *stimulus* values. It is of crucial importance in an "open field" situation because, if the other person fails to elicit sufficient attraction, further contact is not sought. Although the "prospect" in question might be potentially a highly desirable person, the first person—foregoing opportunities for further contact—never finds this out. Consequently, physically unattractive individuals or persons whose stimulus value may be low for certain other individuals (e.g., other races and religions) are unlikely to be seriously considered as marital condidates by a societally determined, high stimulus-value person.

Value comparison stage. If mutual stimulus attraction exists between a man and a woman, they initiate and then increase their interaction so that they enter the second, or *value comparison*, stage. This stage is so named because the individuals assess their value compatibility through verbal interaction.

The couple may compare their attitudes towards life, politics, religion, sex, and the role of men and women in society and marriage. The fact that the couple are now interacting also permits more continuous and closer scrutiny of physical appearance, as well as other important factors such as temperament, "style" of perceiving the world, and ability to relate to others.

It is possible that closer appraisal of physical qualities and temperament will lead to a change of opinion regarding the desirability of the partner, and this in turn may result in an attempt to terminate the contact as soon as gracefully possible. If contact has been made on the basis of strong stimulus attraction, however, it is more likely that the couple will remain in the second stage, continuing to assess the compatibility of their values.

Should the couple find that they hold similar value orientations in important areas, they are apt to develop much stronger positive feelings for each other than they experienced in the stimulus stage. One reason for this is that when an individual encounters another who holds similar values, he gains support for the conclusion that his own values are correct; his views are given social validation. Providing we have a reasonably positive self-image, we tend to be attracted to those persons whom we perceive as validating it. Also, perceived similarity of values may lead to the assumption that the other likes us, and there is empirical evidence that we like those individuals who we think like us (1).

Last, we may note that persons who have similar values are likely to engage in similar activities and thus reward each other by validating each other's commitment to the activity. Moreover, because these activities are similar, they are apt to have similar reward value in the world at large. Thus, they further draw the couple together, since the two persons have equal status in their milieu. In sum, the holding of similar values should be a major factor in drawing two individuals together.

Role stage. It is possible that the couple may decide to marry on the basis of stimulus attraction and verbalized value similarity. However, for most persons these are necessary but not sufficient conditions for marriage. It is also important that the couple be able to *function* in compatible roles. By *role* is meant "the behavior that is characteristic and expected of the occupant of a defined position in a group" (5, p. 488). A role is thus a norm for a particular relationship and for particular situations. The role of husband, for example, may be perceived by the wife as embodying tenderness and acceptance of her. This role, however, does not necessarily clash with another role of the husband, that of his ability to aggressively maintain the economic security of the family. There are, in short, a multiplicity of roles for the different kinds of situations that one encounters.

In the premarital phase, however, the partner's ability to function in the desired role is not so readily observable as his verbalized expression of views on religion, economics, politics, and how men should treat women. Knowing, for example, how much emotional support the partner will give when the individual fails a school examination presupposes an advanced stage of intimacy. It is for this reason that the role stage is placed last in the time sequence leading to marital choice.

There are a large number of role expectations, the mutual fulfillment of which often determines whether the couple will marry. The content of these expectations, which have been researched and supported within the framework of SRV theory, includes the ability to satisfy personality and sexual needs, the ability to relate well to parents and peers, mutual high or low self-esteem, the ability of the woman to confirm and predict the man's self- and ideal-self image, and the comparable mental health of the partners.

We have to this point considered the situation as it arises when the couple meet in an "open field." Some individuals, however, meet in a "closed field." By this I mean a situation such as, for example, a classroom seminar in which two individuals experience a certain amount of nonstereotyped interaction regardless of whether they are initially drawn to each other. The effect is to weaken the influence of stimulus variables on marital choice and to maximize the influence of the second-stage or verbal-interaction variables. Thus, the individual who might never have been approached in an "open field" because she is of modest physical attraction, or the "wrong" religion or color, may become quite attractive to her coworker as a result of luncheon conversations in the office cafeteria which reveal her intelligence, sensitivity, and the similarity of her value-orientation to his own.

EXCHANGE PRINCIPLE

Although romantics may believe that love overrides all material considerations, the second principle of SVR theory holds that love depends on equality of exchange. The exchange principle as applied to social behavior follows pioneering efforts by Thibaut and Kelley (20) and Homans (9).

Essentially, these approaches maintain that each person tries to make social interaction as profitable as possible, *profit* being defined as the rewards he gains from the interaction minus the costs he must pay. By *rewards* are meant the pleasures, benefits, and gratifications an individual gains from a relationship. *Costs* are factors that inhibit or deter the performance of preferred behaviors. A young man living in the Bronx, for example, might like a young lady from Brooklyn whom he met while both were at a resort. Back in the city, however, he may doubt that the rewards he might gain from the relationship would be worth the costs in time and fatigue or two-hour subway rides to Brooklyn.

Closely allied to rewards and costs are assets and liabilities. *Assets* are the commodities (behaviors or qualities) possessed by the individual, which are capable of rewarding others and, in return, causing others to reciprocate by rewarding the individual. *Liabilities* are the individual's behaviors or qualities which are costly to others and thus, by reciprocity, costly also to the self.

A man who is physically unattractive (liability), for example, might desire a woman who has the asset of beauty. Assuming, however, that his nonphysical qualities are no more rewarding than hers, she gains less profit from the relationship than he does, and thus his suit is likely to be rejected. Rejection is a cost to him because it may lower his self-esteem and increase his fear of failure in future encounters so that he may decide to avoid attempting to court women who he perceives as much above him in attractiveness.

Contrariwise, he is likely to feel highly confident of success if he tries to date a woman even less attractive than himself, whereby risking little chance of rejection (low cost). However, the reward value of such a move is also low. As a consequence, an experienced individual is likely to express a maximum degree of effort, and also obtain the greatest reward at the least cost, when he directs his efforts toward someone of approximately equal physical attraction, assuming all other variables are constant.

During the first moments of contact, the individual may attempt to supplement his visual impression of the other with information regarding the other's role in society, professional aspirations, and background. Thus, persons attracted to each other are likely to be balanced for the total weighted amalgam of stimulus characterisitics even though, for a given trait, gross disparities may exist. Men, for example, tend to weigh physical attractiveness in a partner more than women do, whereas women give greater weight to professional aspiration in the partner. Accordingly, although physical attraction may play a leading role, it is hypothesized that the weighted pool of stimulus attractions that each possesses for the other will be approximately equal if individuals are to progress in courtship.

SVR THEORY AND INTERRACIAL MARRIAGE

We have already alluded to the fact that blacks as "lower status" people do not often pass the stimulus stage for whites. To the extent that the "black is beautiful" slogan has been accepted by blacks, whites would similarly fail to pass the stimulus stage for blacks. In view of the prejudices existing against color differences, it may be presumed that most black-white marriages are the result of "closed field" interactions in which the stimulus effect is minimized and the value and role stages emphasized.

Regarding compatibility of values between blacks and whites, there is little in the way of empirical research. From surveys on sexual attitudes and styles of life, though, it appears that the differences for many members of both races are not completely reducible to differences in socioeconomic status and education. If that is so, the few black-white couples who pass the stimulus stage may well founder at the value stage.

Role functioning offers perhaps the least hindrance to black-white couples negotiating the first two stages successfully. Roles to some extent are open to choice, depending on the structure of personality as well as on the demands of the environment. Yet, roles are also influenced by the mores of society and the effects of child rearing. Because the discrimination in jobs has fallen most heavily on the black male, his role in the family has often been more tenuous than that of the white male. On the other hand, the extended family (grandparents, cousins, nephews, aunts, uncles, nieces) has traditionally been much closer in black families. Thus the difference in cultural role prescriptions between blacks and whites could represent an additional problem for the longevity of black-white couple relationship.

ANOTHER LOOK AT EXCHANGE

In the face of the difficulties outlined above, it is scarcely surprising to note that the black-white marriage percentage for the country as a whole reported in the 1960 census was 0.15 percent. But what of this tiny fraction of one percent—the exceptions? Are these individuals insensitive to color so that they interact simply as two people? I wish to suggest that few persons, if any, are insensitive to color, and that *whites marrying blacks profit from segregation consciously or unconsciously by marrying partners with higher marital assets than they themselves possess.*

Although Merton's use of the exchange model did not result in support for his hypothesis, the difficulty may have rested in his choice of socioeconomic class as the variable on which to base his exchange theory. Marrying a person of another class is a rare occurrence because it raises the specter of intrafamilial dissension through a clash in the different values associated with class—a view expressed earlier by Davis and by Merton himself.

Merton would have been on firmer ground had he predicted that although class is homogamously selective for black-white marriage, it is not as selective as it is for all-white or all-black marriages. He might then have noted that *when* there are differences in status, they are in the direction of black superiority and white inferiority with respect to the average of each race.

There is little reliable evidence to support this view with respect to class, but it is supported by the data on education taken from the 1960 census as shown in Table 1.

An examination of this table indicates that the black husband of a white wife possesses an education superior to that of the black husband of a black wife, but not to that of the white husband of a white wife. Likewise, the black wife of a white husband typically has an education superior to that of the black wife of a black husband, but not to that of the white wife of a white husband. In short, compared to all-black marriages, black-white marriages are completely in accord with the exchange theory predictions. Compared to the white educational levels, however, black-white marriages do not support the predictions because the educational level of the black is always lower than that of his same sex counterpart in an all-white marriage.

In comparing educational levels, however, we should keep in mind that blacks average less education than whites. If we assume that races are approximately equal in intelligence, then the absolute level of education for a black might tend to downgrade his intelligence; hence a white marrying a black with a slightly inferior education might actually be marrying an individual slightly superior in intellectual level. Perhaps a fairer test of educational status might be to compare each person with the norm for his race rather than to consider the absolute level of education attained. In any event, if one takes cognizance of the difference in educational levels between the races, Table 1 generally supports the exchange theory.

There is another variable influencing the exchange balance in marriage which should be considered—the sex factor. SVR theory

TABLE 1

Percent Distribution by Years of School Completed by
Husband and Wife, by Race of Husband and Wife: United States, 1960

Years of school completed by husband and wife	White husband		Negro husband	
	White wife	Negro wife	White wife	Negro wife
All married couples*	100.0	100.0	100.0	100.0
Husband:				
No high school (0-8)	16.9	34.4	30.2	40.0
High school (9-12)	54.2	48.1	49.7	49.9
College (13 or more)	28.9	17.5	20.1	10.1
Wife:				
No high school	11.3	24.8	25.4	27.0
High school	68.4	60.6	59.1	62.3
College	20.3	14.6	15.4	10.7

Source: U.S. Bureau of the Census, *U.S. Census of Population: 1960, Subject Reports, Marital Status,* Final Report PC(2)-4E, table 12.

*Married couples with husband and wife in first marriage, married between 1950 and 1960, and excluding couples with either spouse other than white or Negro.

has postulated, and research confirmed, that men at present possess more power in marital choice than women. It follows, therefore, that men ought to be better able to traverse the color barrier than women; accordingly, more black men should marry white women than black women marry white men. Data on recent marriages in the 1960 census supported this assumption in that, for the sample studies, there were 7,534 marriages of the first kind and 6,082 of the second.

It is also noteworthy that the proportion of black man-white woman marriages of the total black-white marriages was highest in the North and West (62 percent) compared to the South, where it was only 42 percent (3). If we make the reasonable assumption that the black man enjoys more status in the West and North than in the South, then the figures are consistent with the exchange theory.

There is another variable which probably is not so homogamously selective as socioeconomic class or education, and would therefore be more readily available for "trading" to achieve equal exchange in interracial marriage. This is physical attractiveness, which, perhaps because it was not a sociological or psychological variable, has been ignored until recently by most researchers in these disciplines. According to the exchange component of SVR theory, an individual possessing higher race status might select a partner with a lower race status who is more attractive than a partner he might obtain within his own race. Regrettably, this hypothesis has not yet been put to empirical test.

There is some evidence, however, which indicates that physical attractiveness itself is strongly influenced by status. A study was undertaken in which three photos each of black men, black women, white men, and white women were judged for physical attractiveness by black and white judges of both sexes (18). Each picture represented a gradation of culturally acknowledged racial characteristics. The picture of the extreme black type, for example, depicted an individual with thicker lips, wider nose, and more prominent cheekbones than the other pictures. The photograph of the most extreme white type presented an individual with thinner lips, narrower nose, and smoother cheekbones than the other types. Both white and black men preferred the extreme white type, whereas black and white women showed no such preference.

If we assume that preferences for physical types are culturally learned rather than innate, then these differences suggest the effect of higher white status on standards of sexual attractiveness. The lower black women's ratings of sexual attraction to both black and white types may reflect the dual handicap of being black and a woman. These twin handicaps on the one hand may generally dampen the probability of black women-white men marriages and reduce black women's sexual interest in white men. On the other hand, black woman may feel resentment against black men because, as men, they have the option, and sometimes exercise it, of courting white women.

The power of color in mate selection is also seen in another recent study which investigates the effect of lightness of color on educational level, occupation, and socioeconomic mobility within black marriages (21). For long-standing marriages, lightness of skin color is positively associated with higher educational level, occupation, and mobility for both sexes. For more recent marriages, darkness of skin color for the man is positively associated with these variables, whereas women still continue to show a positive association between lightness of skin and these variables. Not surprisingly, therefore, whereas light-skinned men and women were highly likely to be paired in earlier marriages, the more recent marriges show more dark-skinned men paired with light-skinned women. These data, collected in the latter part of 1965, from a Washington, D.C., sample, suggests that for that sample and time period at least, black was more beautiful for men than for women.

There are a number of other largely psychological factors which are apparently associated with interracial marriage but for which not enough is at present known to integrate them into an exchange model. The information about them stems from observations, interviews, and case studies rather than from firm empirical data. Moreover, these factors are highly variable from person to person and are not so readily measurable as class, education, or even physical attractiveness. I shall therefore only briefly list them as fodder for future research.

OTHER PSYCHOLOGICAL FACTORS INFLUENCING INTERRACIAL MARRIAGE

BLACK SEXUALITY

The Negro has acquired the reputation of being the personification of sex. The black woman's sexual needs, say many white men, are insatiable. This *imago* is no doubt a projection of the sexual exploitation of the black woman by the Southern white man in antebellum and postbellum days. If the black woman is seen as constantly in rut, then the white man feels less guilty about his actions. He is only serving as a stud.

The black man, according to his *imago*, is so happy-go-lucky, so natural, so rhythmic, that he feels and expresses nature's urges without the least inhibitions. The white man thinks of all the lewd thoughts that ever crossed his mind and imagines the black man acting them out without his own inhibitions. And that penis!

> The black man's sword is a sword. When he has thrust it into your wife, she has really felt something. It is a revelation. In the chasm that it has left, your little toy is lost. Pump away until the room is awash with your sweat, you might as well just be singing. *This is good-by.* . . . Four Negroes with their penises exposed would fill a cathedral. They would be unable to leave the building until their erections had subsided; and in such close quarters that would not be a simple matter (6, p. 169).

There is, however, neither a shred of evidence to indicate that blacks are any differently endowed sexually from whites, nor that there is any difference in size of sexual organs. Someone actually has taken the trouble of measuring the penises of African black men and reported a mean of 4.6244 inches, which was just about the same figure arrived at by another researcher for European men (6). Those who can only be satisfied by blacks are therefore suffering from a fetish just as are those who can only be satisfied by a partner wearing cowboy boots.

GUILT

Some whites feel very guilty about the wrongs white has perpetrated against blacks. To punish themselves for having been born white, they marry a black, and because guilt is not an augur of success in marriage, they thereby visit punishment on two people. The black counterpart is the black man who, in order to strike back at "whitey," sleeps with his women to humiliate him. Usually, however, the revenge motive doesn't necessarily go so far as marrying the white woman. When it does, the consequences are disastrous.

REBELLION AGAINST PARENTS

In *Portnoy's Complaint*, Portnoy fantasized "a soft white Protestant ass on the toilet seat." If a different religion and physical type can have so much attraction within the Caucasian race, it should not be difficult to imagine the attraction and excitement for someone of another color. There is some evidence that highly secure people, who are confident of not being rejected, are more apt to seek out dissimilar persons than those who lack confidence (1). It is possible, therefore, that interracial marriage for such persons provides an extra stimulation, given that the partners are also compatible in other respects.

A black psychiatrist, Dr. John Osmundsen, however, commenting on interracial marriage some years ago, stated that "deep-seated psychological sicknesses of various sorts underlie the 'vast majority' of marriages between white persons and Negroes. . . . The participants make use of the unique opportunity that socially opposed or forbidden interracial sex offers for acting out their personal problems" (17, p. 73).

It is of course true that the divorce rate for black-white marriage is higher than that for intrawhite marriage. Whether, however, this fact is due to the state of mental health of those entering interracial marriage or whether it is due to the opposition of society to this mésalliance is a moot point.

CONCLUSIONS AND PROGNOSTICATIONS FOR THE FUTURE

We have seen that interracial marriage was not included in the earlier traditional theories of marital choice. Merton's suggestion of an exchange theory of marital choice was a step in the right direction, but he failed to take into account the selective, homogamous effect of socioeconomic class that inhibits marriage between disparate classes, and other variables that might more readily serve as exchange factors.

I have suggested that we consider interracial marriage as involving a twofold set of probabilities. The first set measures the probability that a black and a white will ever come into contact with each other as marriage eligibles. It was shown that the black population within an area, residential segregation, and socioeconomic level are each highly related to the degree of intermarriage. In the second probability set, SVR theory accounted for the likelihood that a black and white would marry if they met as marriageable eligibles. To the extent that prejudice exists against a race, that race becomes a negative weight in the compilation of marital assets and liabilities; hence the relatively greater education of blacks and relative inferior education of the whites they marry. The fact that recent marriages show a greater number of black male-white female marriages compared to black female-white male marriages is said to be due to the greater marital asset that maleness carries compared to femaleness. It is believed that physical attractiveness as an important marital asset should be more heavily present for blacks as compared to whites, since it would compensate for the negative weight assigned by society to color. Obviously, these weights are in a continous state of modification. To the extent that "black is beautiful" is really believed by blacks and by whites, it would diminish the effects found earlier.

Relatively recent polls do not suggest an imminent disappearance of racial prejudice. In a Gallup Poll of 1965, some 48 percent of Americans approved of the then-existing laws making intermarriage a crime. In 1968, a similar poll found that only 20 percent of

Americans approved of marriages between whites and nonwhites.

The prognostication, nevertheless, is for a continually rising intermarriage rate. One reason is that the attitude toward acceptance of blacks as equals is increasing even though majority opinion, as we have seen, is still against intermarriage. Slowly but steadily, advertisements and dramas on television show an increasing number of scenes depicting blacks interacting as equals with whites. Movies treat black-white marriage in a positive tone, and indices of segregation, such as busing and "separate but equal schools," draw more opposition than heretofore.

Inhibitions against interracial contact, in short, are breaking down. Heer has empirically demonstrated that residential segregation by race is less than a few years ago, and the ratio of black to white white-collar workers is rising (7). Since the time studied, 1953–1963, it appears that factors facilitating intermarriage have increased rather than decreased, but this can no longer be demonstrated by state records, since in most states race is no longer recorded on marriage licenses.

Although interracial marriage is increasing, it is not likely to become an avalanche given present negative attitudes of blacks and whites toward each other and given the economic status difference and cultural life styles that separate them. However, the goal of most progressives is not mass intermarriage as an antidote for racial strife. Rather, the hope is for a climate of mutual acceptance in which those of different races who wish to marry can do so without the hardships —legal, overt, or subtle—imposed by society. Perhaps in the near future the color of an individual will become of much less concern than the kind of person he is. In such an age, when a white man is asked, "Would you want your daughter to marry a Negro?" he might calmly reply, "Which Negro did you have in mind?" (22).

3

CAROLINE B. ROSE, M.A.

Potential Role Conflicts in Black-White Marriages

What do sociologists know about the differences between black and white cultures in the United States? How are these differences reflected in marital conflict? Mrs. Rose uses her extensive, intimate contact with both cultures to make predictions about the future of interracial marriage within the context of changing attitudes that characterize American society today. Her investigation and optimistic conclusions represent a valuable summary of assumptions and predictions in this critical area, a blueprint for social action, and a pointer to future social trends.

THE USEFULNESS of science depends in part upon its ability to predict accurately. This chapter is an exercise in prediction: on the basis of what sociologists know about marital conflict and about the differences between black and white cultures. I will try to predict some of the problems that may occur in marriages between young blacks and young whites.

Underlying the predictions are some assumptions based on what we know about black-white marriages in the past:

Assumption 1: There will be an increase in black-white marriages. This is a safe prediction; there have been so few black-white marriages in the past that they will increase solely on the basis of the population increase in the marriageable ages. A greater increase than this can be expected, however, for the following reasons:

1. Until 1967, sixteen states had laws forbidding interracial marriages. These laws are now unconstitutional. Although people could marry in the past by going to states where interracial marriages were legal, the difficulties this involved, both physical and psychological, undoubtedly hampered interracial marriage.

2. Marriage occurs among groups whose members have frequent, equal status contacts. The increase of integration in schools, particularly in colleges, and in offices and other work places where young adults are employed will provide more opportunity for young blacks and whites of marriageable age to meet.

3. Urban life breaks down ethnocentrism and increases intimate contacts across ethnic and racial groupings. By 1969, 70 percent of blacks and 64 percent of whites lived in metropolitan areas (13).

Assumption 2: Black-white marriages in the past have occurred mainly among celebrities, bohemians, and in the lower economic classes. In the future, the great majority of such marriages are likely to occur among middle-class young people. The reasons for this are the same as the reasons listed under Assumption 1. Middle-class young people—those in urban schools and colleges and those working in white-collar and technical and professional jobs—will be drawn more heavily in the future from the black community, thus increasing equal status contacts in the marriageable ages. As discrimination decreases and as the class structure of the Negro community comes to resemble that of the white community, marriage between blacks and whites should be more like marriages within each community. Studies show that in general, in terms of economic and social status, homogamy prevails; (9, ch. 13) and we should expect this pattern to prevail in future black-white marriages.

Assumption 3: In the past Negro men have married white women far more often than white men have married Negro women. The most usual explanation for this is that the white woman exchanges her superior caste position for either the superior class position of the black man or for his personal traits superior to those of white men available to her. On the other hand, since white men have had sexual access to black women without marriage, they do not so often marry black women. A second explanation is that because black men have been barred by law and custom from sexual access to white women, they desire this more, and so are moved more often to marriage, even though the white woman is inferior in class position and personal traits to available black women.

Our assumption is that this pattern will change in accord with the arguments presented above and, therefore, that black-white marriages will follow patterns similar to those that prevail within either the black or white communities; that is, in the future, we would expect an increase in marriages where the husband is white and the wife black.

Unfortunately, there is very little case material on black-white marriage to provide information about how interracial couples get along. An article in *Ebony* in 1968 presented five case studies (12). In three of these marriages the husband was black, and the other two the wives were black. Albert Gordon in his book *Intermarriage* reported in detail on five interracial marriages (6).* In four of these marriages the man was black, in the fifth the wife was black. Two of Gordon's couples had been divorced, one after twenty-four years of marriage and two children; the other after two years of marriage.

On December 20, 1969, David Susskind interviewed four interracial couples on his TV show. All four couples were dating, but only two were planning marriage. All were exceptionally frank in discussing their situation. I took detailed notes on what these couples said. Among these couples, two of the men and two of the women were black. Of the two couples intending to marry, the woman was white in one case, black in the other. In an article in June, 1968, William Barry Furlong also described some interracial marriages, but not in great detail (5).

These case studies are not representative in the statistical sense; moreover, there is no way of knowing whether or not they are typical of a large percentage of black-white marriages. The questions asked the couples, or at least those they talked about, covered areas often identified in the past as major sources of conflict in interracial marriages. The evidence from these marriages, without exception, does not support the idea that the following problem areas are frequent sources of conflict:

1. *Lack of friends.* All of the couples, including the dating couples, said they had no lack of friends. They dropped—or were dropped by—those who disapproved, but found other couples, all black, all white, or mixed, without any trouble.

2. *Disapproval of family.* In a number of cases the families disapproved of the marriage, several times to the point of ostracism of the couple. But either the couple had anticipated this and was able to adjust to it, or the spouse whose family did the rejecting was already far from his or her family, both physically and emotionally.

3. *Conflicts in the children's minds.* In harmony with the prevailing American custom, all the children were considered black, raised as black, and had to meet the same difficulties that all black American children must meet. The idea that the child of a mixed

---

*Gordon included a sixth case in which the wife was racially white, although she had always considered herself a Negro and had been raised in a Negro community. Since this writer regards race as a social, not a biological category, this case was not included.

marriage is in some no-man's land, neither black nor white, is a fairy tale based on the idea that race is a physical, not a social, characteristic.

4. *Economics.* Some couples reported financial difficulties, in a few cases because the black wage earner either met discrimination or had few skills. In no case was this the result of the intermarriage, and in no case did money troubles seem to cause more difficulties than they do in any marriage.

5. *Housing.* A number of the couples reported difficulty in finding suitable housing, but not because they were intermarried; the couple met discrimination because one of them was black. This again did not cause much conflict. Some of the couples were well-to-do and found no difficulty.

6. *Religion.* In addition to racial intermarriage, some of the couples were religiously intermarried. Again, there was no evidence of conflict. Sometimes, both spouses were only weakly religious and did not seem to be particularly concerned with the religious issue. Sometimes, one member of the pair converted to the other's religion. Differences in religion were handled very much in the same way as married couples of the same race handle them.

In summary, on the evidence of these case studies, racially intermarried couples seem to face the same problems that confront couples who are of the same race, and their solution does not seem to be hindered by the racial mixture of the marriage. It is true that intermarried couples, particularly if the husband is black, meet some problems that not all white couples meet, but this is the result of discrimination against blacks and not directly the result of mixing the races in marriage.

In the rest of this chapter we want to look at some attitudes that members of the black and white communities carry with them, consciously or unconsciously, into an intermarriage and which would not be present in marriages between people of the same race.

Marriage involves acting out new roles—those of husband, wife, and, usually, parents. It is not clear where one learns marriage roles, but it has been assumed that this learning usually occurs in the family one is raised in. Although many young people consciously reject parental models, unconsciously they may follow them. The generation gap is loudly announced today, but it may actually be no greater than it has been in the past in a country where there has always been great mobility, both geographic and social; where there has always had to be a great deal of improvisation in marital roles because parental models did not fit new situations. Nevertheless, nobody throws off entirely his childhood experiences or his remembrances of how his parents behaved under certain circumstances. Faced with problems in marriage, even those openly hostile to their parents may act out marital roles as their parents did.

On the assumption that this may happen in interracial as well as in intraracial marriages, what kinds of role conflicts are likely to stem from traditional differences in marital roles in the two communities? More explicitly (since the writer feels that there is not much difference in how the roles have been played), what conflicts can arise from the feeling or belief that marital roles in the black community are different from those in the white community?

In a great deal of recent literature on the black community, much has been made of the large number of black families headed by women. From this fact, a whole series of assumptions and consequences has been deduced:

1. Black families have been disorganized ever since the days of slavery because marriage among slaves was prohibited or arbitrarily broken. The black family under slavery consisted of mother and children, with the father frequently absent.

2. Black men cannot get jobs paying enough to support families; therefore, they are unable to assume familial responsibility. Where relief payments are available to women and children only, the men often leave their families to enable them to get a decent income.

3. The inability of the black man to provide for his family and, even more devastating, his inability to protect black women from unwelcome sexual advances from the white man, has harmed the black man's concept of his own masculinity.

Even if all these assumptions and consequences are true, let's remember that only 28 percent of black families are female-headed (14). Seventy-two percent have both parents present. If, as we predict, most intermarried couples in the future will be middle class, at least by achievement, it is not likely that more of the black spouses than of the white spouses will have come from the lower class, female-headed families. (It is, of course, possible that female-headed families are not lower class, but it is rare.)

Despite the fact that almost three-fourths of black families provide both husband-wife and mother-father family role models, the idea that the black man has been and is subordinate to the black woman has very deep roots in the black culture. My black students, when faced with the arguments just presented, insist that even if the father is present, he is subordinate in the family. Several hundred autobiographies from these same students, however, reveal—at least to a white, middle-class professor—as much paternal dominance as one would expect in white families.

There are several reasons why blacks believe that black women are more dominant in the family roles than white women are. First, the role models within the black community, among the richer and the better-educated, are extremely paternalistic compared to husband-wife roles in the same stratum of white society. The middle-class black has been segregated from many of the changes that have taken place in the last fifty years in white marriage patterns (10, pp. 250–259). Middle-class blacks, now in their forties and fifties, were educated in all-black schools, and they were raised in a much more severe religious climate than comparably educated whites. The black middle class, therefore, offers to the rising lower class very strict, paternalistic marital roles.

If the black middle class has been isolated from whites by segregation, the black lower class has been even more so. Most young blacks have no idea of how whites live except from what they glean from the cinema and TV. In particular, they have no realistic idea of the variety of life styles among whites. Their concept that the white man is powerful and dominant in business and politics compared to the black man tends to color their perception of the role of the white husband and father. As the blacks long for political and economic equality with the white man, so they aspire to fill the same kind of family roles the whites are thought to play.

The idea that the black man has been subordinate and should now try to be dominant even in his marital roles is widely held and practiced. Among black militants, especially those who are most interested in the African heritage, male dominance is acted out with great clarity. Women walk behind the men and defer to them conspicuously.

On the other hand, among the white middle class, men and women are assuming more equalitarian roles. Among young, college-educated whites, men are not only willing for their wives to work, but glad to have someone share the responsibility of earning enough to support a middle-class standard of living. In return, young white men are willing to share household and child-rearing tasks as well as decision making about how money should be spent (8, pp. 194–196).

Dominance in the family, we think, will be one of the most likely areas of conflict between black men and white women in an interracial marriage. The patterns of equality commonplace to white women for at least two generations may seem threatening to a black man peculiarly sensitive to the need for strength in his male roles. Strain between white men and black women may be less acute in these areas, but present nevertheless. Black women too have a distorted idea of white life and may expect to have less responsibility, particularly financial responsibility, than their husbands expect.

People have unconscious as well as conscious motives for their actions, marriage included. Expressed or not, it is likely that white members of interracial marriages may feel that they are doing something virtuous, that they are giving clear evidence of lack of prejudice, and contributing to harmony and to a better world. Such attitudes may be openly expressed; often whites first meet blacks in civil rights organizations and may be very clear and articulate about the right to and social values of interracial marriage. There is nothing incompatible with seeing one's marriage as a social good and at the same time having intimate and romantic feelings toward husband or wife and, later, children.

The question we would rather ask is whether the failure to believe in the social values of interracial marriage can affect the marriage negatively. Failure may result from a change in the social climate: blacks may have made sufficient progress so that interracial affairs are no longer important social problems; conversely, blacks may give up on white America and accept voluntary segregation. Either way, the white partner will have lost one motive—conscious or unconscious—for the marriage, although personal ones may still be strong.

If the black community becomes more segregated, the white

spouse will face strong hostility. In general, in the past, this has not been true; white partners in interracial marriages have been welcomed by the black community. But there is now potential hostility in the black community, particularly among black women and black militants of both sexes.

In the weeks following the publication of the article on intermarriage in *Ebony*, mentioned earlier, a large number of letters antagonistic to interracial marriage were published in the letters columns (4). I quote from some of them: ". . . I think it is high time black women and white men took revenge on those traitors to their race who pass them over in favor of non-sisters and black men! . . ." ". . . Why can't those black men who have married white women admit to themselves . . . soul brother prefers the Caucasian female —simply because this 'treasure' has been denied him so long . . . [and] stop blaming this union on 'love' . . ."

A similar article in an earlier issue was followed by this letter among others: ". . . I am not a racist but white women are a threat to black women. In the near future there aren't going to be enough nice black men around for us to marry . . ." (3).

Not all of the letters were hostile, and there is no way of knowing which ones the editors of *Ebony* chose to print, but the point I wish to make is not that everybody is hostile, but that there is potential hostility.

It is unlikely that marriages will take place solely because the white member feels that he is making a social contribution to better race relations, even though much interracial dating is thus motivated (1). Unless some personal attraction and some reasonable chances of compatibility arise, the whites turn elsewhere or the blacks reject them as marriage partners. Nevertheless, in many marriages there is likely to be a self-righteous component on the part of whites, which adds an extra burden to those marriages where it exists, particularly if it is not rewarded by success in the marriage, acceptance by the black community, and a minimum of "gratitude" on the part of the black partner. It is easy to visualize a quarrel in which the white partner expects concessions solely on the basis of his righteousness. If the black partner senses that his or her white spouse feels this way, he is likely to resent it. Not everybody has as good a sense of humor as the white husband and black wife in the following conversation. White man: "I think at first there's a feeling of pride for the white person—that you've brought somebody in the world, that you've given her a chance that she wouldn't have had otherwise."

Black woman's rejoinder: "Dear, don't you think at first you were trying hard to impress Negroes with how liberal you were?"

It is also possible that both partners believe that they are contributing to better race relations; such an attitude should solidify the marriage because it constitutes a shared feeling and goal. It is also possible—but not likely, given the widespread and long-continued attitude on the part of white society that blacks are inferior—that the black partner would feel that he or she is the one who makes a social contribution by entering into an interracial marriage. The black partner is more likely to be defensive since there is some feeling against interracial marriages among blacks; but if he does feel that he is improving the world solely by the fact of his interracial marriage, this attitude would operate against harmony in the marriage in the same way as if the white partner felt this way.

In the classical literature on race relations, much was made of the sexual barriers between blacks and whites, enforced by law and by the mores. Myrdal felt that the core of anti-black feeling in the South was the idea that blacks were biologically inferior and that children of mixed parentage must be kept in the black group; hence the taboo not on sexual relations, but no black male-white female sexual relations (11, vol. I, ch. 3).

Many sociologists did not take this explanation seriously, but some literature, written by angry and outspoken blacks, gives ample evidence that blacks perceived the regulations enforcing the caste system in just this way: that the greatest taboo, and the most highly enforced, was the prohibition of black male-white female sex relations. As a consequence, white women became tempting to black men far out of proportion to any personal attractions they might possess. Eldridge Cleaver expresses this feeling, "I believe if a leader wanted to unite the Negroes in a solid unity, he could do so very easily. . . . All he'd have to do is promise every black man a white woman and every black woman a white man. . . . He would have so many followers he wouldn't know what to do with them" (2, p. 14).

The desire to attain a white woman as wife and to erase from his mind forever the idea that a black man is so biologically inferior that he should not pass on his genetic potential is undoubtedly deep in some black men. In my opinion the presence of this feeling should solidify interracial marriages between black men and white women. The black man has what he wants, what many black men have been denied, brutally and violently, and the fulfillment of which has played a large part in black humor and in private informal discussion.

The feeling that white women are more sexually desirable than black women has two possible dimensions. It may result solely from the historical taboos we have mentioned, and be satisfied by marriage. Or it may result from group self-hatred: that is, from the feeling that the physical traits of blacks are ugly and those of whites are beautiful. There is far less of this among young blacks than among older people, but it persists. To detest the group from which you come and in whose biological traits you share is a serious psychological disability which hampers self-confidence and accomplishment. A black man who marries a white woman because he is suffering from hatred of his own group is likely to feel tremendous guilt in his marriage.

Black females, as well as black males, may suffer from group self-hatred. This can be even more devastating to women than to men because of the higher premium on physical appearance set for women than for men in our society, coupled with the impossibility for a black woman to look like a white woman. The toll that group self-hatred takes of black women is graphically described in William H. Grier and Price M. Cobbs's *Black Rage* (7, ch. 3).

The question arises as to how many of the people entering into interracial marriage are suffering from group self-hatred. It may be postulated that more men than women harbor this feeling, and that this might well be a motivation toward such marriages for men. As far as black women are concerned, those who feel physically inferior are less likely to take the unconventional step of marrying a white man.

The young people in the David Susskind interviews frankly discussed problems of group self-hatred and the taboos against sexual relations between black men and white women. How past history can manifest itself in the daily lives of young people is shown by some of the attitudes they expressed.

Milton, a black man, spoke about his own conflicts; he said he had always, even in high school, dated only white girls. These dates were always clandestine, then he thought it exciting, but now he wonders why he put up with it. He finds black girls unattractive and wonders if he has an obligation to date black girls. He is an actor, and he emphasized that he did not work in the black theater. He summed up his feeling by saying that he knew something was wrong with his attitudes toward women, and that he was thinking about it and trying to understand and resolve his problems.

The other black man interviewed that night was Calvin, a Columbia student. He was extremely militant and admitted that his friends were putting great pressure on him to stop dating his white girl friend, Bernadette. He accepted the militants' argument that black men had been brainwashed into preferring white women, but even so he was not able to give up his white girl. When one of the black girls on the program (Stephanie) said, "Do you notice that every black militant has a white girl?" Calvin objected strongly that this was not so. Stephanie was dating a white man.

This evidence is slim, although the writer has frequently heard similar discussions among young blacks. Faced with new situations for which the past gives little guidance, they must work out ways of carrying on intimate relations with young whites, and it is natural they should experience conflict. Young whites also experience conflicts, but it is undoubtedly less difficult for a member of the dominant majority to adjust than for a member of an oppressed minority.

Even though the writer is predicting some conflicts in future interracial marriages, there is no reason to think that they will founder on these conflicts. Interracial marriages should have as good a chance of succeeding as any other marriages in which circumstances other than the racial background of the participants are favorable. Conflict and problems occur in all marriages; a successful marriage is one in which they are solved. It was the universal testimony of all the interracial marriage partners whose stories were reported that hostility from the outside world made them feel closer to each other. It is possible that the necessity of finding some solution to the conflicts we have just been discussing may bring future interracial marriage partners closer together.

4

VLADIMIR PISKACEK, M.D.
and MARLENE GOLUB, M.S.W.

Children of Interracial Marriages

In the chapter that follows, Dr. Vladimir Piskacek and Mrs. Marlene Golub address themselves to the manifold problems that face the children of biracial marriages. In order to develop their sense of identity, these children must overcome some very special difficulties that confront them. All children face difficulties in developing a clear and stable self-image, but as the authors point out, the problems of the black-white child are especially acute.

Drawing on their clinical experiences, the contributors present, in brief, some of the difficulties faced by several interracial couples and by their children. These biracial families represent a microcosm of America's racially troubled society of which they are such a significant part.

We emerge from the reading of this chapter with a greater awareness and understanding, and a larger and deeper feeling, for both the issues and the opportunities.

THE BURDEN of the black child is a heavy one. The burden of the black-white child is infinitely greater. In present-day society the children of interracial marriages grow up to a unique destiny. They are poised between two worlds, two sets of expectations, and they are sometimes ravaged by conflict. Pigment is a fate in a society in which different shades of skin color have such tremendous social significance.

Skin color, a mere physical characteristic, becomes significant only because society assigns arbitrary meanings or values to it. Interracial families and their children have to come to grips with this social factor and cope with a myriad of complexities, given that, within the same family, each child may be born with a different skin tone. Each child must cope with identity problems and with adjustment problems connected with the psychological resolution of social contradictions.

Such a child is in conflict with parents, with society, and with himself. How well he is able to resolve this struggle depends upon his parents' awareness of the problems and how well the parents can integrate this conflict for the child. Failure to accomplish this integration leads to severe unhappiness and, in many instances, to the referral to a child guidance clinic. This chapter describes problem families that come to the attention of clinicians. It must be kept in mind that what we are discussing is a selective sample that is not representative of interracial marriages in general. The racial problem is not a causal factor related to any specific clinical maladjustment, but, rather, a stress factor that affects general problems of living and creates additional pressures on the children and their families. Thus a greater strength is required of a biracial family in order to achieve the same level of adjustment that is required of a uniracial family. According to Spiegel, children who manifest emotional disturbances belong to families in which parents unwittingly involve them in their own conflicts (2). In general, families have a variety of conflicts. In our families the culture-value conflict is most important. If this conflict is profound and prolonged, and if the children cannot escape emotional participation and, particularly, if the children are vulnerable, then behavioral and emotional problems will follow.

Healthy families that manage to work out their problems should also be studied since they accomplish the seemingly impossible—the integration of conflicting attitudes. Unfortunately, there is little data available to illuminate the dynamics of such successful resolution, since such families never present themselves at mental health clinics. However, we can describe one family with whom we are personally familiar. The husband, a black accountant, and his white wife met while both were at the university. Both of them came from apparently emotionally stable families. The Harrises were able to anticipate and to openly discuss with their respective families problems that might arise from their union. When problems did arise, they were prepared to view them with some objectivity and to seek workable compromises. They never allowed themselves to use race as a weapon. Instead, each was flexible enough to make the necessary adjustments to strengthen the relationship. An important factor that contributed to their success was the positive feedback they received from both of their families and the mutual respect they had for each other. When their daughter was born, they had already resolved many of their conflicts. She grew up relatively secure, accepted by both sets of grandparents. The successful outcome was related to a minimum of ambivalence, to conflict resolution, and to acceptance by both the nuclear and the extended families. The parents provided secure role models with which the child could identify. Above all, the parents' maturity united them in a common perception of their child. Thus, they were able to provide her with a consistent reinforcement of her value as a person in terms of sameness and continuity in time. Identity is a life-long process. Although identity is not fully crystallized prior to puberty, the awareness of self, e.g., awareness of racial and sexual identity, is already established by the age of four or five. A sense of identity as a dynamic process is fostered by positive interaction between the parents, the child, and society, as illustrated in the above example. Also illustrated is that this girl was spared role conflict; the inputs she received were free of double messages, double binds, and double expectations.

In contrast, Richard and Brenda Johnson, a couple in their early thirties, had become increasingly aware of their marital difficulties and their inability to communicate. Mr. Johnson, an attractive black professional man, and Mrs. Johnson, an equally attractive white woman, had been married for seven years and had both been married before. They had a six-year-old boy who was extremely sensitive and was doing very poorly in school. The teacher reported that the child was sullen, had difficulty in learning, and, at times, put his head down and refused to do his work. His sister, a bright five-year old, was hyperactive and excessively clinging. Both parents were troubled by their children's behavior, and found it difficult to comprehend. Both parents were intelligent, well educated, and prided themselves on their progressive views. The Johnsons placed emphasis on social advancement and achievement. One might describe them as autonomous personalities, capable of breaking conformity patterns in their search for self-realization. In this family, there were several levels of conflict. On one level, there was conflict with the parents on both sides, who had not accepted their marriage. The color identity of the children became an important issue in the household. There was rivalry for the loyalties of the children and disagreement as to what constituted the children's racial identity. The problems were not resolved, and the question of color and race was used as a defensive displacement.

The Warrens became known to our clinic as a result of their thirteen-year-old daughter's school problems and hyperactivity. Mr. Warren was a successful black businessman. His wife was a registered nurse. The daughter tended to identify more strongly with her black father and openly preferred her paternal relatives. Her father's family had always been more accepting of her, while her white grandparents were rejecting. Despite this, the mother had maintained a close relationship with her parents and would at times go home alone for visits, where she played the role of a single woman. The Warrens had been married for 15 years. Although outwardly they appeared to be functioning as a family, inwardly they were each quite isolated from the others. Mrs. Warren felt rejected by her daughter, and, in an effort to compensate, at times she attempted to get close to her husband. At other times, she felt also rejected by her husband and attempted to get close to his mother or sister. Essentially, she was always seeking some close relationship which eluded her. The Warrens were like the two porcupines in Schopenhauer's story who attempted to comfort one another but were unable to get close because their spines got in the way, and they always ended up hurting each other.

In both these families, the Johnsons and the Warrens, there are shifting alliances set up by each member of the family which served as protective maneuvers, each person defending himself against feelings of isolation. In both instances there is painful awareness of deep intrafamilial conflicts, accompanied by feelings of helplessness. Each of the parents is struggling with problems greater than the person's capacity to solve them. Unlike the Harrises, each partner came to the marriage unprepared to accept the complexities of an interracial marriage. Instead of taking a realistic view of their situation and attempting to cope with it, they tended to deny that problems would arise.

It is interesting to note that of the three families described, only the Harrises lived in an interracial neighborhood. The other two families lived in all black communities. Mrs. Johnson and Mrs. Warren both attempted to assimilate into the black community, and were not successful. They were not accepted to a degree that would make them comfortable. They, in turn, had many negative feelings toward their black neighbors, and thus tended to view them with suspicion, anticipating rejection. Each woman complained that she could not comfortably invite her white friends and relatives to visit, and therefore she felt apart from both communities. However, neither discussed this feeling with her husband, unlike Mrs. Harris who openly stated that she wanted to live in an interracial neighborhood and maintain relationships with her friends and family.

According to the Johnsons, their marriage functioned on a fairly even keel until they had children. It was then that many of their conflicts came to the surface. For example, when their first child was born and the nurse in the hospital brought the baby to his mother for the first time, she made a mistake and brought to Mrs. Johnson a white baby. This precipitated a series of emotional reactions: the awakening of her own unresolved feelings followed by depression; resentment toward her husband, whom she blamed for the fact that her parents were not there; refusal to nurse her baby at that time; displacement of anger to both her husband and child.

The introduction of a child into a situation such as the one described above often brings about a state of marital disequilibrium from which the couple never fully recovers. They live parallel lives where mutual sharing by all family members is at a minimum. There is often competition for the loyalty of the child who is manipulated by both parents. He is used as a sounding board onto which they project their own insecurities. For example, a father may lecture his son on the history and suffering of the black people. He extracts from the boy declarations of racial loyalty again and again. Actually, the father is attempting to gain his wife's approval through the boy because he is really never sure that he has been unconditionally accepted by her as a man in general, or as a black man in particular. These insecurities stem in many cases from unresolved infantile conflicts. Often the mother has had great difficulties in relating to her own mother and keeps seeking a mother substitute. This type of woman often has not successfully come to terms with many of her own feelings, especially those of racial prejudice, and therefore cannot accept her child's dual racial identity. She may therefore unconsciously seek to alter her child's identity and make him into a white child. If she perceives herself as unsuccessful in accomplishing this, she may begin to feel alienated from her child, and she may act this out to the extent of rejecting and abandoning her child. She may do so in actuality or only emotionally. If the wife does actually abandon the family, the paternal grandmother may step in and assume the role of mother to the child.

The way a child perceives himself depends upon how his parents perceive him. If they are unified in their perception of him, he is more likely to have an integrated sense of self. This is clearly demonstrated in the instance of the Harris family. The child's sense of self was not fragmented. She had a good sense of who she was and what she was. At times she did probe the subject of her identity, but the feedback from her parents was a positive and united one which served to strengthen her identity.

The sense of self is derived from identification with one's parents. As the child grows up, the peer relationships and the relationship with society strengthen and maintain the sense of self. If there is a contradiction between these factors, the child's sense of identity is weakened. This is experienced by the child as uncertainty about himself, his roles, his way of relating to other people. We can refer to this state as identity confusion. The child often asks, "Who am I?" The identity confusion is most acute when one parent tells the child that he is white and the other parent tells him that he is black.

In one interview, the Johnsons were observed having a verbal clash over the children: Mr. Johnson insisted that the children were not half-white, as his wife perceived them, but that they were all-black. His wife shook her head in dismay, unable to comprehend his position. Mr. Johnson tried to substantiate his argument by declaring that society viewed his children as being black, and therefore he felt it necessary to prepare them for a black identity. The mother felt that her husband was negating her very being. Often a racial role assignment is not verbalized so clearly, but it is unconsciously asserted. Mrs. Johnson could even pay lip service to the idea that her children were black, but she would continue to relate to them with a white value system and its expectations. This is very confusing to a child, particularly if he sees the other siblings having a different role assignment, based upon the differences of the skin color. One mother reported how much easier it would be if all her children were of the same skin tone.

Often a clash arises between the child's choice of identification and parental racial identity assignment. This conflict can be diminished, however, if the child is left with one parent, although a residue may continue to persist. For example, a ten-year-old boy, who was being sent to a residential treatment center, was overheard questioning his white mother about his racial identity. He said, "Am I black or white? I want to be a Negro." He also inquired about his father's birth place, though he had not seen his father for many years. Clearly, this child had not escaped the procrustean beds of arbitrary molds.

In other instances child and parent may concur regarding the child's racial identity, but society may not agree with them.

An adolescent girl who had been in treatment said, "My problem is that I am Italian and Irish, but I don't look it." She added hesitantly, "I might be one-eighth Negro." She complained that black boys asked her for dates and that no one understood her. The girl felt discriminated against by both whites and blacks, and that she had no one to turn to. Instead, she turned to compulsive promiscuity in a frantic search for belongingness. Through intensive treatment, she was able to work out her feelings of inner void and despair.

The cry "Who am I?" is frequently heard from children of interracial parents at our treatment center. One bright college student told us, "I don't know who I am." It is perhaps not coincidental that he places such a great premium on learning. At times of identity crisis, the vacillation between two introjected identities in the ego of the child is betrayed by the vacillation of his behavior. In one of our cases for example, an adolescent girl used to come to interviews in two distinct hairstyles. At times she would wear an Afro hairdo and would discuss popular black leaders, music, etc. At other times she would come with her hair straightened and her whole aspect reflecting her white identification. Another example is represented by the young student described earlier, who, after the summer, came to treatment with a deep suntan and described to us the deeper meaning underlying his change in appearance.

An organism cannot tolerate a permanent state of tension. If there is no resolution and integration, there is maladjustment and neurosis, or a fixation and characterological problems, or a giving up in psychosis. A youngster who is unable to integrate his experiences may enter into a state of conflict with his parents (rebellion), or with society (alienation), or with himself (identity crisis). The black-white child is left to his own devices. He is truly representative of a class of one. He cannot be supported by the defenses that the culture provides. He cannot profit from the experiences of his parents and share their defenses since they are the product of a different, homogeneous background and will never be able to experience his position. A black mother, however, can at least protect her child emotionally against racial prejudice, which a white mother is not equipped to do. Recall for instance the case of the Johnsons. Mr. Johnson angrily reproached his wife for not being able to accept the fact that their children were black according to the criteria of society, and needed to be prepared.

What compensatory mechanisms are then available to the child? What real choices are open to him? He may choose to overidentify with one race as a defense against identity diffusion, which might paradoxically lead to an actual loss of identity. Another solution is negative identification, with rejection of one part of identity; for example, de-evaluation of all black attributes. There is also a standstill solution leading to alienation and depersonalization, resulting in final distortion of personality.

[In general, social scientists have popularized the conception of the "marginal man" for people who live between two cultures or two subcultures and who live in boundaries of different economic, religious, ethnic, or racial groups. In actuality, these people belong to none. Some of them are not able to integrate their fragments of cultural values. Others, however, are successful and have reached cultural or political prominence. Some characteristics of these people may be described as self-hate, insecurity, defensiveness, self-pity, isolation, and ambivalence. These characteristics are therefore not unique of black-white children. In this sense, in our present schizoid age with its widespread alienation, we all are "black-white children."

Let us consider now a very expressive description of the black-white child's experience as transcribed from a therapy session of the student we referred to earlier. He came to us for help because of difficulties in school. He said he felt mentally inferior to white students and physically inferior to black students.

"I used to be very polite, very conscious of myself, so conscious of what I had to say next that I wouldn't even listen to what other people had to say . . . I was afraid to get involved with people. If I get involved with people, I might get hurt." He does not like radicals. "They put on a big hustle if I do not agree with them . . . I don't try to convince anybody. . . . Anything that bothers me I try to avoid." He said that he is afraid that he may lose his girl friend. He is afraid to talk too much because "if I committed myself too much I might say too much . . . I hate to generalize. . . . People want to label me." He prefers to talk on the telephone instead of in person. "The telephone protects me. . . . They do not see me. I can hang up any time. I let people win arguments. Sometimes I don't know what to do with myself . . . I have a fear of hearing my own voice, like everybody's listening . . . I get shy. . . . If I would see somebody on the street drop money, I couldn't say anything. . . . Sometimes I feel everybody is out to hurt me physically or mentally." He avoids having sexual relations with his girl friend, who has the same skin color he has, because he respects her. He secretly enjoys sex with a very dark girl. He's aware of his double standard, but is incapable of doing anything about it.

He expresses feelings about his state of mind which he calls an "identity crisis." "I don't know what I am. I search for who I am . . . I blame it on my mother." When asked what is the worst thing that could happen to him, he said, "Not to be able mentally to cope with the situation. . . . In school I was black. I was black because it was politically great to be black. If they called me Spanish, they could. . . . I would be what they wanted me to be. I was moderate, leaning both ways. Yet it bothered me, what my identity was. It depended on with whom I was. Someone once asked my mother what we are. She said, 'People!' My girl friend does not know what to call herself and I don't know what to call myself. Two blind people in a dark room . . . I don't know what she is, and I never ask." He doesn't feel at ease at a white party. Nor does he feel at ease at a black party. He does feel at ease at a party where there are whites and a few blacks.

The black-white child's struggle with himself, his parents, society, and with his past and present elicits our respect, admiration, and compassion. The interracial family is a microcosm of race relations, and should be intensively studied in order to understand many variables—social conflict in general and identity formation in early childhood in particular. These families' successes are our hopes—their failures our warnings.

5

PAUL L. ADAMS, M.D.

Counseling with Interracial Couples and Their Children in the South

In an important humanistic contribution, Dr. Paul L. Adams offers us a philosophy of counseling with interracial couples and their children that comes from long personal experience in the South. Examining such counseling within the cultural context of the South, Dr. Adams considers racism not solely as a state of mind but as an institution and as an ideology. He also considers sexual exploitation and romantic love, and shows to what extent all of these factors affect the role of the counselor and determine the outcome of his work.

It will be clear to the reader that what Dr. Adams has to say about the South applies in many ways to our larger society. The techniques that he examines and evaluates have application in the everyday work of those whose responsibility it is to help biracial parents, wherever they may be located, work out their own problems and those of their children.

SOUTHERN CULTURE AND INTERRACIAL PROBLEMS

Miscegenation—the biological mixing of the genes of two different stocks, breeds, or races—is not a rare case. Especially in the South of the United States, transracial breeding has occurred ever since different ethnic groups encountered each other upon the arrival of the first Europeans. And, in our Southern history, Caucasoid economic exploitation has been attended by Caucasoid sexual exploitation. This is not uniquely Southern, naturally, but it represents an important ingredient of the Southern cultural reality in which all Southerners "live, move and have their being." The fusion of racism and sexual exploitation is a crucial part of Southern culture.

The history of the South shows that both Indians and Africans—even when exploited economically—have been sex partners of Southern whites, with only a modicum of that constricting physical repugnance that Northerners frequently have felt toward nonwhite peoples. Miscegenation is as Southern as sweet potato pie. It is the process that has converted many people, otherwise "black," into brown or "bright." It is, moreover, the process whereby many pass from being socially defined as "black" into being defined as "white." Given the human proclivity for paradox, Southern whites have pronounced the most elaborate denunciations of miscegenation, have outlawed it, adduced Scripture to condemn it, have passed laws to delegitimize it, and at the very same time they have practiced it liberally.

But the mixing of biological stocks represents only a minor part of the story of the interracial sexual contacts that occur in the South. Thanks to truly effective contraceptives, biological mixing has declined, and there has been an increase in nonprocreative heterosexual contacts of every kind, including interracial ones. Furthermore, homosexual contacts between whites and blacks are on the upswing. In one Southern state, early in the 1960's, there occurred a rather extensive, well-documented epidemic of venereal disease among homosexual males. The intricate pattern traced by the transfer and arborization of infections through transracial homosexual contacts made a striking graph. No, Southern lust is no respecter of race, on occasion. Sexual activity across race lines will increase, it would appear, because general sexual taboos are relaxing, and because contraceptive advances promote and enable sexual activity for pleasure, not procreation.

Interracial cohabitation or copulation, of the heterosexual variety, is many times more frequent than is interracial marriage. Marriages across race lines are seldom seen in the South. But the same infrequency holds true for marriages of Jew (or Catholic) with Protestant, or rich with poor. In this chapter comprehensiveness will be sacrificed to relevance, and we will look almost exclusively at marriages of blacks with whites. Black with white is what we mean by "interracial." The South's relative lack of modernity, its slowness in becoming as industrialized and smog-ridden as the remainder of the nation, and its long experience of a racist, "biracial" society, have tended to lead Southern white Anglo-Saxon Protestants to know, sleep with, love, and marry . . . primarily Wasps. In the same way, blacks have copulated principally with blacks, and have married almost exclusively blacks. Endogamy, operating in the final analysis *as an incest equivalent,* is culturally reinforced by Jew and Gentile, and by black and white in the United States.

The function of endogamy, after all is said and done, is to create an equilibrium, as nondynamic as possible, wherein a man, being dissuaded from marrying his biological sister, is urged to marry the *cultural* cognate of precisely his sister.

Only in the year 1967, more than a century after the Civil War, did the Supreme Court of the United States definitively strike down laws prohibiting marriage between blacks and whites. The 1967 decision of the Supreme Court was unanimous, and that tended to compensate, perhaps, for the fact that the decision had been given so belatedly. At the time of the Supreme Court's decision there were still sixteen states which were holding out in proscribing miscegenation, meaning *marriage* of white and black, and as late as 1971, several states kept on "enforcing" the old Black Codes forbidding racial intermarriage until a formal legal action would challenge the old state law. This is states' rights to the bitter end. The United States has had a lot of experience with "deliberate speed," and deliberate foot dragging, where racial equality is the issue.

In Southern racist society, interracial humanism seems to lie dormant in most of daily life's activities—the reality systems that engage people throughout their purposive waking lives. Not so, when one knows the psychiatric picture of some of the South after dark, in the South that sleeps and dreams. At night, there is an odd integration. Black men dream lustfully of white women, and white men dream erotically of black women. Also, white women dream of black men, and black women dream of white men. One's own wild and savage sexuality is carried in dreams as *the other race, the other sex.* Those are the vicissitudes of racism, eroding its way into the inner lives of racists, both black and white. The dreaded fantasied sexual excesses of both blacks and whites are projected in dreams as *not me but them*—bad, unrestrained, perverse, and enticingly despicable overall.

The culture of the South provides the setting for both maddening and healing. It provides both the problems and the solutions. The part of the culture which psychiatrists and counselors contend with is the personal and familial version, the individual's perspective as mediated through his family of origin. It is this arena, the family sphere, that we will look at. For a biracial pair it is enough at the beginning to be able to cope with their two families. Later, they might be able to afford a fuller view of the entire culture. Anyway, racism in its more abstract forms takes on clearer meaning when one approaches it from the base of how racism operated in one's own small family of origin. I will attempt in the following pages to document the ways in which Southern culture affects live people—the men, women, and children of interracial marriages—by shaping their lives and fortunes, not in the abstract but within familial relationships.

COUNSELING WITH BIRACIAL COUPLES

Northern white liberals in particular, view the South as extraordinarily repressive. And when white Northerners move south, they enter into a classical know-nothing, do-nothing stance with respect to black people. My own conclusion is that the biggest cowards are Northern liberals transplanted to the South. They are among the most "unnatural" and "uptight" people when they are thrown with either blacks or interracial couples containing one black member. They are edgy about what they can and cannot do. In contrast, Southern white conservatives are frequently much more accepting of interracial pairs. Sifting out the essences from all the fears and prejudices is not an easy matter.

In my own private life as a Southerner I have known perhaps an unusually large number of interracial couples. As a psychiatrist I have worked with only a small group, although, as every clinician might discover, over the years the cases will add up to dozens. In the South, Orientals and Indians and blacks are all married to whites, and in increasing numbers. In the past two decades, a large number of Southern white males have acquired Japanese brides. Still, the most frequent intermarriage seen by a psychiatrist is that involving a white Jew and a white non-Jew, a union fraught with racism even if it is not *interracial* in any rational sense of the term. It is, however, the marriage of white with black that really sets the South on edge.

If a psychiatrist or other counselor in the South were to seek out the couples who are at highest risk, who will most likely develop mental symptoms, he should look not among interracial couples but, instead, among the average endogamous uniracial pairs. The latter are the people who make up counselors' clientele. The reasons for this are many, but only a few of them will be dealt with in this discussion. The undeniable fact is that the average white or the average black uniracial married couple is the one most likely to apply to the marriage counselor for help, and to go back later, and to spread the word to friends and relatives. Counseling in actual practice is a middle class service, and the conformists go for it most enthusiastically.

A biracial couple is more likely to be marginal with respect to the Establishment, including the marriage counseling Establishment. A biracial couple has a wider empathy than most counselors have. Moreover, an interracial pair, even if neurotically conflicted, is more prone to have made commitments that defy convention more fully than the person who readily turns to a bourgeois counselor for help. A biracial couple is "on to" the marriage counselor and has made strides in seeing through conventions that most marriage counselors have never even imagined.

The interracial couple usually senses that people transcend stereotypes and that, even if black is beautiful, *all* blacks are not always personally attractive or lovable. Comforting, although illusory, generalizations are not very appropriate for the biracially wed. Interracial couples appear to furnish a happy reminder that all deviance is not madness: some kinds of nonconformity can be wholesome and creative.

The typical counselor is conventional, oriented toward "social truths," cautiously conformist, and eager to "help" people to fit into societal norms. The run-of-the-mill counselor is indeed square, steeped in illusion, and obsessed with making man fit the Sabbath, not the Sabbath fit man. For these counselors therapy is not a liberating change, but only a shrewd cop-out training course. Such counseling, far from being disalienting, is itself alienated and conducive to a more profound alienation. Interracial couples wisely give wide berth to such counselors. This kind of counselor converts all differences into *deficiencies.* Consequently, difference itself is never praised, and the world—uniracial and unidimensional—is pasted up in the paper-thin image of . . . the counselor.

There are five human roles for which a biracial pair might seek professional help: *premarital, marital, prenatal, preadoptive,* and *parental.* Stresses and strains that in themselves have little to do with the racial factor can drive an interracial couple to get professional counsel. Also, some couples may seek help for problems related to the respective families of origin—"his folks" and "her folks." These are often "racial" problems in important ways. "Who wants his daughter (or son) to marry a nigger?" is, after all, a family-related question. If there were only one area in which marital counseling could ever be called for, it would be in helping the two members of a biracial marital pair to understand how their respective families of origin had helped to shape their values and attitudes, and trained them for the new marriage. This puts us into the heart of premarital counseling with biracial couples.

PREMARITAL COUNSELING

Premarital counseling has *not* been made available for all young people, although that was the forecast often made thirty or forty years ago. Premarriage counseling is shunned by the majority of young people in the United States, north or south, and regardless of color. That there was more premarital counseling twenty years ago than there is today does not pertain to race so much as to sexuality. In the past, there were problems about premarital chastity and sex for fun, and those were the burning issues requiring counseling. Nowadays, the sexual hangups seem to have diminished and rarely does a young couple—interracial or not—check in wondering about sexual matters.

Premarital counseling could be helpful to an interracial couple who expect to live on romantic love. If a young biracial couple appeared, contemplating a marriage that was grounded exclusively on romantic love, I would regard them as needing premarital counseling, and even discouragement. But my own views are against the romantic grain, and for that reason should perhaps be made more explicit.

The big problem here is that romantic love is the only popular warrant, the only acceptable ideological support, given for interracial marriage. The end result is that "romantic delusions" are in the popular mind the only justification for interracial marriage: if they don't fall head over heels in love, then why don't they stick to their own kind? For the man on the street it is only a deep irrational "love that conquers all" that can give any justification to an interracial marriage. In the writings of marriage counselors, too, the pieties of romantic love are often set forth as the only argument in support of biracial marriage. The writers appear to consider the biracial marriage as something strange and fantastic, justifiable only by thoughts and words that are equally extravagant, emotional, and antirational. A successful marriage based exclusively upon romance is an unlikely probability of which the interracial pair really ought to be forewarned. Marriage requires a better love than the romantic variety.

If a young biracial couple did want to obtain counseling concerning the racial aspects of their hopes and doubts, the average marriage counselor in the southern United States might take up a highly cautious or outrightly opposing line. An undue sensitivity to racist ideology drives the ordinary marriage counselor to warn a biracial prospective couple of many racially based hazards and obstacles to their happiness. In the service of this sensitivity, the many racist clichés are hauled out: What are you trying to prove? Don't you want to try to find one of your own kind for a mate? But what will it mean to your children? Do you realize that minority groups are also very much opposed to intermarriage nowadays? The weighty stupidity of centuries lies in these questions, and it is a tribute to rebellious, energetic young biracial lovers that they show it all up as irrationality and blather. They have the courage to say no to both the culture and the Cult of Adapatation.

Indeed, it *is* more challenging to dare to marry someone outside of one's own subculture, but it does not automatically doom one to an incessant agony. To my personal knowledge, biracial couples, largely without premarital counseling, do find apartments and homes and friendly acquaintances, they even raise healthy children, and ultimately—banking in the interim on the higher acceptance by nonwhites—"make their peace" with their Caucasoid as well as non-white families of origin. For the student of intermarriage, it is of some interest that biracial couples exert a humanizing and "radicalizing" influence on both of their families of origin. The parents do come around, and sometimes attest to finding their lives enriched as a consequence.

Nonetheless, the families of origin (his and hers) are not fully decisive factors for middle-class couples who are planning a romantic marriage and seeking counseling. For working-class families the orig-inal families *are* much more decisive, but counseling is both most useful and least available for working-class persons. It is an unhappy example of how helping resources are improperly allocated in the United States.

MARITAL COUNSELING

If during the premarital stage there has not been an understanding of diversity and an acceptance of realistic differences in the two original families' styles, then problems will ensue during the mar-riage. For some of these problems the interracial couple may seek counseling. In my experience, the most helpful counseling focus is on family patterns and styles, even in newly wed couples. It has been jokingly asserted that race, politics, religion, and sexual appetites are not at the heart and soul of a good marriage, insofar as what really counts is the divergence of tastes in matters such as garlic in food, bedroom temperature, and whether one of the pair is an inordinately early riser! Little things make and break even interracial marriages. The great philosophical and social debates seem to take second place to these petty, practical concerns of daily living.

The peculiar thing about biracial couples is that they are alerted and ready to make all of these practical discussions refer in some way to *the racial angle.* Given a society of institutionalized racism, this race-conscious pattern of argumentation lies close at hand and keeps marital conflict hot and heavy. The Jewish spouse, or the non-Jewish one, will pull out the ace up his sleeve: antisemitism or antigentilism, prejudice or counterprejudice. The black spouse finds it both an easy and a devastating weapon to condemn his white wife as not only white but antiblack in her very bones. The foolish equation becomes "to disagree with me = to hate my race." Marriage counseling can be relevant here.

Romantic love notions presume that only one mate is suitable. Counselors often presume that, aside from race differences, anyone can be happily married to anyone else. Psychodynamic theory in particular does not jibe well with ideas of romantic love. The supposition of depth psychology is that neurotic fantasies outweight realities in the causation of human problems, and that by some form of therapy or counseling the fantasies will be squared off against reality. That kind of assumption allows the counselor to proceed in helping the client to clear up the neurotic and to accept the real, and to put Ego where Id used to be. The idea that realism and rationality have an important place in a healthy life is quite sound, but we know nowadays that "reality problems" can be formidable, even overpowering, in the form of war, discrimination, poverty, and alienation. All problems are not "just in our minds."

In marriage as in any strong heterosexual relationship, irrespective of its legality, there are two principles that an interracial couple will observe if the relationship is to be a good one. First of all, *each has no desire to change the partner;* each accepts the other without having the good American's preoccupations with control, domination, and possession. Both are accepting. They endorse each other. Neither desires to convert or to reform the other, and each can celebrate the lovable humanity that resides in diversity as embodied in the other. Obviously, there is no wish to change the other's religion or politics. This can be done without the silly romantic fervor that quite often peaks into mutual jealousy, suspicion, and the end of love.

A second criterion for the interracial couple, as indeed for all couples, is that *each sees something of himself in the other.* For the interracial couple, this says that the white spouse has seen himself or herself as the "wicked, sloppy, malicious, instinctual, biological-sexual-sensual-genital-nigger." These words are from Frantz Fanon, a black psychiatrist who was married to a white woman. For the part of the nonwhite spouse, there must be some recognition of whatever is "honky-whitey-ofay-Simon Legree-racist" in himself or herself.

With empathy and flexibility, an interracial pair can build a good marriage—in which their respective childhoods are both integrated and transcended.

PRENATAL COUNSELING

Even if a successful marriage has been established before pregnancy occurs, there still may arise some emotional and practical disturbances at the time of the first pregnancy. The pregnant woman may experience a recrudescence of archaic, truly infantile prejudices that concern race. When motherhood impends, there is a harking back to the family of origin. A revival of old racist worries and obsessions might come "from the blue" to a young woman who sees herself as free from racism. She might suddenly feel that if her baby's complexion is "too dark," she will hate it. Shading of color will suddenly loom up as being very important. The primiparous white woman might become obsessively concerned about the facial prospects ahead of her unborn child, and she might elect an abortion instead of a pregnancy: "Do I have a right to bring a child onto this scene?" "I accept being an interracial marriage partner, but I cannot accept being an interracial parent." We could assume that her black husband will keep her attuned to all the racist overtones of her reluctance, and that the counselor can thus be free to focus more upon her legitimate rights to her own body, including her womb.

On the other hand, out of the interchange set off by pregnancy there can come newer understandings and a keener respect for values of all sorts. The pregnancy can become a time of new challenges, and of new learnings, that enrich both the marriage relationship and the personal lives of the biracial spouses.

If the young couple do decide to go on with the pregnancy, they may benefit from good general medical advice as well as from marital counseling. The latter is occasioned, in my experience, by a recurrent cathexis of one's own parents when one's own parenthood is in process. For the interracial pair, any return to their families of origin is racially charged.

A cosmic concern arises fleetingly even in the most blasé of young couples who face having a baby. It looks as if they wanted to square away their stand toward the generations preceding them at the very time in life when their own generativity is being called to fruition. The recurrence of attention to their own parents gives them the wrap-up needed to enhance their own parenthood. Especially the mother-to-be must come to some "tenable truce" with her own mother, if she can be so very lucky, even if mother and daughter have lived theretofore in considerable opposition and animosity. A young woman needs to come to some decent terms with her own mother, even if her mother has said nasty things about the interracial marriage.

PREADOPTIVE COUNSELING

A disproportionately large number of black babies are available for adoption in the United States. It appears that black-white couples will increasingly adopt, rather than deliver, black children. There is no big problem if the parents desire to adopt a black baby—which is what their own natural child would be—but the rub comes if for some reason they choose to adopt a white or Oriental child.

Many adoption agencies make it difficult for any "mixing" of race and religion to occur during adoption. In fact, ethnocentrism became so profound in one instance known to me personally that an agency sought for a baby whose natural parents had both been Southern Jews, adoptive parents who also were Southern Jews! In a culture that tries diligently to preserve "Jewish purity," we can guess what lengths will be covered when it comes to color matchings.

The marriage counselor can help an interracial couple in all the decisions they have to make concerning the adoption. The counselor can also assist the prospective interracial parents to find adoption resources that will meet their particular needs.

PARENTAL COUNSELING

When biracial couples seek counseling concerning problems with their children, or problems in being parents, generally they are concerned with problems that pertain much more to their parental roles than to their special racial backgrounds. By this time in their lives their real difficulty is more likely to be getting some pleasure from parenthood, and the concern over race becomes secondary.

The enjoyment of parenthood is not something one prepares for in formal courses. But courses are hardly needed when that most efficient training school, the original family, exists. All the varied modes of therapy, counseling, and casework seem pale compared to the informal training derived from living in infancy in a family. Interaction of parent and child is the most humanizing of interactions for both child and parent. The child learns how to be a child and how to prepare for parenthood; the parent learns how to be a parent *for real* and at the same time reexperiences his own childhood. These same themes of growth, caring, and identification characterize the biracial as well as the uniracial family, in the South as well as in the North. Wherever racism is most rampant, the manmade suffering is greatest for the parent and for the child in an interracial family.

Since parental counseling often accompanies child counseling or child therapy, I will have occasion to return to the interracial parents when I discuss counseling with the children of interracial marriages.

HELPING THE CHILDREN OF INTERRACIAL COUPLES

In the social order of the United States, children of one black parent are regarded as black. Moreover, they almost always end up by regarding themselves as black. This is the result of a system whereby any known or asserted blackness leads to one's being considered as a black person. But children with one white and one black parent do not accept this system automatically. The learning of the culture, and of its racist canons, develops over a span of time in one's childhood, and is characterized by the variations of individual idiosyncracy against the more stable backdrop of the cultural patterns. The culture may call a female child black because her father is partially black, but the little girl may have strong identifications with her mother's whiteness. Even if she eventually "adapts," it will take time. The inner life has riches which the folkways may not hold, and may even disallow.

My experience with the children of Southern biracial couples leads me to the conviction that the children of one black and one white parent act and think more like Southern black than like Southern white children. To carry the point one step further, I do feel that the children of these interracial couples have a broader perspective than the mass of either white or black children. They are, it might be said, like very keenly imaginative and perceptive black children in their world view, but more astute socially, more clever than either the average black or the average white child. Perhaps there is something about the "unhappy mulatto" condition that has greater promise than the pathos of conventional myth would have it. To know from one's birth and to grow up with parents who have broken some conventions and who have not observed the taboos may conceivably give one some advantages for living in the world of today.

PRESCHOOL CHILDREN

A child of any color who is wanted by his mother, and who is considered by his mother as worthwhile, good, and full of promise, will develop a favorable self-concept. If the mother has reservations, doubts, and hatreds for either herself or her baby, the child will lack a feeling of confidence and trust. The child will sense the maternal attitude of acceptance or rejection by his "reading" of the mother's muscular tone, vocal tension, breathing, and heart rate. If the mother, black or white, resents her baby's skin color—as do many black and white mothers who have been enculturated in racism—the baby will sense that something is amiss, and he will learn that his mother is "color struck." This threatens the security of the mother-child relationship and the child's own favorable self-esteem.

Basic self-esteem or self-regard, whether favorable or unfavorable, is firmly laid down by 18–24 months of age. Also one's awareness of his sex (gender) is firmly implanted by that age. The child with one or both black parents has incorporated the general evaluations (attitudes) of his mother concerning skin color. Initially, the child has a race awareness that is generic rather than racial, fused to the general self-regarding sentiments. If lucky, he feels wanted, he feels that he is a "good egg."

By age three, the child is aware of color differences within his own family, and by age four or five, he will talk to others (including a psychiatrist) about skin color and will display color preferences with dolls as well as with boys and girls. Even by age five or six, the child will not know all of the race cues—and will not converse with complete coherence, accuracy, or consistency about race. Nonetheless, the counselor need not shy away from talk of race. For example, in an interview between a four-year-old boy with a black mother and a white father, and a counselor:

BOY: Your skin's not black.

COUNSELOR: That's right. It's not black as yours is.

BOY: Do you think my skin is beautiful?

COUNSELOR: I think your skin is very beautiful. What do you think?

BOY: You think black is beautiful?

Enculturation has occurred here, not only for some concern about color but also for a specific vogue in terminology!

ELEMENTARY SCHOOL CHILDREN

While older children are more reticent, or "discreet," about their interracial families, they are certainly wiser than preschool children. Their erudition on matters racial will become very obvious as they loosen up in a relationship with a counselor.

The children of interfaith marriages, by contrast, talk with relative ease and apparent involvement about Jew and non-Jew. It is quite routine for these children to inquire if the counselor is a Jew, and only silliness can justify not answering first, then, later, asking questions. Perhaps this is only one man's opinion.

As the children of interracial couples progress through elementary school, they "blacken" apace with their socialization in the Negro community, where their parents usually find a haven. Also their age-mates of all colors are ossifying in all of their racial stereotypes. Peers are becoming increasingly important as the children get older.

I forecast that within the next twenty years it will be easier for the children of interracial marriages to find acceptance, as do their parents, among both blacks and whites. Some stirring prospects for genuine integration exist in the South—in schools and other public facilities and perhaps, after a century or more, *even* in churches and synagogues! *Northern* racism probably affords a grimmer forecast.

ADOLESCENTS

The teenager from an interracial family has the problems that his compeers have in the South, plus some especially poignant twists to the task of finding his identity as an adult, that originate in a biracial family in a racist and segregated society.

Even in interracial families whose growing children were spared the grosser impacts of discrimination, adolescents may present unusually serious difficulties. This, of course, is the very same story in uniracial families—the adolescents surprise everyone, themselves also.

Even adolescents who have been spared discrimination in their earlier years, begin to feel it acutely when they buck up against the social processes of dating and assortative mating. The closenesses in interpersonal relations are reshuffled. Latent racism in one's acquaintances comes to the fore, and old friends reject the black. In addition, ordinary personal slights without racial meaning are given a racial slant. The "protective paranoia" of minority status is called upon for protection.

Pathetically, adolescents from interracial families may become antiblack, in much the same manner that adolescents from interfaith families may become antisemitic, and those from liberal families may become Nazis. The adolescent's yearning to be rid of subjugation *is* pathetic . . . if one has none of the militancy and apparatus needed to get the job done. In this regard, the civil rights and Black Power movements have been extremely wholesome from a psychiatric standpoint.

In the midst of his strong, but ambivalent, emotions the adolescent from a biracial family can "let his parents have it" with an expertness that defies description. The adolescent plays "poor, pitiful mulatto," "lynch the black parent," and "see how I can make you sorry." His gamesmanship is fantastic. The counselor is not spared the put-on and gross-out either.

The counselor stands fairly secure, in my experience, when he can genuinely convey to the teenager that he approves of the adolescent's interracial family, even though he may not approve of *everything* about the adolescent's parents. Ultimately, acceptance of self coincides with a wordly-wise acceptance of the interracial parents.

The adolescent is helped best by a counselor who explores "the racial thing," who accepts the "black" adolescent unreservedly, and who is willing to say, "O.K., now, *other than the race thing* you have some problems I might help with."

SUMMARY

Racism is not just a state of mind that exists in people's thoughts only. Racism in the South is not solely a matter of prejudices and mental phenomena. Instead, racism is also a way of life, things that masters did to slaves and that whites do to blacks. It is institutionalized—in work, in schools, in politics, in social esteem and honor, in property and economic advantages, and even in recreation and religion. Racism operates twenty-four hours a day, and it "does in" black people for the advantage of certain white people. One of the corollaries of racism is an ideology against biracial marriages.

To understand the sociopsychiatric climate of the contemporary South, the student must understand racism, and sexism, and romantic love. Just as racism "does in" blacks, sexism "does in" women, and romance "does in" a rational, loving family system. It is in early life, in one's original family, that most racism is enculturated for the Southerner. It is also in that time and place that most counselors learned their racist thoughts and deeds.

Counseling with interracial couples and their children in the South occurs in a cognitive and political mode that opposes racism, sexism, and the romantic fallacy. If the counselor is not himself dominated and paralyzed by socioneurotic distortion, or "false consciousness," he can be of some assistance to interracial pairs premaritally, or when marriage problems arise—especially with problems concerning adoption and rearing of children. In addition, the non-alienated counselor can help the growing children of black-white and Jew-Gentile couples. No meaningful work—South or North—is done by rote, or very easily, or with much popular acclaim. Meaningful work is both scientifically sound and existentially sound. It demands much, and the "popular" rewards are few. But if counseling, or education, or therapy can engage our reason and our loving commitments, we cannot require more from our work lives.

6

WARREN D. TENHOUTEN, Ph.D.

Race and Family Power Structure: A Critical Analysis of the Black Matriarchy Thesis

Central to much U. S. Government planning for the black community has been The Negro Family: The Case for National Action, *a federal publication whose principal author was Daniel Patrick Moynihan. It is precisely this report's group of formulations, and the conclusions based on them, that the chapter by Dr. Warren D. TenHouten critically examines and evaluates.*

TenHouten first analyzes the so-called Moynihan thesis— that at the heart of the deterioration of black society is the deterioration of the Negro family, seen as highly unstable and with the wife in the dominant role. He then undertakes an important and useful empirical study of black and white families to test the validity of the Moynihan thesis.

Professor TenHouten concludes, on the basis of his study, that his data do not support the measures of family disorganization of the black family indicated by the Moynihan Report —illegitimacy rates, female-headed families, and unemployment—and he seriously questions their validity as indicators of a "black family pathology."

The goal of his inquiry is to invite a fresh and helpful look at one of the dominant ideas on which much public policy has been based.

IT IS A widely held view that there are pronounced differences in the structures of black and white families in the United States. The white family is seen as patriarchal, with the wife subdominant to the husband, or egalitarian, with the husband and wife exercising equal power. The black family is viewed as matriarchal, the wife being the dominant and stable member, and the husband subdominant. This stereotype of the black family is held by numerous social scientists and social planners and has been given wide exposure in mass media and nontechnical publications.

In the great migration of blacks from the South to the urban North during the early decades of this century, the maternal family was viewed by Frazier as unable to cope with an urban environment, becoming dependent on charity, and having its children run amuck —with sons joining delinquent gangs and daughters bearing illegitimate children (7, 8).

Explanations offered for the development of such pathological black families are *historical* and *socioeconomic.* The historical argument describes the black female as traditionally the most permanent and dependable member of black society. Burgess and Locke (6, p. 62), in a typical statement from a textbook on the American family, write:

This research was supported by an NIMH Grant, HD–02405–02, and an OEO Contract, B99–4891. Computing assistance was obtained from the Health Science Computing Facility at UCLA, sponsored by NIH Grant FR-3. The author is indebted to Diane Dimperio of UCLA for her contributions to the sampling design and field procedures. A more elaborate statement of this research is presented in "The Black Family: Myth and Reality," *Psychiatry* 33 (1970):145–173.

Under slavery the mother remained the important figure in the family. The affectional relations of mother and child developed deep and permanent attachment. Frequently, also, the father was a member of the family group, but often the relationship was casual and easily broken. . . . Then, too, Negro husbands were sold more often. These and other factors contributed to the development of a matricentric form of the family during slavery.

In modern urban society the hypothesized subdominance of the black husband to the wife is attributed to economic status. The female in the black home has a better chance to find work than does her husband, who is at an extreme disadvantage in economic competition. Since the husband is defined as having low economic "value" in society relative to his wife, the black woman has greater control of economic resources (money, economic security, and occupational status), and brings more resources *into* the family unit.As a result of the wife's contribution to the family and the husband's lack of contribution—so the argument goes— the wife wields *power* in the family and plays the dominant role. Rainwater, in elaborating this argument, writes that in such a circumstance the husband (and the wife) may "turn to others," and the husband is more apt to drink and become involved with his peers at the family's expense (20, p. 192). The result of this behavior is seen as desertion and divorce.

The stereotype of the female-dominated (matriarchal) black family was given attention by a 1965 U.S. Government publication, *The Negro Family: The Case for National Action*, whose major author is D. P. Moynihan, and which is widely known as the Moynihan Report. His description of the black family draws on both "causal" arguments—the supposed historical tradition of matriarchy, and the economic dependence of black males. Moynihan's contention is that:

At the heart of the deterioration of the fabric of Negro society is the deterioration of the Negro family.

The white family has achieved a high degree of stability and is maintaining that stability.

By contrast, the family structure of lower-class Negroes is highly unstable, and in many centers is approaching complete breakdown. [15, p. 5]

He adds that:

> . . . the Negro community has been forced into a matriarchal
> structure which, because it is so out of line with the rest of Ameri-
> can society, seriously retards the progress of the group as a whole,
> and imposes a crushing burden on the Negro male. [15, p. 29]

Moynihan's position thus reiterates Frazier's conceptualization
of the maternal family in the black community. But it also implies
that the black family's adverse position has become *self-sustaining*
by its own internal dynamics of *family role deviancy.* Parker and
Kleiner state that Moynihan's writings carry such an implication (18,
p. 500ff.), and cite the following statement:

> The cumulative results of unemployment and low income, and
> probably also of excessive dependence upon the income of women,
> has produced an unmistakable crisis in the Negro family, and raises
> the serious question of whether this crisis is beginning to create
> conditions which tend to reinforce the cycle that produced it in the
> first instance. [16, p. 147]

Parker and Kleiner conclude that there are indeed problems in
the black family, but that these problems appear to be created and
maintained not by a family structure that deviates from white "normality," but by social and personal consequences of unemployment
and discrimination. As a result of being unable to attain success in an
economic system largely controlled by whites, blacks may be apt to
feel that they are not successful in family role performance (18,
p. 507).

The political consequences of this dispute about black family
pathology are obvious. If the Moynihan thesis is valid, then it may
not be possible to "help" the black community through changing
institutional and informal racism in *white* society; it would instead
be necessary to intervene directly in the family in *black* society.
That is, if black families are pathological because of their deviant
organization, then a rationale would exist for intervention in the
black family. If, however, black families are not pathologically
matriarchal and disorganized, then no such rationale exists, and
the problem is racism in white society. To a large extent, the
Moynihan thesis constitutes policy, and many U.S. Government
programs are oriented to rehabilitating the black family: Aid to
Dependent Children, Head Start, and Day Care Centers are examples. Certainly the efficacy of such programs in combatting
poverty depends on the validity of the assumption of black family

pathology. It is the purpose of this chapter to evaluate critically the Moynihan thesis.

THE BLACK MATRIARCHY THESIS: AN EVALUATION

The Moynihan thesis can be evaluated both as an *analytic concept* and as an *empirical generalization*. First, there exists some lack of clarity about the meaning of matriarchy. A family can be defined as matriarchal if the wife is dominant and the husband subdominant. The wife can dominate either the husband-wife (conjugal) relationship, or the parent-child relationship. Conjugal matriarchy would mean that the wife is dominant and the husband subdominant in their relations with each other. Parental matriarchy would mean that the wife plays a dominant role in parent-child relations (control and child rearing). It may be that conjugal matriarchy exists in black families, but that parental matriarchy does not, or the obverse could be the case. And it could be the case that black families are characterized by neither conjugal nor parental matriarchy.

Female dominance in black families is seen as pathological by Moynihan *because* it differs from the male dominance of the white and middle-class black family. The inference that such deviance from the more frequent type is pathological is expressed explicitly by Moynihan in his statement that matriarchal structure retards the progress of blacks "because it is so out of line with the rest of American society" (15, p. 29). The *causal* connection between the plight of black communities and the assumed matriarchy is not explained: certainly it cannot be assumed to be the case.

There are other factors related to the thesis of matriarchy which must be considered in any empirical evaluation. Differences between blacks and whites may reflect differences in socioeconomic level (roughly, "lower-class" as contrasted with "middle-class") as much as or more than race. Thus, social class level represents an important *specification* of the thesis of matriarchy in the black family. Frazier claims that lower-class black families are matriarchal. Moynihan's view of the black family is consistent with this opinion. He is explicit in stating that the deterioration of the black family is most intense in lower-class black families . He contends that the family structure of lower-class black families is highly unstable and that in many urban centers it is approaching complete breakdown.

He feels at the same time that the middle-class black family "is steadily growing stronger and more successful" and "puts a higher premium on family stability and the conserving of family resources than does the white middle class family" (15, pp. 5-6). Since blacks are disproportionately represented in the lower strata of society, it follows from the specified thesis that, for an overall black-white comparison, black families are more unstable and more matriarchal than white families.

As a final analytic comment, female dominance in *any* family relationship cannot be *assumed* to be disadvantageous for the particular group to which it refers. Since groups differ in their relations to the economy and to society, it may be that differing family patterns are appropriate to different social contexts.

The Moynihan thesis can also be evaluated as an empirical generalization. In the following section, measures of family "instability" and "pathology" used in the report are critically examined. The variables to be considered are illegitimacy rates, percentages of female-headed families, and unemployment rates.*

ILLEGITIMACY RATES

Illegitimacy rates can be defined in a number of ways. In the Moynihan Report, illegitimacy rates are defined as *1000 times the ratio of illegitimate births to all live births.* Moynihan uses these rates as measures of family pathology. This interpretation can be questioned on a number of grounds: the statistical properties of the data, including the definition of illegitimacy; the substantive explanation of illegitimate births; the relevance of data on illegitimacy for the measurement of family pathology; and the lack of control of the variable family socioeconomic status.

The illegitimacy rates in 1940 were, by Moynihan's definition, 20 for whites and 168 for nonwhites. (Since over 90 percent of nonwhites in the United States are blacks, the nonwhite rates are used to estimate the black rates.) By 1963, the rates for whites had increased to 31, and the rates for nonwhites to 236. Thus there has been an increase in both groups. As Moynihan observes, the total increase for whites is 11, as compared to 68 for nonwhites. But these

---

*Moynihan also employs statistics on participation in the Aid to Dependent Children program, failure to pass armed forces mental tests, delinquency rates, and crime to describe the "tangle of pathology" in the black community.

increases can be given a second interpretation, which takes into account the 1940 base figures. As a proportion of this base, the rate has increased 55 percent among whites, as compared to 40 percent among blacks. The nonwhite figure rises more rapidly in absolute terms in part because its initial level is higher.

Thus, the claim that black families are *increasingly* disorganized in comparison to white families is supported if the absolute increase is used as the measure of family disorganization. But if the ratio of the later rate to the earlier rate is used, the data show that white families may be increasingly disorganized in comparison to black families.

In addition, there are two difficulties with the definition of illegitimacy used in the Moynihan Report, both of which create biases toward higher rates for nonwhites. First, black women have absolutely higher birth rates, whether married or not. Second, the proportion of women who are unmarried and of child-bearing age (15 through 44) is higher for blacks than for whites. If the illegitimacy rate is defined as *1000 times the number of illegitimate births per thousand unmarried women 15–44 years of age*, (26, p. 447) illegitimacy is related to the population of women *at risk*, and non-white-white comparisons are more meaningful. By this measure the 1940 rates were 36 for nonwhites and 3.6 for whites, a nonwhite-white ratio of 10 to 1. This ratio increased until 1950, at which time it was 12 to 1. But since 1950 the ratio of nonwhite to white illegitimacy rates has declined, so that by 1960 the rates were non-whites 92 and whites 12, a ratio of less than 8 to 1 (26, p. 447). *If these rates could be defined as valid measures of family pathology, one would conclude that the white family is becoming more pathological and the black family less pathological.*

There is some basis for believing that illegitimate black births are more apt to be recorded as such than are illegitimate births for whites. Ventura points out that ". . . it is probable . . . that variations in reporting accuracy exist among different segments of the population. For example, it is likely that women in higher socioeconomic groups have more opportunity to under-report the incidence of illegitimate births" (26, p. 446). Since blacks are less apt to have high socioeconomic status than are whites, this socioeconomic effect also leads to more probable reporting of black illegitimate births as opposed to white illegitimate births. Thus the data that *are* available are of questionable quality; and (as of 1966) there are no data from 16 states and 30 percent of the population.

In considering other possible explanations of the illegitimacy rates, one finds that there are no reliable data indicating that unmarried black women have more active sex lives than do unmarried white women: there is no evidence of a "morality gap" between the black and the white community. Since nonmarital sex is frequent in both groups, any difference in illegitimacy may depend on the greater access to birth control by white women (and men). Whites are more apt to know what birth control *is*, are better able to afford and use it,* and have greater access to abortion as a means of birth control. It is this writer's opinion that much of the race difference in illegitimacy results from this factor, and that the decline in nonwhite illegitimacy will be greater as birth control becomes more available in the black community.

The higher rate of illegitimacy reported in the black community may also reflect the greater extent to which illegitimate black babies are incorporated into the family unit, rather than being expelled and concealed from the family and community. Black people in the United States are apparently far more accepting of illegitimate children and are more apt to care for them than whites. Perhaps it is a *pathology of white values* that lowers the frequency of illegitimate births accepted as members of the family. At any rate, there is an ethnocentric bias in regarding black acceptance of illegitimate babies as pathological because this is not done in the white family and deviates from white "normality."

The word "legitimate," after all, means only that a certificate of legitimation of a birth is registered with some municipal officer (usually for a fixed fee). This, per se, says nothing about a commitment to take responsibility for, and care for, and express loyalty to a child. In the black family there are norms that the *entire* family will take responsibility for a child. In the white community, this is somewhat less apt to be the case if a child is illegitimate.

Ventura indicates that socioeconomic level is itself an important factor contributing to nonwhite-white differences in illegitimacy (26,

---

*Ventura (26, p. 448) uses research by Whelpton, Campbell and Patterson (27) to conclude that is is likely that white couples involved in premarital sex relations are more apt to use contraceptives than are black couples.

p. 448). She writes: "It is likely that if it were possible to control for social class, much of the difference between the two groups would disappear." That is, blacks are more apt to be in a lower class than whites, lower-class people are more apt to have illegitimate children, and these factors, per se, may constitute an explanation for the higher illegitimacy rates in the black group. The data on illegitimacy rates collected before 1968 contain no information on the parents' socioeconomic status. Thus, until the later data are analyzed, there is no way to know that black-white differences are not a consequence of social class membership. A limited amount of data suggests that much of the difference in illegitimacy rates between blacks and whites disappears in comparisons within the same social class levels. Pakter *et al.* (17), for example, find the illegitimacy rates of blacks to be 38 in Central Harlem (poor black) but only 9 in Pelham Bay (nonpoor black). Herzog states that comparisons between poor and nonpoor census tracts show illegitimacy rates to be higher in poorer tracts (12).

For all these reasons, data on illegitimacy are inappropriate for testing the Moynihan thesis of pathology among lower-class blacks.

FEMALE-HEADED FAMILIES

The percentage of women with husbands absent has been stable among whites from 1950 to 1960, but has increased somewhat for blacks. Among women of child-bearing age, in the decade from 1950 to 1960, the percentages of female-headed homes for nonwhites and whites, respectively are 33 and 8 for urban areas, 15 and 6 for rural nonfarm areas, and 10 and 3 for rural farm areas. Overall, the 1960 percentages are nonwhite families 21 and white families 9 (15, p. 11). Thus in both urban and rural areas, female-headed families are more prevalent among blacks than among whites.

The percentage of female-headed families among blacks (as distinct from nonwhites) gradually rose from 19 in 1940 to 24 in 1959. The overall rise from 1949 to 1965 for blacks is about one-third of one percent per year (12, pp. 25–26). But from 1959 through 1965, there has been no rise, and the 1965 percentage is 24 (as compared to 9 for whites). Thus the census data show that the level of female-headed families is not rising for blacks. If the percentage of female-headed families could be defined as a valid measure of family pathology, one would not conclude that the black family is becoming more pathological. As with illegitimacy rates (by Ventura's defini-tion), this outcome does not support the Moynihan thesis of increas-ing deterioration in the black family.

The most common family structure among blacks is one in which both husband and wife are present in the home. In urban areas, where the black family is alleged to be rapidly deteriorating, the percentage of such families is 65. Of the remaining 35 percent, only 18 are headed by the wife (4). The increase in female-headed homes for blacks may in part be a consequence of urban migration, rather than family disorganization. For, as Moynihan points out, blacks are more urban than whites, and black families in cities are more apt to be headed by a woman than are black families in the country.

Since the Moynihan thesis states that matriarchy is characteristic of lower-class urban black families, data comparing urban blacks and whites are necessary. If the percentage of female-headed families is a valid measure of family pathology and matriarchy, the percentages for the lower-class black group should be higher than those for other groups. The 1960 census data show the following: for families with children that have annual incomes under $3,000, the percentages are blacks 47 and whites 38; for families with incomes of $3,000 or more, blacks 8 and whites 4. Thus blacks at both income levels are more apt to have female-headed families, but the black-white differ-ences within income groups are only 9 and 4 percent (20). Further, percentages of female-headed families are far more closely related to income level than to race: among blacks, the low-income families are 39 percent more apt to have female-headed families; among whites, 34 percent. Thus the effects of income level are about five times more characteristic of poor families than of black families.

One reason why black women (both poor and nonpoor) are more apt to head families is differential access to adoption. Most white women who have illegitimate babies are able to have them adopted. But since the demand for black babies is so low, black women have comparatively limited opportunity to have their illegitimate babies adopted, and thus are apt to keep them (9, p. 482ff.).

The data on female-headed homes in black and poor communi-ties undoubtedly exaggerate the extent to which the fathers are not present. Substitute-father laws and welfare requirements often make financial aid contingent on there being no father in the home. This of course creates a strong economic incentive to conceal the presence of the husband, and also contributes to husbands' motivation to leave the family unit.

The Moynihan thesis implies that black men are emasculated and subdominant in their homes. There is, however, no evidence showing that black men who leave their wives do so *because* they were unable to exert power over their wives or children. To say a man is powerless because he is *absent* reduces the meaning of power to that of triviality. Further, as regards the approximately 60 percent of black homes with a husband present, there is no convincing evidence that these husbands are, in comparison to white husbands, emasculated and powerless.

UNEMPLOYMENT RATES

Moynihan writes that ". . . unemployment among Negroes outside the South has persisted at a catastrophic level since the first statistics were gathered in 1930" (15, p. 20). The high level of unemployment among blacks is certainly a sad commentary on the performance of the American economy. But black unemployment has *not* increased. The data presented for the years 1930, 1940, 1950, and 1960 indicate that 1960 is the year of least unemployment for blacks. Unemployment among blacks also declined slightly from 1960 to 1964. Unemployment among both races has decreased, and, further, the decrease has been more rapid among blacks than among whites.

It is argued that unemployment causes instability in the home (a study of white families is cited by Moynihan [3]). It is further argued that unemployment has more deleterious effects on the black home than on the white home. But the two conclusions imply that the decrease in black unemployment levels should *increase* family stability, just as decreased white unemployment should stabilize white families. Since unemployment has decreased faster for blacks than for whites, black homes should be increasingly stable vis-à-vis white homes. To support his thesis, Moynihan relies on data showing that between 1960 and 1964 the number of new Aid to Dependent Children cases rose. But the other data used in the report as measures of family instability did not show such a rise. Marital separation, for example, continued to parallel unemployment. Valentine states that Moynihan ignores other evidence in the report, such as the *decline* of family income relative to white income (25, p. 32). Valentine concludes that there is in the report more evidence to support the

interpretation that family structure measures are caused by economic factors that to support the opposite interpretation. It may be
too strong a statement to say that these data contradict Moynihan's
argument, but any support given to the thesis of black matriarchy
and family pathology is, at best, equivocal.

As with illegitimacy rates and female-headed families, the instability of employment of blacks as opposed to whites reflects social
class as well as race. Lower-class persons work at jobs that are unstable in comparison to the jobs of the middle class. Thus, part of the
instability of employment behavior for blacks derives from the fact
that they are more apt to be lower class than whites. When comparisons are made within social class levels, much of the race difference
in employment behavior is removed (10).

In summary, the evidence for deterioration of the black family
is derived from demographic data rather than from data on family
dynamics, and does not support the conclusions drawn from it. As
Geismar and Gerhart write, "The act of inferring functioning patterns from such structural and official, recorded behavioral characteristics, is not so much the articulation of a theoretical position as it
is a form of research which grasps at available straws" (9, p. 480).

Of course, it *could* be the case that data derived from family
research would show disorganization, pathology, and male power-
lessness in the black family. The balance of the chapter presents a
study designed for such an analysis, and cites relevant data from
other studies.

AN EMPIRICAL STUDY OF BLACK AND WHITE FAMILIES

THE STUDY DESIGN

A major objective in the design of the study was to control not only
the statuses of the families, but of the neighborhoods from which the
families were selected. To this end, a technique was developed
which employed a sampling population that balanced the social
status (measured by median home values and median family income
in the sampling units) of the black and white families. The sampling
method, along with characteristics of the population and sample, is
described in detail elsewhere (23, pp. 155–159).

A second major objective in the method for the study was to

construct a sample in which the structure of black and white families was controlled. It was necessary to construct a population of families for which the distribution of conjugal and parental power *in* the family could be studied comparatively. To this end, a decision was made to study complete families consisting of two parents and two or more dependent children. To facilitate such comparisons, it was also decided not to include interracial families.

The study's main hypothesis was that if control of neighborhood status, family status, and family structure did not remove differences in conjugal and parental power of black and white husbands and wives, then support might be obtained for the thesis of matriarchy in the lower-class black family. But if no systematic differences remained after the imposition of these controls, then the Moynihan thesis would not be supported, and its credibility would be contingent upon further research with comparable controls.

The basic element of the study was, then, the *nuclear family*, consisting of husband, wife, and dependent children. Intensive interviews were conducted with the husband and wife, and with the two oldest unmarried children living at home, between the ages of 15 and 23.

Interviewing. In order to attain an appropriate level of rapport between interviewers and respondents, it was decided to use indigenous interviewers, blacks interviewing black families and whites interviewing white families. The interviews for the husband and wife were ordinarily completed in 45 minutes each. The children's interviews in general took from 75 to 90 minutes each.

The interviews were used to gather data on the families' socioeconomic, migratory, and structural histories, social patterns pertaining to children's educational and occupational plans and aspirations, and on values and attitudes relevant to child rearing. A two-year follow-up study was carried out, in which the children were reinterviewed to obtain data on their present educational plans and aspirations, their involvement with their neighborhoods and communities, and their political values and behavior (24). The first study was carried out in the fall of 1967; the second in the summer of 1969.

Family socioeconomic status. The index of socioeconomic status (SES) for each family was based on three criteria: the occupational status of the husband; the mean number of years of schooling completed by the husband and wife; the total family income in the year preceding the field study. The final measure was the mean of three scores, giving each indicator equal weight. Although the concept of "social class" is more complex than this measure, the family SES score is used as a measure of social class, with lower SES families considered "lower class" and higher SES families "middle class."

The sample. The sample was drawn from a population confined to Los Angeles County. A probability sample was employed consisting of 148 black families and 138 white families, with four interviews obtained in all but a few of the families. A total of 293 black and 267 white children were interviewed.

DATA ON CONJUGAL POWER

The data presented in this section pertain to three dimensions of conjugal power. First, a number of items are used as measures of the extent to which the husband and wife value male dominance and female submissiveness in their conjugal relations. These items are used to measure the variable *male dominance ideology.* The second dimension employs parents' perceptions of power over eight major family decisions: these decision-making spheres are called *conjugal decision-making power.* Third, children's perceptions of the extent to which the mother bosses the father and the father bosses the mother are used to construct a model of *conjugal power structure.*

Male dominance ideology. Nine items were selected to construct a measure of male dominance. The husbands and wives were asked to "strongly agree," "agree," "disagree," or "strongly disagree" with the following statements:

1. A man ought to feel free to relax when he gets home from work.

2. Some equality in marriage is a good thing, but by and large the husband ought to have the main say-so in family matters.

3. It goes against human nature to place women in authority over men.

4. Men should make the really important decisions in the family.

5. Husbands should be more strict with their wives.

6. Marriage is the best career for a woman.

7. The wife should fit her life to her husband's.

8. A wife should let her husband decide most things.

9. The husband should control the family's money.

According to the Moynihan thesis, black males are emasculated and live in wife-dominated homes. As a consequence of this thesis, it could be predicted that the level of male dominance ideology would be higher for whites than for blacks. It is further contended in this thesis that the pathological matriarchy of black families—the husband being subdominant to the wife—is most pronounced in *lower-class* black families. According to this specification of the thesis, it could be predicted that male dominance ideology would be lowest among low SES blacks.

TABLE 1

Measures of Male Dominance Ideology: Percentages of Husbands and
Wives* with "High" Responses, by Race and Family Socioeconomic Status

	Lower SES		Higher SES		Total	
	Black	White	Black	White	Black	White
Measure of Male Dominance	N=196	N=92	N=89	N=169	N=285	N=261
Man free to relax	95	93	92	85	94	88
Husband has main say-so	84	70	72	69	80	67
Woman's authority less	80	69	66	69	76	69
Men make big decisions	73	64	70	42	72	50
Husbands strict with wives	44	25	29	22	39	24
Marriage career of women	83	75	68	62	78	74
Wife fit life to husband's	87	82	80	80	84	80
Husband decides most things	57	46	42	37	53	40
Husband controls money	44	34	41	28	45	30
Mean scale score	5.1	4.3	4.2	3.9	4.8	4.0

*Responses of husbands and wives are not differentiated here

Table 1 shows the data on male dominance ideology. In this table, for separate items, responses of "strongly agree" and "agree" are scored "high." For the total sample, blacks are higher than whites on each of the nine items. These differences range from 4 percent to 22 percent. The larger differences are concentrated in items stating that the husband should make decisions and control the family's money. The scale scores show a race difference in the same direction: the mean scores are blacks 4.8 and whites 4.0. Blacks are significantly higher on male dominance ideology than are whites.

Division of the sample into lower SES and higher SES groups for each race provides information of the effects of "social class" upon endorsement of male dominance. There is a consistent difference between SES groups within both races, with male dominance ideology higher in the lower SES groups. For blacks, this is true for every item, with a mean difference of 9 percent and a difference of .9 in the scale score. For whites, this is the case for eight of nine items, with the mean difference of 7 percent and a difference of .4 in the scale score. Thus the data show that male dominance ideology may characterize blacks more than whites, and lower-class families more than middle-class families. Male dominance is most pronounced in the lower SES black group, and least in the middle-class white group. This general outcome is in direct opposition to the Moynihan thesis. Further, the group defined as setting the "norm" in family patterns, the middle-class whites, is *lowest* on male dominance.

Conjugal decision-making power. There are numerous collective family decisions that a husband and wife must make. Blood and Wolfe selected eight decisions to assess the relative balance of power between husband and wife (5, p. 19). Both husbands and wives were asked who would make the *final* decision about:

1. What job the husband should take
2. What car to buy
3. Whether or not to buy life insurance
4. Where to go on a vacation
5. What apartment or house to take
6. Whether the wife should go to work
7. What doctor to have
8. How much money the family should spend on food each week

The alternative responses to the questions were "husband always," "husband more than wife," "husband and wife exactly the same," "wife more than husband," and "wife always."

Unlike the items for male dominance ideology, which were regarded as forming a scale, these spheres of decision making do not form a scale, and the items were consequently regarded as eight separate variables.

For each sphere of conjugal power, responses of "husband always" and "husband more than wife" can be regarded as "high" on husband's power. A high percentage of "high" scores for a group, then, indicates a low level of male emasculation and subdominance. Given this measure, it could then be predicted—by the Moynihan thesis—that black males would be less powerful within their families than white males, and would, therefore, have lower percentages of "high" scores for the eight decisions. The specification of the thesis would lead to the further claim that the percentages of "high" responses would be lowest in the lower SES black group.

Table 2 shows the data for conjugal decision-making power. There are no consistent differences by race in response to these items. White husbands have as high or higher scores for each item, but none of these differences is significant. For the summary measure —the mean of the percentages of "highs" for the eight items—the percentages are blacks 30 and whites 33.

Division of the sample by SES groups shows no significant interaction between the control variables, race and socioeconomic status. According to Moynihan, lower-class black husbands tend to be *powerless* in their families. The data do not support this hypothesis.*

Conjugal power structure. Families can be described as patriarchal if the husband dominates the wife and matriarchal if the wife dominates the husband. If neither the husband nor the wife dominates the other, the family is egalitarian. As Straus points out, power can be shared in two distinct ways (21). First, it may be that *neither* the husband nor the wife makes power assertions over the other: Herbst calls such families *autonomic.* (11). Second, it may be that *both* the husband and the wife make power assertions over each other, and simultaneously attempt to dominate. Straus calls this the *conflict* family.

Straus uses these distinctions to construct a model of conjugal power. To measure the extent to which power assertions are made, children are asked:

1. Does your mother boss your father?
2. Does your father boss your mother?

---

*These outcomes are not directionally consistent with the Blood and Wolfe study of 731 wives in the Detroit metropolitan area (5), nor are they directionally consistent with the data employing this measure presented by Aldous (2). The results of the Aldous study are based on a relatively small sample and are not in general statistically significant. Blood and Wolfe find husbands most powerful in higher SES families, though the reported differences are not dramatic. They find that the percentages of wife-dominated families are 44 for blacks and 20 for whites. A second measure of husband's conjugal power, based on a ten-point scale, shows a mean score of 4.4 for blacks and 5.2 for whites, a mean difference of only .8. Further, the authors indicate that the black husbands are low on conjugal power in part because the black wives in the sample were at the time being exploited by an insurance scheme, and hence were scored as "powerful" for this decision. This item is left in the scale, which erodes its validity. Hyman and Reed contend that even if the differences are valid, a reasonable interpretation is that the average white family is slightly patriarchal and the black family egalitarian (13, p. 348 ff.).

TABLE 2

Percentages* of Husbands High on Conjugal Power For Eight
Family Decisions, by Race and Family Socioeconomic Status

	Lower SES		Higher SES		Total	
	Black	White	Black	White	Black	White
Family Decision	% (N)	% (N)	% (N)	% (N)	% (N)	% (N)
Job husband should take	92 (94)	94 (45)	94 (44)	98 (83)	92 (138)	97 (128)
What car to buy	50 (94)	61 (45)	56 (44)	56 (83)	52 (138)	58 (128)
Buy life insurance	36 (94)	40 (45)	40 (42)	41 (83)	37 (136)	41 (128)
Where to vacation	15 (94)	16 (44)	7 (41)	16 (83)	13 (135)	16 (127)
Apartment, house to take	7 (94)	9 (45)	7 (44)	7 (83)	7 (138)	8 (128)
Should wife work	20 (94)	33 (45)	22 (44)	23 (83)	20 (138)	27 (128)
What doctor to have	8 (94)	3 (45)	6 (44)	8 (83)	7 (138)	7 (128)
Money to spend on food	8 (94)	11 (45)	9 (43)	8 (82)	8 (137)	9 (127)
Mean for eight decisions	30	33	30	32	30	33

*Based on pooled responses of husband and wife: percent of families with both scoring
husband "high," plus .5 times the percent of families with husband or wife but not
both scoring husband "high."

In this study the response categories "often," "sometimes," "seldom," and "never" were used. "Often" and "sometimes" were
combined for the "high" category. The model has the following
form:

FREQUENCY OF		
Mother	*Father*	RESULTING
Bossing	*Bossing*	FAMILY
Father	*Mother*	TYPE
Low	Low	Autonomic
High	High	Conflict
Low	High	Husband-dominated
High	Low	Wife-dominated

According to the Moynihan thesis, the black family is wife-
dominated. The white family and the middle-class black family are
by contrast seen as egalitarian (here, autonomic or conflict) or husband-dominated. It could therefore be predicted that the wife-
dominated family type would be more frequent among the lower
SES black families than among white families and higher SES black
families. Further, husband-dominated families should be less frequent among lower SES blacks than among families in the other
three groups.

For conjugal power structure, as perceived by children—unlike
male dominance ideology and husband's power as perceived by hus-

bands and wives—the problem of validity of response is germane. Since the child does not participate in the conjugal relationship, disagreement between children on conjugal power makes it difficult to categorize the actual family power structure. For this reason a family's conjugal type is regarded as measured adequately only if both children report the same type. Thus each observation in Table 3 represents a *shared* perception of the two oldest children who live at home.

TABLE 3

Percentages of Family Types, From Responses by Two Oldest Children, by Race and Family Socioeconomic Status

| | Lower SES | | Higher SES | |
Conjugal Type	*Black* N= 96	*White* N= 46	*Black* N= 50	*White* N= 66
Autonomic	67	30	64	61
Conflict	12	9	20	12
Husband-dominant	19	56	12	24
Wife-dominant	2	4	4	3

The data show that the wife-dominated family is an infrequent pattern in all four groups. The Moynihan thesis implies that this type is most frequent among lower-class blacks. But Table 3 indicates that the percentage of wife-dominated types among the four race-SES groups is insignificant, so the data show no differences for this type. Certainly they do not indicate that lower-class black families are matriarchal.

If wife-dominated families are excluded, there is a significant dependence on family type by race-SES group. This is a weak effect, however, and little variation in family type is accounted for by race-SES group. What the data *do* show is that one group differs from the other three. The lower SES white families are far less apt to have an autonomic pattern, and far more apt to have a husband-dominated pattern. About two-thirds of the families in the three other groups are autonomic (lower SES blacks 67, higher SES blacks 64, higher SES whites 61), as compared to only 30 percent for lower SES whites. Also, the percentages of husband-dominated families in both socio-economic groups are higher for whites than for blacks, but are far higher for the lower SES whites (56 percent) than for any other group. Thus the most prevalent family type is autonomic for lower

SES blacks, higher SES blacks, and higher SES whites; and husband-dominated for lower SES whites.

In sum, the data in the three tables lend no support to the stereotype of the lower-class black husband as powerless in his conjugal relations. Lower-class black husbands are highest on male dominance ideology, about the same as whites on conjugal decision power, and similar to middle-class blacks and whites on family type. Lower-class whites, on the other hand, are not higher on male dominance ideology, but are higher on husband-dominated families than the other three groups.*

The thesis of rapid deterioration of lower-class black families is thus not supported by these data. Any male subdominance, matriarchy, and pathology that may be present in these families do not appear to be concentrated in conjugal relations. Parental relations provide a second major class of family interactions, and a second place to look for the supposedly crumbling lower-class black family. In the next section the distribution of parental power in the sample families will be explored.

DATA ON PARENTAL POWER

In this section dimensions of parental power are considered. First, parents' response to an item concerning the mother's responsibility for child rearing served as a measure of *mother's parental power.* Second, children were asked questions to measure their mother's and father's parent-child *decision power.* Third, children were asked five questions pertaining to *parental control* of their social activities. Fourth, children were asked about their contacts with their parents

---

*Further data on conjugal decision-making power are presented in Hyman and Reed (13), from survey data made available from a national survey carried out by Almond and Verba (2). A random sample of persons over 18 years of age were asked questions about their family of origin and, if married, about their family of procreation. First, respondents were asked which parent in their family of origin, if either, made the important decisions. For 93 blacks, the percentages are father 28 and mother 14; for 852 whites, father 22 and mother 13. Second, married respondents were asked if they or their spouses made the important family decisions. For 67 blacks, the percentages are husband 9 and wife 10; for 628 whites, husband 6 and wife 7. The data show virtually no race difference, either for the family of origin or of procreation. Third, Almond and Verba asked a question on whether the husband or wife, if either, decided how they should vote. For 66 blacks, the percentages are husband 11 and wife 2; for 627 whites, husband 7 and wife 0. Again, the race difference is negligible. The Almond and Verba survey thus lends no support to the claim that black husbands are powerless in their conjugal roles. In fact, for each of the three measures, black husbands are scored higher on conjugal power than white husbands.

about their educational plans. The questions in this last group were used to assess *parental resources*—expressive support and instrumental means—in helping the children attain their *educational goals.*

Mothers' parental power. To assess the extent to which the parental role is defined as a female role, husband and wives were asked to "strongly agree," "agree," or "strongly disagree" with the statement that raising a child is more a mother's job than a father's. This item is regarded as a measure of female dominance ideology for the parental role.

If black women are powerful and black men powerless in their parental roles, it could be anticipated that the proportion showing agreement with this statement would be higher for blacks than for whites. Further, if female dominance is particularly characteristic of lower-class black families, then the largest percentages scored "high" (agreement) should be found among the lower SES black families.

The percentages of parents who "strongly agree" or "agree" that mothers should dominate the parental role are: lower SES blacks, 40% (N = actual number = 196); lower SES whites, 40% (N = 92); higher SES blacks, 16% (N = 95); and higher SES whites, 15% (N = 205). Thus the data show that family socioeconomic status has a strong effect, but that race has no effect. For both races, lower SES persons are more apt to agree than are higher SES persons. This outcome is consistent with Table 1, which shows that, for both races, the lower-class families are higher on male dominance ideology for the *conjugal* role than the middle-class families. But the hypothesis that the mother's parental power would be greater in lower-class *black* families receives no support from these data.

Parental decision power. The children in the sample families were asked two questions on parent-child decision making:

1. In general, how are most decisions between you and your *father* made?

2. In general, how are most decisions between you and your *mother* made?

Of six response categories, the following three were judged "high" for father's decision power: "father just tells," "father listens but tells," and "father has the final word." The following responses were scored "low": "opinions equal," "respondent has the final word," and "respondent makes decision." The same scoring procedure was used for mother's decision power.

If black men are emasculated and powerless for *parental* roles, it could be expected that the percentages scored "high" on parent-child decision power would be lower for blacks than for whites, and lowest for lower-class blacks.

TABLE 4

Percentages of Children Perceiving Mothers and Fathers as Dominating Parent-Child Decisions, by Race and Family Socioeconomic Status

| Decision | Lower SES | | Higher SES | | Total | |
	Black N=204	White N=92	Black N=87	White N=163	Black N=291	White N=255
Mother-child	47	35	55	41	52	37
Father-child	38	36	46	52	43	42

The data for the two items are shown in Table 4. Few differences are seen in the parent-child power of the mother and the father. For the total sample, 43 percent of the fathers and 45 percent of the mothers are scored "high" on decision power. The higher SES parents are, for every race-SES group, more powerful than the corresponding lower SES groups. For the total sample, differences in the race variable do occur for mother-child decision: the percentages for black and white fathers are 43 and 42; for black and white mothers, 52 and 37. Thus black mothers appear to be more powerful in parent-child roles than white mothers, and also more powerful than black fathers. The differences between black and white mothers is found in both higher and lower SES groups, but is slightly more pronounced in the higher SES groups. Comparisons of the black and white fathers similarly show a greater difference in the higher SES groups.

The specification of the Moynihan thesis that fathers are powerless and mothers powerful in lower-class black families is not supported by the data in Table 4.

Parental control. The parental power described *in general* above is complemented by questions on parents' control over a number of *specific* activities. Just after the foregoing questions, children were told:

Let's look at a few specific rules your parents might have for you to see who makes the rules for you, your *mother,* your *father, both* parents, or *neither* parent:

1. Who decides how late you can stay out?
2. Who decides how much spending money you have?
3. Who decides what friends you go around with?
4. Who decides what shows, movies, or parties you can go to?
5. Who decides about things like after-school activities?

Although the items do not form a scale, a single measure was used to facilitate summarizing the results. This overall measure is the mean of the percentages of responses for the father, for the combined neither-both category, and for the mother.

TABLE 5

Percentages of Children Perceiving Fathers, Neither Parent or Both,
or Mothers as Making Rules, by Race and Family Socioeconomic Status

	Lower SES						Higher SES						Total					
	Black			White			Black			White			Black			White		
Activity	N=203			N=92			N=89			N=163			N=292			N=255		
	Fa	N-B	Mo	Fa	N-B	Mo	Fa	N-B	Mo	Fa	N-B	Mo	Fa	N-B	Mo	Fa	N-B	Mo
Stay out late	15	65	20	26	62	12	15	68	17	12	75	13	15	66	19	17	70	13
Spending money	9	70	21	12	74	14	9	70	21	9	69	21	9	70	21	11	70	19
Choice of friends	3	76	21	9	80	11	7	77	16	5	88	7	3	76	21	9	80	11
Shows, parties	2	79	19	12	82	6	8	77	15	3	87	10	2	79	19	12	81	7
After school activities	3	76	22	4	76	20	5	72	23	5	79	16	3	75	22	4	77	19
Mean for five activities	6	73	21	13	73	13	9	73	18	7	79	13	7	73	20	9	77	13

The data on parental control are shown in Table 5. For all four race-SES groups, about three-fourths of the families are egalitarian, so that neither parent exerts a disproportionate amount of control over the child's activities.

The effects of socioeconomic level observed in Table 4 are not apparent here. Among blacks there are virtually no effects for the SES variable. For whites there is a small difference, with fathers slightly more powerful in the lower class, as compared to the more egalitarian middle-class families. As in the previous tables, lower-class white fathers are comparatively more powerful than other fathers, with 13 percent, as opposed to 6, 9, and 7 percent for lower SES blacks, higher SES blacks, and higher SES whites.

Mothers are more powerful in the black group than in the white group—8 percent more in the lower SES families and 5 percent more in the higher SES families. Also, mothers exert more control than fathers in all but the lower SES white families, where there is no difference.

The Moynihan thesis of male subdominance and female dominance among lower-class black families, however, receives weak support from these data. For the five activities, the mean percentages of black fathers making decisions (6 percent) is lower than for any other group of fathers. Further, the mean percentage of black mothers making decisions (21 percent) is higher than in the other groups of mothers.

Thus, the results of Tables 4 and 5 are not entirely consistent, indicating that any overall support for Moynihan is equivocal.*

Parental contributions to educational goals. In addition to exerting control over the children, the parental role includes facilitating the child's achievement outside of the family. In particular, the father and mother contribute to the child's level of educational attainment through parent-child relations. Data were obtained on the child's perceptions of *expressive support* for educational attainment, and the *instrumental means* of actually helping the child attain the educational goals. Of these two contributions, support is generally regarded as more appropriate to the "female role," and instrumentality more appropriate to the "male role." At the same time, both support and instrumentality are resources for the child, so that encouragement from fathers and help from mothers can also contribute to achievement.

Expressive support for educational attainment was measured by responses to the questions:

*The national survey by Almond and Verba mentioned in the footnote on p. 101 provides related data on which parent, if either, was or is responsible for parental discipline. For families of origin, the percentages for 97 blacks are father 16 and mother 28; for 85 whites, father 19 and mother 25. For families of procreation, the percentages for 56 married blacks are husband 4 and wife 37; for 474 married whites, father 7 and wife 28. The outcomes are weak, but, for families of procreation, do lend limited support to a view of powerful black mothers. The data do *not* show that black husbands are powerless, as in both comparisons the percentages of fathers scored high on discipline are only 3 percent higher for whites than for blacks.

Do you feel that your *mother (father)* approves of your getting more education? Does she (he) strongly approve, approve, disapprove, or strongly disapprove? Responses of "strongly approve" and "approve" were scored "high" for parents' expressive support. Instrumentality was measured by responses to the questions:

1. In your own words, could you describe in what ways your *mother (father)* has the *ability* to help you attain your educational goal?

2. In general, would you say she (he) has a lot of ability, some ability, little ability, or no ability at all?

Responses of "a lot" or "some" ability were scored "high" in instrumental means for the data, which are shown in Table 6.

TABLE 6

Children's Perceptions of Expressive Support and Instrumental
Means from Mothers and Fathers in Attaining Educational
Goals, by Race and Family Socioeconomic Status

	Lower SES				*Higher SES*				*Total*			
	Black		*White*		*Black*		*White*		*Black*		*White*	
	%	*(N)*	%	*(N)*	%	*(N)*	%	*(N)*	%	*(N)*	%	*(N)*
Expressive support												
Mother	91	(202)	88	(92)	94	(89)	91	(163)	92	(291)	90	(255)
Father	73	(204)	66	(92)	78	(89)	72	(162)	75	(293)	74	(254)
Instrumental means												
Mother	58	(193)	40	(79)	74	(88)	49	(149)	63	(281)	46	(228)
Father	51	(172)	46	(69)	74	(84)	63	(137)	59	(256)	57	(206)

For the first questions, there is almost no difference in expressive support by race: 91 percent of all the mothers are highly expressive, and 75 percent of the fathers. For instrumentality, there is no race difference for fathers (blacks 59, whites 57), but there is a pronounced difference for mothers. Black mothers are more instrumental (63 percent) in comparison to white mothers (46 percent). In fact, in most categories black mothers are more instrumental than black and white fathers as well. Thus, black youth are apparently able to obtain more instrumental help from *both* parents than white children. Since instrumentality might be regarded as the "male role" (19), this could be interpreted as support of the view that black women are matriarchal in the parental role. It is hard to imagine this as a measure of family pathology, however; on the contrary, help from both parents could be regarded as less pathological than help from the father alone.

Just as black fathers are generally both more supportive and more instrumental than white fathers, black mothers are both more supportive and more instrumental than white mothers. For expressiveness, the differences are small and not significant. But for instrumentality, the differences are large in both socioeconomic levels—18 percent in the lower SES group, and 25 in the higher SES group. In each SES group white mothers are lowest on instrumentality; black mothers are highest in the lower SES group, and tied for highest with black fathers in the higher SES group. This picture of the powerful black mother, for the parental role, is consistent with the Moynihan thesis. But without a correspondingly powerless black father, the data do not imply a matriarchal role structure in which the black man is emasculated and pathologically ineffective as a parent.*

CONCLUSIONS

In this chapter, the Moynihan thesis—that family deterioration constitutes "the fundamental weakness of the Negro community" and that this pathology "is capable of sustaining itself without assistance from the white world"—has been evaluated as an analytic concept and as an empirical generalization. The Moynihan argument is unclear in which roles—conjugal or parental—the black man is sub-

---

*There are almost no data pertaining to the relative influence of the mother and father in black and white families with respect to the development of political values. Hyman and Reed present a comparison based on survey data made available by Jennings from a national sample of about 20,000 high school seniors (13, pp. 350–351). Of these students, 151 blacks and 2,384 whites reported that their mothers and fathers had differing political preferences. The political preferences of the respondents were also measured, so the percentages of respondents having the same preference as their mother or father can be regarded as a measure of the influence of the two parents. If the black father is emasculated and noninfluential, as implied by the Moynihan thesis, the influence of the mother in comparison to the father should be higher for blacks than for whites. The results show no such difference. For blacks, the percentages are father 32 and mother 40; for whites, father 34 and mother 40. These data may have limited validity as measures of parental influence, however, because there is evidence that political party loyalty is a less relevant dimension of political behavior for blacks than for whites (14).

dominant and his wife dominant. Further, Moynihan *assumes* that matriarchy in black families is not functional "because it is so out of line with the rest of American society." No theoretical argument or empirical data are employed to support his assumption.

When the measures of family disorganization used in the Moynihan Report are critically examined, it is found that for illegitimacy rates, female-headed families, and unemployment, the available data do not provide support for the black matriarchy thesis. The accuracy of these data is also questionable, as is their appropriateness as measure of family pathology.

In general, the data from the empirical study reported here do not show lower-class black husbands to be powerless in either their conjugal or their parental roles. Black wives do appear to be powerful in their parental roles, but there is no indication that this emasculates the black husband-father. On the contrary, this can be seen as a positive resource for black youth and as a strength in black families. If the data show any group to be atypical, it may be the lower-class white husbands, who tend to dominate the conjugal role but to play a somewhat smaller role in child socialization.

Perhaps the major limitation of the empirical study is that it was carried out in a single metropolitan area. The validity of the findings, though, is enhanced by data from two national surveys reported in Hyman and Reed (13). The Almond and Verba survey data show no race differences in conjugal power and no differences in parental power for fathers; they also show that black mothers are slightly higher on parental power than are white mothers (2). The Jennings data show no race differences in parental influence over political preferences. Thus, these surveys are consistent with the empirical study reported here, and are not consistent with the Moynihan thesis. The weight of existing evidence suggests that the stereotype of lower-class black families as matriarchal, pathological, and "approaching a state of complete breakdown" may in reality constitute social mythology. The reality is that such a view is not supported by a convincing body of social research.

In a modern technocratic society, marriage is a difficult project. It is even more difficult if the values and cultural experiences of the participants differ. Thus, interracial marriage may be difficult because of cultural differences in the black and white experiences in American society. And these differences are of course exacerbated by racial discrimination and racism. This chapter suggests that radical differences in family structure, however, might not be included among black-white cultural differences. If the stereotype of black families as matriarchies is invalid, then there are no differences by race in the expected power of the husband and wife in their conjugal and parental roles. The personalities of the persons involved in a marriage should be a far more salient determinant of family power structure.

7

HENRY J. KEENAN, JR., M.S.W.

The Interracial Family through Transracial Adoption

At a time when there is a discernible increase in transracial adoption, it is important to know what we can about the life styles of those who adopt children of a different race and about the many factors that are involved in their choice. We also need to know both the opportunities and the problems that transracial adoption affords to those who undertake it.

In the chapter that follows, Mr. Henry J. Keenan, Jr., an expert in group marriage counseling, offers the reader valuable information drawn from his own experience with transracial adoption. But, even more important, he helps the reader understand the basic human factors that are needed for a person to undertake and be successful in the challenging and unfamiliar role of parent in this type of interracial family.

The area is a controversial one, like so much in contemporary American life, and only recently some responsible professional members of the black community have aligned themselves against the placement of black children in white families. These black members feel that no white parents, no matter how intelligent and loving, can give the black child a true sense of his position as a black in American society.

The scope of the chapter is both wide and deep, and the reader is afforded an opportunity to view transracial adoption on a broad canvas painted in clear and sharp lines with a strong humanistic hand.

Creativity and imagination play an important role in the life style of the couple who adopts transracially. These are not the sole character-istics, however. In addition, there are the important factors of self-awareness, motivation, emotional security, need fulfillment of a reciprocal nature, and recognition of the ability to relate in a positive, growth-producing way to a child as a child, not as a black, white, or yellow child. Although these characteristics are present in many couples, when creativity and imagination are applied, they help to differentiate the transracial family via adoption from other more common family groups we experience.

The difference between the couples who adopt transracially and those who do not, seems to be one of practice, or form, if you wish, of life style. Their self-awareness leads them to an acceptance of both their good qualities and their limitations. Their limitations do not pose a threat with which they feel unable to cope. The ability to acknowledge limitations seems to be more pronounced in these cou-ples' patterns of interactions. Idealism is tempered by the realities of social pressures, but not to the point of acting as a deterrent force in their lives. These adoptive parents seem to be able to utilize social and familial pressures to their own best advantage, and to utilize these pressures to increase their determination to cope with their particular problems in creatively effective ways. Their perspective enables them to view these pressures as challenges to be met rather than as dangers to be avoided. Reality testing and acceptance provide one of the foundation stones for nurturing the child and enabling him to progress from infancy through adolescence and into adulthood with the support of loving, tender, and meaningful relationships in the home.

It would certainly be a fallacy to state that anyone could meet all the special needs of the transracially adopted child simply because he is a well-meaning person. Thales, a Greek philosopher, said, "Know thyself." This means knowing oneself in relation to historical, cultural, community, and family relationships impinging upon oneself and one's child. Saying that things will change when one's child is older will not really do much in the way of answering his needs of today or of solving his problems of tomorrow in the schoolyard. Therefore, a sufficient balance must be developed between the realities of today's world and the hopes for the years to come.

Another important characteristic is the willingness to invest oneself in a lifetime of work requiring optimum performance in as many situations as is humanly possible. The ability to love oneself, acknowledge one's own humanity, admit one's own mistakes, and be constantly ready to try harder than before is no small accomplishment in the art of living. In business and professional life many external controls have been instituted to insure constant application of effort to achieve the objectives of success. The system of rewards and controls in the application of a similar type of effort in parenthood is more elusive and difficult to analyze. Yet, such a system must be present in expanding quantity and quality in the parent of the transracially adopted child.

Selfishness and impatience have no place in the constellation of this type of family relationship. Love and open communication are essential. One cannot underestimate the great need for frequent and open discussion between the adoptive parents. This continuing dialogue should explore problems, engage in the discovery of ideas, release feelings, and generally open up common awareness of their total involvement with and commitment to the family. The realization that their family is different, and the imaginative utilization of this difference to build a strong structure of love and togetherness will surely move the family up the ladder of success as a well-functioning unit of society.

"BUT THERE IS SO MUCH TO CONTEND WITH."

As we reflect upon the needs and responses within a family, we come upon many areas of commonality. Families must be thought of in a much wider frame of reference than ever before. This is necessary because of the rapidly changing life styles that are being developed, tested, and followed in America today. Any family, whether it is the customary grouping of parents and their own children or one of the newer communal families, which have only recently received greater attention, must rely upon others in the society to meet needs that the family itself cannot meet alone. Every family, or primary social unit, has to resolve problems, live through experiences, and react to feelings of others with which it is confronted, in context with other units of society, such as the extended family and the community at large.

It is appropriate, therefore, to direct our attention to some of the common problems and feelings about transracial adoption on the part of the adoptive parents themselves, their extended family, and the community in which the couple resides.

No one can justifiably say that his life is uncomplicated. We all live through experiences that are trying and demanding. We all have developed a certain ability to meet life, dependent upon our own strengths and weaknesses. To solve or to avoid problems is a decision that every person must constantly make. In my opinion, success must be measured by our willingness to attempt *something*. Every experience, regardless of the outcome, regardless of the fact that the desired result is achieved or missed, can serve as a basis of awareness and wisdom. To acknowledge the need for assistance and the possibility of being in error is to acknowledge the humanity of our existence. To make superhuman demands of ourselves will certainly place unnecessary frustrations and failures in our path. Our goal should be success—and the teaching of success to our children by our example, by our acceptance of ourselves as human beings capable of learning, capable of error, and often in need of assistance from others.

BETWEEN PARENT AND AGENCY—A PROCESS OF FAMILY
FORMATION

Multiracial familes via adoption have become a more common phenomenon over the last few years. Some of the following information will aid in understanding how such adoptions occur. One of the questions usually found on the adoption application form is, "Would you consider a child whose race is different from yours, mentally and/or physically handicapped, an older child, or other (please specify)?" The greatest percentage of prospective adoptive parents either know or have heard of someone who has adopted such a child. This question has been raised before, and the couple has already discussed a range of possible answers. However, not until the couple is actually faced with placing a written answer on the page does its decision solidify. Do you think you can, or don't you? If they feel that they can, or that they are potentially capable of being the kind of persons described above, then their answer should be YES! There will be time to change their decision, but at least at first they should forge ahead and attempt to meet the challenge facing them. A child is waiting!

Once the prospective parents have filed a written application, and the agency has noted their response to that question, a staff member will call them, generally in a relatively short period of time. By answering yes to the question, they have helped to remove the obstacle of the long waiting list. Then, with the arrangements for an appointment made, the couple has begun its adoptive study. During the adoptive study, the social worker will meet with the husband and wife a number of times to get to know them, to understand the reasons why they feel qualified to adopt a child with special needs, to help them think about some of the areas of concern peculiar to this type of adoption, and, in short, to help them become parents.

Many of the disturbing myths concerning adoption, the study, and the role of the social worker do not need to worry applicants. They are not true. A prospective adoptive couple is viewed as a healthy, well-functioning couple who wants a child for one of many reasons. It may be that the applicants are medically unable to have a child of their own. They may already have one or more biological children and wish to increase the number of children through adoption. Discussion will be directed toward such topics as expectations, interpersonal relationships in marriage, roles of parents, motivation, various techniques of child rearing, general background information, and plans for the future. None of these discussions need to make the couple feel that the social worker is trying to find something wrong.

The social worker is, in point of fact, attempting to meet the potential parents' need for a child as intelligently as possible so that parents and child may gain from their new relationship.

The placement of a multiracial child in the home brings with it many of the same feelings and experiences of any adoption placement—even that of taking Junior home from the hospital. The child embodies the fears, doubts, and responsibilities that have been discussed. There are the questions about whether the parents can "do it," whether they are going to love this child "as their own," and whether the baby will love them. Overshadowing these questions, though, is the feeling of hopeful promise that all things will be worked out well with the application of creative and loving effort on their part. Before they are fully able to realize that last year was made up of 365 days, the required year for formalizing adoption will have passed, and they will be preparing excitedly with their social worker to go to court and have the adoption completed legally. Before this, however, the parents will have met new situations and felt feelings and solved problems that they may have envisioned before the adoption but never experienced. What are some of these?

"WHAT WILL THIS DO TO THE FAMILY?"

The adoptive parents must expect a full range of possible reactions from their families of origin. They should use time, communication, and intelligence during the preadoptive phase to inform significant people of their intentions to adopt a child of another race. The decision to adopt transracially should be communicated prior to the actual placement of the child. Some people may differ with me on this point vehemently; however, I have not seen, nor have I heard, any testimony that would substantially shake the foundation of this belief and approach. To go to the grandparents' home with one's new son or daughter without any previous mention of the fact that the child has special characteristics is to be insensitive to their feelings. Some may argue that presenting information about the racial background burdens grandparents with unnecessary brooding and worry before placement. However, the grandparents' feelings must be handled with consideration and they must be given time to adjust if there is to be minimal disruption of the relationship between the adoptive couple and their parents. One must also consider that the increased intensity of negative feelings caused by a lack of foreknowledge may be sensed by the child. Informing the grandparents early in the adoptive process gives them the opportunity to deal with some of their negative feelings before the child becomes a family member.

When the prospective parents inform the future grandparents of the special qualities of the child being considered for adoption, the couple may encounter the grandparents' outright objection to the idea. The problem then becomes one of deciding what to do if this happens. One alternative can be the avoidance of the grandparents; another can be continued communication even though one-sided. One cannot be so naive as to believe that no rifts have occurred in families because of transracial adoption. The most appropriate solution will be found if the spouses maintain a good relationship with the social worker, keep the channels of communication open, use their intelligence, and base their decision on a well-thought-out plan of action. Similar reactions may arise with other family members, and problem solving may become necessary. Grandparents are given particular attention because of the special nature of their relationship with the adoptive couple.

The grandparents and other relatives may be able to express various degrees of acceptance, tempered with some hesitancy. It is imperative to remember, though, that their age, the social factors of their past experiences, and their present sense of security militate, sometimes strongly, against "choosing" to take on the problems that the interracial adoption involves. Family members express a sincere interest in the parents' and child's future happiness, and desire to see no one suffer unavoidable hurt. They express common conscious feelings of concern for the great social ills of our time; but for their son or daughter to take on the special responsibility of adopting a child—let alone a child of another race, may seem to them inexplicable. They may question whether the child will appreciate his situation when he grows up. Will he resent being adopted? How will he feel about being of another race than his parents? Expressions of concern about the child's, the couple's, and the relatives' acceptance in the community are voiced.

Family members ask what will happen to the child in school or when he begins dating. "When he wants to get married," they ask, "whom will he marry?" "Who will marry him or her?" "How will the child identify with his own race?" "Will he, with his Afro-American ancestry, think of himself as a Caucasian?" "Being white in a black home, will he think of himself as a 'brother'?" "How will the other race relate to and accept him?" No one of us has the power of clairvoyance, and we must accept that our answers are based on hope and on our efforts to realize our hopes.

No matter who he is, no child is born with a written guarantee for success or happiness. No parent can expect his child to be consistently appreciative of him. No parent can predict that his child will do well and be accepted in school, either as a student or as a peer, that he will be considered a good dating partner or a good marriage prospect. Much of the child's acceptance will come by way of his own acceptance of himself and his own well-integrated personality, which he has received through his parents' loving relationship with him in the home. Love alone will not conquer all, but it will make the process of conquest much easier.

Questions about being adopted or about racial identity can only be answered by the individual family; but there are organizations, books, social workers, and other counseling resources that can aid in the search for answers. Half of the solution lies in recognizing that not everyone will be satisfied with the answers that the couple give to the questions raised by their relatives and friends. No one of us is interchangeable with another. Every person is entitled to retain his own integrity and to satisfy his needs peacefully without impinging on the rights of others. If one has decided to adopt a child of another race, he has made a decision based on his perception of himself and of his relationships, needs, and life objectives. Does he not have the right to exercise his own judgment and to determine his own life?

Every effort should be made to give due consideration to the feelings of others. Therefore, if one forces oneself, one's child, or one's ideas on others, it can only lead to unhappiness and further rejection. If relatives and friends are making quiet, reserved efforts to accept the adopted child, then wise use of special occasions can help the process. A couple should be careful and considerate in their choice of godparents for the child. Birthdays can offer a particularly good opportunity for meaningful activities. Little things can go a long way. A cake imprinted with a personal message such as, "My birthday is happy because I am with my family," might do much to soften reluctant hearts. A special party invitation could read:

> Although I am still little and have many inches to grow,
>
>   I'll be a better person because of your love, I know.
>
> Then won't you come and join me on this happy day,
>
>   So I will be able to thank you in my own special way.

The child could then present each of the guests with a small special gift, which, although inexpensive, carries with it an immeasurable wealth of love and meaning given in trust and confidence. An intuitive and thoughtful couple will find countless ways of helping others to release their feelings of love. Not every person who is hesitant to accept the child will respond to such simple acts of love. Therefore, more creative energy will have to be utilized in ways appropriate to these situations.

One of the most elusive traits of the human personality seems to be a lack of genuine sensitivity to others. We often excuse our lack of consideration by saying that we are too busy, too hurried to take time to act in ways that allow for the feelings of others. We seem to forget that we are dealing with other humans' lives. If I say, "I should have done this or that," and never do it, I am failing not only myself, but also my child. If we can make every day a special day by applying our sensitivity to the needs and feelings of others, we and our children will live a richer life. Our children learn to relate to life by our example.

"WHAT ABOUT THE BUTCHER, THE BAKER, THE CANDLESTICK MAKER?"

The adoptive couple must expect the possibility of a wide range of neighborhood reaction, both positive and negative. As with the family and friends of the adoptive couple, reactions from the community may run from outright rejection to well-defined acceptance. If outright rejection is evidenced, conceivably one might take on the monumental task of community re-education. This resolution may have certain justifications, but from this writer's point of view chances for success are extremely limited. There is too much space available in this country for this to be the *only* solution. There are a greater number of communities in which the social climate is amenable to the multiracial family than of those where a negative social climate exists. We are all aware of geographical, demographic, and sociological subgroupings in our country that would add to the problems rather than facilitate the solving of those problems. They can be avoided. The watchwords "careful consideration" should apply to the couple's decisions. Most of the many couples I have talked with agree with the principle that if one expects to be accepted, acceptance is forthcoming. This is one of the principles with which the multiracial family must learn to live.

Alternately, acceptance of the interracial family comes at the other end of the spectrum of reactions. Between the two poles, however, there exist many forms of behavior that are sometimes referred to as the "well almosts" of acceptance by many couples of my acquaintance. One of the most complex, yet enjoyable, experiences of the multiracial family is learning how others spontaneously react to children and parents through different modes of overacceptance. The focus is mainly on the children, although the couple is often the recipient of "odd compliments," for lack of a better term. A few examples will help explain what I mean.

Consider Mrs. Marrel, about sixty years of age, who attends church regularly and embodies all the attributes of the deeply religious, God-fearing woman. Entering the grocery store, she sees a young mother struggling with a grocery cart, a week's grocery order, and three children under three years of age, two of whom are obviously of a different race from that of the mother. Mrs. Marrel approaches, pats the children on their cheeks, and says to the young mother, "Surely God will bless you for your charity, my dear." One can be annoyed with this expression of acceptance only if one is insensitive to the particular makeup of another human being and to the background that formed the person into what he is.

Upon meeting a multiracial family, a handsome, middle-aged pediatrician, who has raised his own family and sees children all day long, pauses and says, "If only we were younger . . ." If he were younger, maybe he would not do anything differently. Then, again, which of us knows for sure?

Many couples express annoyance when relating an encounter of this nature to others, especially in groups formed to support and encourage transracial adoption. These groups are usually comprised of couples who have either adopted transracially or are interested in doing so, and of professionals involved in these placements. The intensity of negative feelings seems to be lower in couples who have the flexibility to see the giver of the "odd compliment" as a well-intentioned person, who, while confused and perhaps slightly rattled by the encounter, musters good feelings that may not be verbally well expressed or meant in quite the way they are interpreted. At other times, it may not be a matter of words awkwardly put together. The person may be expressing sincere feelings which arise because his religious or philosophical precepts dictate that he say positive things in uncomfortable situations.

It would be unfair to leave the impression that the only expressions one hears are postive in tone. We do not live in an idyllic world. At times near-panic and claustrophobia hit one when he is cornered by a person determined to "get something straight." Upsetting, often rude, questions and statements may make it very difficult for someone to come up with the "right" answers and comments. In fact, most of the time *any* answer or comment made is less than satisfactory to the other party.

One of the most frustrating situations occurs when someone expresses negative or uninformed ideas about adoption in front of the adopted child. He may refer to the child by pseudosympathetic, distasteful phrases, such as "the poor little waif "; or may question, in the presence of the child, how you could love him "like your own." Each couple has to come to its own decision on the most suitable way to handle such encounters.

"DON'T TELL ANYONE, BUT . . ." OR, "I WANT YOU TO KNOW . . ."

Under this section I will attempt to bring into focus some attitudes and raise some questions that should be considered by any couple contemplating a transracial adoption.

Right and wrong—Are there absolutes? "I think they are wonderful, and I admire their courage, but I don't think I would take on those problems." A transracial adoption may be all right for some, but what about others? Does any one have the right to say that transracial adoption is absolutely right or wrong at all times and in all circumstances? What are some of the variables?

Normality—Who has the yardstick? "They seem fairly normal to me. What would make them do such a thing?" Are couples who adopt transracially involved in some "cause," or are they really meeting their needs for their own family but in a way that begets surprise on the part of others? Is there a hidden meaning? Are they trying to prove something? If so, they should not; not with another person's life.

Aggression—A place in my life? "One thing you have to face is that you will have to fight for your children. It will not be an easy life." Are parents aware of this, and willing to accept it? Their child will need them. They and he will be hurt. How will they handle their own and their child's hurt?

Racism—Is it all white? "You took away our manhood, deprived us of the exercise of our rights, refused us recognition and education, broke down our family life, and now you are stealing our children!" How do members of both races look at the transracial family? Generalizations, lack of knowledge, and poor communication are dangers here that must be avoided.

"YES, BUT WHAT ABOUT . . . ?" THE PROBLEM-SOLVING PROCESS

As far as has been determined by this writer, the process of problem solving is similar in adoptive and nonadoptive families. If the couple builds their future on today's strong and stable foundations, then it will have the assurance to face the dismal warnings and foreboding of what might come to pass. As previously stated, no child comes with a written guarantee.

The way the family explains to a child that he is adopted has a lot to do with how the family lives with that fact throughout the years of the growth and development of the child. One cannot deny that the explanation is complicated by the visible racial difference between the child and his parents. Again, one's own feelings, attitudes, and beliefs will be communicated to one's child. He will have to cope with his own problems, but not without the support of loving parents. He will have many more advantages in the process of discovery and acceptance of himself as a person of integrity and worth if he has loving, secure parents who share his life than if he were to spend his first eighteen years of life in a series of foster homes, no matter how good they might be.

One hope in writing this chapter is that the reader will not develop the unrealistic expectation that all the questions will be answered in neat packages. The answers to most significant questions of a personal nature must be individualized and specific. No social scientist, psychologist, psychiatrist, or social worker, no individual or group, can lay claim to absolute truths of life and living. There are of course some commonalities between one person's experiences and those of others, but, for the most part, each must develop his own coping mechanisms, make his own decisions, and carry them through into practice—in short, live his own life.

Questions about the future should concern us today because the answers to such questions must be shaped in growth-producing ways today. The transracially adopted child will face the same questions as to whether he will find love and acceptance as a person that we had to resolve for ourselves as children and that we are still answering today. Some questions concern the issue of whether the child will find love and acceptance as a dating or marital partner. "Will the adopted child rebel against me *because* he is of a different race, or will his rebellion in adolescence come about because it is a normal part of human growth and development?" The answer to these questions may simply be that a child who is transracially adopted has to find love and acceptance as a person by methods common to all other human beings. There are, of course, special factors, but they need not be looked at as disadvantages. If one learns to look for acceptance from others, he will find it. If he looks for rejection, his eyes and heart will find it. When looking for acceptance from others, one must act in ways that do not elicit negative responses. In this writer's experience, and in the experiences related by others, this has been found to be generally true. With good planning, trust, and acceptance of self, experience generally demonstrates that the interracial family through transracial adoption is received with a minimum of negativism on the part of the community.

Now we come to the most important question for each one of us.

"WHY NOT US?"

In the course of this chapter, you have followed a rather brief description of sets of experiences, feelings, and discoveries of self. As you reflect on what you have read, it is hoped that you can say to yourself, "They are really not so different, are they?" If you say this and if you believe that you should act as you believe, then call a local family service agency and find out more about interracial families through transracial adoption. Maybe *your* child is waiting!

8

FRANK A. PETRONI, Ph.D.

Interracial Dating —
The Price Is High

Adolescence, a period of emotional and physical growth and stress, is characterized by intense sexual drives. Dr. Petroni has devoted much of his professional career to the study of this age group, particularly to the problems that arise when individuals of different races meet and mingle. He utilizes the results of his extensive investigations of teen-age interracial relations to present, often in their own words, the situations these teen-agers encounter when they find a personal interest in one another.

The result of Dr. Petroni's studies provides us with a wide spectrum of opinions—among daters and their peers, among the parents of the young people, and among various elements of the community—a diversity that is characteristic of the contemporary American scene.

C OME TO my door, baby, face clean and shining black as night. My mother went to answer. You know that you look so fine. Now I could understand your tears and your shame. She called you boy, instead of your name. When she wouldn't let you inside, when she turned and said, "But honey, he's not our kind." She says I can't see you anymore, baby, can't see you anymore. Walk me down to school, baby. Everybody's acting deaf and blind until they turn and say, "Why don't you stick to your own kind?" My teachers all laughed their smirking stares, couldn't keep them out of our affairs. Preachers of equality . . . then why won't they just let us be? They say I can't see you anymore, baby, can't see you anymore. One of these days I'm gonna stop my listening, gonna raise my head up high . . . but that day will have to wait for a while. Baby, I'm only society's child . . .

Janis Ian, "Society's Child"

Over the years, few topics have preoccupied whites, blacks, and others as much as interracial dating and, ultimately, intermarriage. With few exceptions, resistance to integration—in public accommodations, in the neighborhood, or in the school—is implicitly or explicitly motivated, at least in part, by the fear of intimate interracial contact. The line "Guess who's coming to dinner, Mom" evokes fear in a great many households (3). At the same time, in spite of the pressure both at the psychological and at the sociological level on those who date interracially, there is evidence that more couples are involved—or, at least, their involvement is more visible (2).

In part, this may be related to the social movements and programs of the sixties, such as the civil rights movement, the Peace Corps, and VISTA. Each of these activities provided opportunities for the races to mix. Yet, each of these movements attracted mostly the more idealistic youth of our society to their ranks. Thus, while interracial couples are not so invisible and are not forced to meet clandestinely any longer, there is still no stampede (2). Many youths appreciate and acknowledge the problems that the "generation gap" creates in the area of interracial dating, and usually attribute negative attitudes to their parents and grandparents and positive ones to themselves and their age peers; but, in reality, they only profess liberalism (11). A recent Harris Poll on interracial dating reveals the confusion over the subject (2). For example, the poll shows that one out of every five Americans has had a date with someone outside of his or her own race. In the West and among young people—that is, those under 25—the figure is one in three, and in the South the figure is one in ten. While the Harris Poll suggests that interracial dating is not infrequent, the poll also reveals that at least 42 percent of those interviewed knew that interracial couples have difficulties when they appear in public. And of that number, only 57 percent were sympathetic. To further substantiate the ambivalence toward interracial dating, even among the 57 percent who were sympathetic, and thus ostensibly opposed to the community pressures against interracial dating, a full 44 percent contended that it is all right for anyone who honestly believes it is "wrong" to date interracially to express his opinion openly.

The pressures against interracial dating are many and originate from many sources. The results of a poll, while informative and interesting, cannot provide the whole picture. A poll cannot vividly explore the social world of equal-status contacts, the pressures and crosspressures, the groupings and regroupings, the conflicts and alliances, and the overall costs of interracial dating to the participants. For this we need to hear from those who are involved. We need to hear it in their own words. For the words do not easily reduce to numbers. For the social scientist, this is difficult. Without numbers there is reduced confidence, if any at all, in generalization.

Yet, I am impressed with the fact that studies of interracial dating, whether reported in scholarly journals, "pop" social science, *Life, Time, Ebony,* or *Evergreen,* or in a book about interracial dating and marriage among the Maori and Pakeha of New Zealand, show a remarkable consistency with regard to the reported pressures on those who are involved (2, 3, 6, 7, 9, 12).

John Harré, in his study of mixed marriages in New Zealand, wrote the following on the subject of dating:

> There is no doubt that in a vague sort of way the community in general does not fully accept mixed dating. I say vague because reactions are not always consistent, and explanations seldom explicit. They tend to be expressed in such statements as: "It's better to stick to your own race." "It's disgraceful the number of Pakeha girls (white) you see with Maori boys nowadays." "It's just asking for trouble." [6]

At the same time that Harré was collecting data in New Zealand, Julius Lester was interviewing a white woman married to a black in New York City. While the geographical distance involved is immense, the sociological distance is negligible. Lester was told:

> This morning I was taking Michele, the three-year-old, to nursery school. We're walking down the street minding our own business and this woman stops, looks, and says, "She isn't . . ." Her voice just kind of trailed off. I decided I wouldn't help her one damn bit. "Isn't what?" I asked. She wouldn't say it though. She just shook her head and wandered off. [7]

In Minneapolis an incredulous white motorist who spied an interracial couple in the downtown area appeared to have been hypnotized by the experience so that he drove into a parking meter (13). The black man, rather than responding with acrimony, fed the meter a nickel—an unusual expression of hostility, perhaps, but nevertheless hostility.

In Topeka, Kansas, a black high school student, aware of the white community's reactions to white girls who date or talk in public with blacks, refrained from asking a white girl out. The young black man in this case was the son of a professional, was a football letterman, in the student government, and extremely popular.

> In general, I'd say that just the fact that I was taking out a white girl, the imaginations would go wild. They think the moral standards are lower in interracial dating. There's this one white girl I goofed around with a lot. It's gone beyond the friendship state, but we never dated. If I did go out with a white girl, it'd be hard to take her any place. I'd have to think about it for a while before I took out a white girl, because I feel she'd be downgraded. I wouldn't want to ruin her reputation. [9]

That the community does not fully accept interracial dating and that the assumed nonacceptance is often general is seen in the response of another high school student. Only, this time it is a white male who at one time thought of dating a black girl.

> I think if you dated a Negro, you'd lose a lot of so-called friends. But you'd probably gain some Negro friends. I contemplated asking this Negro girl for a date, but I chickened out. I thought where would I take her? The only place where people wouldn't stare at me would be at a drive-in movie, and I don't have a car. If you went to a restaurant, you'd get dirty looks from people. I couldn't take her home and introduce her to my mom; she'd probably kill me. [9]

At times the assumed threat from the community is not expressed by those concerned in such mild ways as saying, "Where would I take her?" Vivid descriptions of anticipated physical harm are not restricted to the Southern states. Most of us have grown up knowing that Southern black men have disappeared, been mutilated, and hanged for making alleged advances toward white women. Few people, however, know that in the 1920's three black men were hanged in downtown Duluth, Minnesota, for the same reason. And few of us know that in 1968 a black journalist from Detroit told a *Time* magazine reporter:

> Off campus no place is really safe. When I have a white girl in my car, I don't stop at red lights, I make sure my car's in good condition with the gas tank full and a good spare. God forbid I should have to stop somewhere with a white girl. [3]

CENSURE OF ONE'S OWN PEOPLE

Generalized community pressure against interracial intimacy, while a deterrent to some blacks and whites who have thought of crossing the color line, is nevertheless a more abstract pressure than the censure of one's own people. It is not the white person only who experiences this pressure—like the white girl who is boycotted by white boys for dating a black (9). The black male who dates across the color line may be viewed by other blacks as a breach in group solidarity for which powerful negative sanctions may be invoked to bring the person in line. These sanctions run the gamut from name calling (such as Uncle Tom) to physical violence (10). Surprisingly, the violence generally does not come from other black men, who may see

interracial dating as a threat to the black movement. It is the black
woman who is more vehemently opposed to interracial dating and
who, in her frustration and anger, may beat up a black male who's
"living a lie" (talking black and dating white).

In some cities, black girls have formed clubs to "Save Our Men."
Black girls stare menacingly at white girls with black dates. *Life*
magazine reported that on campus the sight of an interracial couple
can incite some black women to physical abuse. Often it is the white
girl who is the object of the physical attack. But black men have also
been subjected to intimidation (2). The competition for black males
in the dating-mating process is a source of tension between black and
white girls even at the junior high school level.

> Well, in junior high, the Negro girls resented the fact that I went
> out with a white girl, and they really got onto me. They feel in-
> ferior. The white girls get all the guys. Some hostility between the
> Negro girls and white girls comes from this. The Negro girls kind
> of feel left out. She doesn't have white guys to date, and she doesn't
> have Negro guys to date. She says, "Hey, gal, you dating that
> Negro, and I can't get a date with him." This kind of builds up a
> resentment in her. [9]

This is not too different from what might be heard on a college
campus. One college freshman had this to say when asked about her
hostility toward white girls who take away the only boy friends black
girls may have.

> What's wrong with me? There aren't enough black men to go
> around and he's messing with Charlie's daughter. If the white
> woman was in my position, she'd feel just as threatened. When
> your field of choice is wiped out, your world is torn apart. The
> educated black woman doesn't have anybody out there. [2]

Most observers agree that interracial couples consist mainly of
black men and white women. And as one black girl told me, "There
ain't no reciprocity." Why ain't there no reciprocity? One reason is
that black women do not hunt for white men. It is fairly accepted
now that the image of the poor, innocent white woman as the victim
of aggressive advances by black men is a myth (2, 3). Negro men do
not hunt so often as they are hunted.

> The white man has raised the white woman to believe that she is
> the Queen of the World and I think you underestimate the number

of white women who wear the crown proudly and consider it their obligation to defend it. . . . Maybe you've never noticed those white women walking down the street who let a black man know that he should jump at the opportunity to sleep with her, that he should consider himself blessed. I guess you've never been to one of those parties and watched the white girls try to get the black men away from the black women. It's an ugly, vicious scene. [7]

A black female college student poignantly tells of her anger:

If a black guy walks up to a group of black and white girls in a bar, the white chick makes her move before he can open his mouth. She monopolizes the conversation. What can you do—say, "Hey, let me talk, too?" So you sit there awkwardly. At the end of the evening he says, "What're you so quiet about?" Then he's out the door with the honky and you end up going home alone. [2]

Even if white males take the aggressive lead, there are other deterrents for the black girl. Many black girls say they are haunted by the image of the white "massa" coming down the hill to take his pick of slave women.

Fear for one's reputation is also a very real factor for girls who wish to date interracially, whether they are black or white. A black high school student had little doubt about this and was certain that the motives of white males who asked her for a date were questionable.

Any white boy who asked me out, I'd know what he wants. For a Negro boy to have a white girl is some sort of status symbol, but if a white boy asked me out, it'd be a step-down for him. I'd think he wants something I'm not about to give him. [9]

A 24-year-old career girl from New York said the same thing as the previous teenager from a small, Midwest community, but perhaps more poetically: "For many white males, my skin is still a badge that identifies me as a sexual plaything" (3).

From a study of high school students in a desegregated school, we found that black girls were dissuaded from dating white boys because of parental disapproval (12). This was particularly true among "elite" blacks. Most of the black girls from this stratum said their parents would not tolerate interracial dating. The parents expected them to compete with white students, but not for white dates. Other black girls reportedly refuse to date white men because they lack "soul" (3).

Frazier found that women of the black bourgeoisie were particularly handicapped, but that lower-class black women are apparently immune.

> Among the women of the black bourgeoisie there is an intense fear of the competition of white women for Negro men. They often attempt to rationalize their fear by saying that the Negro man always occupies an inferior position in relation to the white woman or that he marries much below his "social" status. They come nearer to the source of their fear when they confess that there are not many eligible Negro men and that these should marry Negro women. That such rationalizations conceal deep-seated insecurity is revealed by the fact that generally they have no objection to the marriage of white men to Negro women, especially if the white man is reputed to be wealthy. In fact, they take pride in the fact and attribute these marriages to the "peculiar" charms of Negro women. [4]

Among "elite" black girls in the high school study, competition from white girls for black dates was heightened by the fact that their parents would also not permit them to date blacks from a lower class, and, in some cases, blacks with a darker skin. Ironically, the black female college student furthers her disadvantage by increasing the gap in education between herself and black men. Although college improves her economic and social status, each year of school above the ninth grade reduces her chances of finding a black marriage partner (2).

But even if black girls would date whites, white boys may be reluctant because of assumed differences in culture.

> Well, there're cultural differences, and their attitudes are different. I think that's what makes the difference. They're easy going. They like to have a lot of fun. They don't think about the future, about things that are important like getting a job, or supporting a family. They don't try for grades. They're just out to have a good time. [9]

Still other black girls see the white boys' reluctance to date blacks as essentially a matter of status considerations. If the belief that *all* whites are better than *all* blacks is general in this society, then the words of a black high school girl, who was given the highest academic award the school has to offer, make sense.

White boys would be scared to ask us out anyway. The Negro boys will ask white girls out, but white boys will never ask Negro girls out. For a Negro boy, going out with a white girl is an accomplishment; it raises his status, even if the white girl is lower class. All white kids are supposed to be better than Negro kids. If a white boy dated a Negro, even if the white boy was one of the "trashy" kind, and the girl was, say, me, his status would drop. They'd ask him if he was hard-up or something. White boys would be stepping down if they asked Negro girls for dates. [9, 12]

BLACK MEN AND WHITE WOMEN

The overwhelmingly prevalent pattern in interracial dating is black boy with white girl. Why? Are white girls less conservative than white boys? Are they out for kicks? Is it because "black is in this year"? One black male college student told a *Time* reporter, "They pass me around. They think I'm this potent black Adonis, this ebony god"(3).

Lewis Yablonsky, a sociologist, said, "If a white girl wants to do her parents in, the classic pattern is to go out with someone black"(3). And some high school students told me that white girls who date interracially are trying "to spit in the eye of society."

What is interesting about the process is that the most logical motive for interracial dating is generally ignored in favor of a psychological reason or, worse yet, a deviant label. Couldn't it be that we are asking the wrong question? Why, when we see an interracial couple, instead of asking why, don't we ask why not? Is it not possible that two people, one white and one black, may just like one another? A white girl from the University of Minnesota spoke of her interracial dating in these terms.

He's just like any other guy I've ever dated, only his skin is black. I've never felt self-conscious with him. He's a good conversationalist and we always have fun, going to shows or just listening to records. [2]

From Topeka, Kansas, the words of a high school student tell us just how expensive it is to date a black student. And the expense is partially there because of the reluctance to accept an interracial couple's motives at face value.

Around Christmas time, I got to know this colored guy real well and wanted to date him. There was a big mixup; my parents didn't like it. My parents put a lot of pressure on me not to go out with him. They are the type people, like Dad, who says he's not prejudiced. He even has *them* working in his office, but he wants them to stay in their place. At school there was a lot of talking behind my back and snickering when I walked down the hallway. I tried to tell myself it didn't matter what people thought, but it still hurt. It hurt an awful lot. My parents made me feel so guilty. They made me feel so cheap. They worried about what people would say. They made me feel like two pieces of dirt. You know, I never thought interracial dating was a good idea, but when I met this colored guy, it changed me. I never went with anyone I really liked before. I think this changes your outlook. It gives you hope, when you find someone you really like. [9]

SEX AND DATING

That sexual intercourse is automatically associated with interracial dating is indicated by the fact that a common reaction is to question the girl's moral standards. Even black girls who have not ventured into the world of interracial dating imagine that this will occur. White boys and girls—because they are responsible, in large part, for the labeling—know that one of the social costs for interracial dating is the white girl's reputation. Prior to dating a black, the girl's personal conduct is rarely mentioned. Perhaps the rationalization that the girl is immoral is one way for members of the white community to cope with the disbelief that a white girl would occasionally prefer dating a black.

In New Zealand too, sex is associated with interracial dating. Harré wrote:

> Several of my informants said that while their relationship with members of the other race had been casual their parents had accepted it with equanimity. The transition to courting had drawn forth criticism. . . . Many Pakehas attribute to Maoris a low standard of sexual morality and fear that a regular relationship . . . may result in a pregnancy. This reaction is strongest when the Pakeha is a girl. . . .[6]

A white girl does not have to actually date a black to have others question her morality. Talking in public to a black man can result in the same labeling process.

> One day we were talking to some Black Power students in front of school. Some adults going by in cars made some filthy remarks.

> You can imagine what they think of white women hanging around
> talking to Negroes. They shot it right out as they drove by. These
> are the good, white middle class people. [9, 12]

A very articulate young Negro described a similar incident in which
he was talking to a white girl.

> One time I was walking down the stairs outside school. I was
> standing with this white girl, and we were talking. About six white
> kids drove by and yelled, "White trash, you're nothing but white
> trash." I guess because she was white and I'm black, and we were
> talking, she was white trash.

White parents eye black boy friends warily; they fear interracial
sex almost as much as interracial marriage. A white college-sorority
girl's comments on this point probably depict what a great many
parents feel.

> Whenever people see a mixed couple, they immediately assume
> they're sleeping together. Nobody ever considers maybe they're
> just having a Coke or happen to dig Fellini films. [2]

There is a tendency to attribute such stereotyped attitudes to the
"community," which is like saying that a corporation is responsible
for losing an investor's money, and not the officers of the corporation.
The latter is a legal fiction and the former a social fiction. Such
stereotyped assumptions are present even among peers, so that the
theory of a generation gap cannot explain the illiberalism. When one
white college freshman told roommates she had accepted a date with
a black football player, her roommates handed her three sex manuals
(2).

A white high school student explains her disgust for fellow students who had reacted stereotypically to another student who was
dating a black.

> I got kind of sick of the kids throwing her to the dogs. There were
> times when you had to take a stand. You either turned the other
> cheek, or you fought back for her. They thought she was cheap,
> and they said nasty things about her. Even the guy I'm dating, he's
> that way too. [9]

WHITE "BOYCOTT"

White girls who date across the color line find themselves unaccepta-
ble to white boys. Most of the students agree that to date interracially

limits the girl's field of potential dates. For many white girls, knowledge of this reaction on the part of white boys serves as a deterrent to interracial dating. Nevertheless, a number of white girls told us they were attracted to certain young black men. One of the girls who did defy her society said, "When I was dating him, I was surprised at how many girls wanted to date colored guys. They would come up to me and ask me things. They really wanted to date colored guys, but they were afraid."

The white "boycott" can persist after the interracial couple no longer dates, but generally only among white boys still in school. Girls who break off their relationship with blacks may be dated by older whites in the community. But our research shows that to regain admission as an acceptable date among the high school boys, a girl would have to change schools or move to a new community.

College students are perhaps more tolerant, so the boycott may not be so great a problem. But even among college students, interracial dating tends to be associated automatically with interracial sex. A white girl who is known as an interracial dater cannot be sure that her new white beau does not expect more permissiveness than he would from another girl. Even black men, who should be rightfully embittered by the dehumanizing implications of the myth of their supersexuality, regard middle-class white girls as more permissive than middle-class black girls, and expect their white dates to permit intimacy sooner than girls of their own race (2).

PARENTAL PRESSURE

The threat of losing one's reputation and losing favor among white boys prevents many white girls, particularly those in high school, from dating blacks. Yet the pressures do not end there. Interracial dating is a test of the white liberal's commitment to civil rights—a test that few have passed. White parents, after all, have acquired the evaluations of black that sociologists like to attribute to a nonperson such as the "community." Parents with a liberal self-conception, who talk integration but in the final analysis are prejudiced—at least on the issue of interracial dating—may find themselves a disappointment to their children.

> This Negro friend of mine gets along beautifully with my mother, but not my father. He senses this too. After meeting my father, he said my father didn't like him. This is something new for me be-

cause my father and mother have always been liberal. Now that
he's been over to my house a couple of times, my father is acting
strange. I guess I'm learning something about him I didn't know
before. [9]

Sometimes the parental reaction is not just a subtle one that
elicits the feeling that one's father doesn't approve. A white college
student remembers that in her first letter from home after telling her
parents she was dating a black, they called her a slut (2). At times,
white families turn to society's gatekeepers when their daughters
date blacks. A Seattle family sent their daughter to a psychiatrist
when they found out she had dated a black student. And the parents
of another girl turned her over to juvenile authorities as "ungoverna-
ble." A white girl from New York labeled her mother's inconsistency
as "clandestine bigotry" (3).

A black high school student told us what happened to a white girl
who dated her ex-boy friend.

> For many Negro boys, dating white girls is their way of showing
> their superiority, their way of trying to hurt the white man. This
> boy I used to date went with a white girl once. She went through
> hell with her parents and everyone else to go out with him. But he
> didn't really care. He was just showing off. Her father even spit in
> her face. Her parents attacked her; they beat her and called her
> a slut. [9]

Acts of physical aggression such as the above may be the exception. Verbal aggression and mental cruelty are far more frequent. In
an interview for *Evergreen*, Julius Lester asked a white woman how
her parents reacted to her marrying a black man, and was told:

> Like Spencer Tracy and Katherine Hepburn. They didn't like it
> one bit . . . when I told them we were getting married, they flipped.
> They knew we were living together and that didn't bother them.
> Like I said, they're liberal. . . . We'd been living together for six
> months and they hadn't minded. I couldn't understand them. Be
> a whore, but don't get married. They flew into town and tried
> every trick in the book. [7]

Parental disapproval of interracial dating is not restricted to
whites. Like the black father in "Guess Who's Coming to Dinner,"
black parents and grandparents do not wholeheartedly approve of
interracial dating. The motives, however, may be different. Within
the black culture, there is the knowledge, whether from direct or

indirect experience, that black males have been treated with a brutality seldom seen in Western civilization for acts that often turned out to be no more than false accusations. Fear for one's male children is a motive with which few in the white world, or any world for that matter, can take issue. By and large, however, black teenagers agree that mixed couples should have that choice without interference from members of the adult community, be they parents (black, white, or brown), teachers, counselors, school administrators, or members of the community at large (12).

Chicano parents seem to differ very little on this issue from whites or blacks. An outspoken Chicano girl student articulated the Mexican parents' position very well. Her words reveal the confusion parental inconsistencies can create in a young person.

> Mom always said have your fun as long as you're young, and as long as you marry a Mexican. I don't feel that way. If I fall in love with a Negro, I'll marry him. If I fall in love with a white, I'll marry a white. My parents would frown on us dating a Negro, even if he has higher standards than the Mexicans we date now: even if the Negro's father was a lawyer or a doctor, and he was a better person than many of the lower class Mexicans we date now. I don't understand it. They would rather see us go out with white people who aren't as good, just because of skin color. They say they want the best for us; if the best meant going out with a Negro, they would say no. [9]

When Louis Harris and Associates asked a cross-section of Americans, "Do you think most *adults* get upset when they see an interracial couple?" 81 percent said yes. When the same people were asked, "Does it upset young people?" 54 percent answered no (2). The results of the Harris Poll seem to support the young, who do not deny completely their illiberalism, but prefer to emphasize that their parents are even more illiberal. In another touchy question, Harris asked the national sample which combination of sexes is most disturbing to adults. By six to one, they said a black man with a white girl.

Although, as I have said earlier, opposition to interracial dating is not uniquely white, the Harris Poll shows black parents to be less opposed. Fifty-eight percent of the black parents were opposed compared to 72 percent of all people interviewed (2).

PRESSURES FROM THE EDUCATIONAL ADMINISTRATION

As if the pressures of peers, parents, and the community were not enough, violators of the proscription against interracial dating must also cope with teachers, counselors, and school administrators (at least in the desegregated secondary school). How do these molders of human minds and spirits react? Is it with dispassion and objectivity? Is it with support and understanding? Is it with fairness and equanimity? No. These caretakers of our children by and large believe that boy-girl relationships *ought to be* white-white, black-black, or brown-brown, and not variations on a theme.

In a recent discussion on this topic with a college class, I was told of an incident which took place at one of the affluent all-white schools in Tucson, Arizona. Two black males from another school, while visiting two girls from the all-white school, were asked to leave. One of the irate girls was told that nonstudents (whether black, white, or brown) are prohibited from visiting the public school. The class reaction was, "Bullshit!" One student from Chicago said, "That's so transparent. If the guys were white, they couldn't tell if they went to that school or not." It only goes to show that you can fool some of the people some of the time, but not all of the people all of the time.

Out of material collected in 1968 from a desegregated high school in the community which was the object of the 1954 Supreme Court's Brown decision, we found that teachers, counselors, and school administrators do not interfere with all interracial couples. The amount of pressure is proportional to the white girl's social status. If the interference is selective, what message can such behavior transmit to members of the minority community? The words of a black girl provide a partial answer.

> I think it's their business, not the school's. She was crazy about him, and he was crazy about her. They went to school to get an education, and that's what the school should be concerned with: giving them an education. Instead, they threatened him, they said he wouldn't get an athletic scholarship. I felt this was entirely wrong for the school to interfere. It's not the school's affair to concern itself with whether or not the students have companionship. It's their business to teach. These kids aren't the only couple at school. But she's somebody. With some of the other couples, the girls aren't important. In fact, one of the other girls is just white "trash." They don't say too much to these others; it's the important ones they want to save. [12]

Another girl left little doubt of the black person's hurt which was aggravated by the school's policy of selectively interfering with interracial dating.

> If you're a low white person, the administration couldn't care less, but if you're a higher white person, they're worried that you might be dragged down by a Negro.

Another possible answer, then, is that such a policy can represent another attack on the black man's self-esteem. While this may not be the intention of the behavior, we can be almost certain that if things are perceived as real, they are real in their consequences. There is a possibility that the school's policy is dictated by the realities of the situation. What can the school officials do to low-status students who date across the color line? Very little. The parents may be informed but, in most cases, the parents already know. One other course of action is to expel low-status students for slight rule infractions, and, at times, this is what happens. High-status students are more vulnerable. Removal from the team or being assigned to the bench can either completely or almost completely cut off one's chances for an athletic scholarship. High-status white girls also provide school officials with some means of social control. It is they who most often run for school offices, seek eligibility on the cheerleader squad or positions in a variety of extra-curricular activities. Ironically, those who work hardest to achieve the prizes the system has to offer provide the system with the means of control should they deviate from the accepted patterns of mating-dating.

The extent to which our caretakers will go knows no boundaries, and at times not even propriety. Thus, a white high school senior student found unhappily that her daily escort between classes was not her black boy friend but her counselor. The same black young man, thinking things would be better in college, two years later (1970) found himself face-to-face with the college president who asked, "Why don't you date the black girls we have here for you?" Can you imagine, now that some of us have melted—not in this melting pot of ours, but in this cauldron—being called in by a college president and asked, "Why don't you date the (German, Scotch, Irish, Danish, Swedish, Italian, French, English, Canadian, or what-have-you) girls we have here for you?"

SUMMARY AND CONCLUSION

There are few topics on which everyone seems to have an opinion. And fewer yet on which it is easy to elicit the opinion. Interracial dating does not fall in this category. In a study of high school students in a desegregated school, we found the students eager to talk about interracial dating. At the same time, we found this to be one of the most emotionally charged subjects in our discussions. Recent reports in journals of mass appeal *(Time, Life,* and the now defunct *Look)* bear this out. Each of these reports indicates an eagerness on the part of those interviewed that survey researchers have seldom known.

The data seems to indicate that the frequency of interracial dating has increased. Younger people are not so intolerant of interracial couples as their parents, grandparents, and society's gatekeepers and caretakers. But this is not to say they are completely tolerant. Youth, in its idealism, often assumes vast generational differences, where there are none or where the differences are slight. It is psychologically easier to project illiberalism, particularly onto parents with whom many youths are at war.

I can offer numerous examples of this phenomenon, which is the subject of one of my papers (11). The following words were spoken by a student in the peace movement and should suffice to highlight the point. Generally, "Peaceniks" lean toward tolerance, so their prejudices may be more subtle. Nevertheless, the prejudices surface as part of the "they" phenomenon.

> Everytime I think of Negroes, I can't really think of individual Negroes. When I think of Negroes, this group image comes to my mind of people who think alike and talk alike. I really think of Negroes as a group. Maybe they're just like us, with parents who disapprove of them. And maybe they're just like us in other ways. But I find it hard to think of Negroes as individuals.

Basically, the student who spoke these words thought he was tolerant of individual and of racial and ethnic differences. Yet, he did not recognize individual differences in blacks. To him, blacks are an undifferentiated mass. This same person, when asked to focus on his parents' attitudes on racial integration, implied they are more prejudiced.

> There aren't any blacks where my parents live. They live in the blocks away from us. I think there's a big gap between myself and my parents on issues like Vietnam, drugs, homosexuality, and race;

although we never talk about it. Even my brother, who's ten years older, is an entrenched conservative. He's a veteran, lives in an expensive apartment, drives a Cadillac, and thinks Washington knows all.

The prevailing pattern of interracial dating is black boy with white girl. The Harris Poll shows that this is the pattern Americans abhor most. Because of its sheer frequency, however, Americans may abhor what they see most. Of course, there are historical factors as well. The sexual exploitation of black women by white Americans is a fact. This is not to imply that the few white men who choose to date blacks at present have the "massa" syndrome, but only that to most Americans this pattern may seem more "legitimate."

Within the secondary school, the black male who dates a white girl is often a high-status athlete. High status, in the sense used here, is unrelated to his father's socioeconomic position in the community. This may, or may not, be high; in most cases, it is not.

The fact that black students with prestige may turn to white girls is one thing that enrages black girls and is a source of tension between black and white girls. The black girl in college also experiences the rage. Ironically, the anger generated may drive potential black suitors away, thereby setting up a "vicious cycle." A black graduate student, who dates white women exclusively, told a *Life* reporter.

> I wouldn't go out with one of those nigger bitches for all the money in the world. They're mean, they're evil, they're hard to get along with. [2]

More than her male counterpart, the black girl preaches separatism. Some students, particularly at the high school level, think this is because girls do not have as many opportunities to share a sports activity such as that shared by black and white boys. Perhaps, but since there is very little evidence of interracial camaraderie off the playing field between athletes, the competition for high-status blacks in the dating-mating complex seems to explain more plausibly the friction between white and black girls. Although we were told that "there ain't no reciprocity," it is unlikely that black girls would date whites in large numbers, if given the chance. Most black women are opposed to interracial dating, which they view as a contradiction for a true black person (2, 8).

Those who date interracially pay a price. In the game of imputing motives, few are convinced that the daters merely like one another. Rarely is the couple not accused of promiscuity. Given the double standard in our society, the cost here is heaviest for the female. Some black women imagine this to be a penalty for dating interracially, and many white women *know* that it is.

One's peers, while prone to lip-service on equality between the races, have nevertheless acquired the stereotypes and evaluations of the blacks held by the dominant society. It is not unusual for whites who date interracially to find themselves in a situation with a high attrition rate among "friends." Or, perhaps worse, the girl (since it is most often a girl) will find herself the object of much unsolicited advice. Even on an initial date, a girl may be told, "But think of the children!" How absurd such advice would appear (to the giver as well) particularly on the first date, if the date was white! There is absolutely no evidence that interracial daters are more serious on the first date than noninterracial daters.

Parents are another source of pressure. In some cases the pressure is physical abuse, though verbal abuse is more commonplace. It is intriguing that the same parents who ask their daughters to think of the neighbors, the family, and the family's social position, use phrases that clearly indicate that they are not thinking of the child but of themselves. Following this kind of barrage in which the white girl, like her black boy friend, is treated as a nonperson, the parent may say, "We are only thinking about what's best for you." I am reminded of the Chicano student who told me, "They say they want the best for us; if the best meant going out with a Negro, they would say no!" There can be little doubt about the "double bind" quality of parental communications in such instances. When parents stop seeing interracial dating as ego devastating for themselves, perhaps such vacuous communications will become history.

As we have seen, additional payment is exacted by the caretakers of our schools and members of the community at large. Both, however, are rarely a part of the dater's reference group. Because of this, their slings and arrows may carry less sting. But when young people are concerned about where they can go without people staring at them, neither is the price insignificant. The caretakers will often say their behavior is a consequence of public opinion to which they must bow since they are agents of the community. However, the community also demands propriety, which, as we have seen, is at times violated by school officials. Further, it is a moot question who is the setter of public opinion and who is set by it. When school officials interfere with interracial dating, they help perpetuate prejudice. Whether the consequence is intended or unintended is for sociological argumentation. It is still a consequence.

A cartoon in the August, 1970 issue of *Ebony*, if taken seriously, may help dissipate the paranoia which manifests itself on the issue of interracial dating. A white father during a clinical session with his psychiatrist says, "And then I found out that most of them don't even want to marry my daughter!"

9

JAMES D. BRUCE, Ph.D. and HYMAN RODMAN, Ph.D.

Black-White Marriages in the United States: A Review of the Empirical Literature

A great deal of the information that we have about black-white unions in the United States is largely impressionistic, and at present there is really no comprehensive study of such marriages. There is, fortunately, a growing body of empirical literature concerning biracial unions, and Dr. James D. Bruce and Dr. Hyman Rodman review it for us in the following chapter.

Their evaluation of the available empirical data makes clear that the formation of biracial unions is affected by a wide range of factors, such as time, place, and conditions of living. Their study also shows that, though the number of interracial marriages in the United States is still slim, their rate appears to be increasing.

There are reasons to believe that changing opinions and feelings about biracial unions, which reflect the ever-wider rate of current social change, are beginning to have some impact on interracial marriages.

The authors' review of the literature raises many questions in our minds, and although the answers provided may be few, this study represents a valuable guideline for the thoughtful reader.

THERE HAS been a long history of black-white miscegenation in the United States. As a result, most blacks and many whites are racially mixed. This may come as a surprise to some whites (including many who are themselves racially mixed without knowing it) because our categorial thinking places everyone into either a black or a white box.

Black-white marriage has also contributed to biological mingling, although it has been less important. State laws and widespread prejudice have minimized the number of black-white marriages. At one time as many as thirty states, primarily Southern and Western, had laws prohibiting black-white marriage. The patent discrimination of these laws gradually led to their repeal outside the Southern states, so that by the time the United States Supreme Court ruled unanimously, in 1967, that such laws were unconstitutional, the number of states that still had such laws had been reduced to sixteen.

To date there has been no comprehensive study of black-white marriages in the United States. Most of the researchers who have undertaken studies in this area have stated that there are only limited and unsatisfactory data available on black-white marriages (27). It has only been in the last three decades that some attempt has been made to obtain more than just frequency statistics on black-white marriages.

The purpose of this chapter is to review and summarize the data in the available literature on black-white marriages. Many of the existing discussions and propositions concerning black-white intermarriage have been based on limited and inconclusive surveys. By presenting a descriptive analysis of the studies done on black-white marriages in the United States, we will try to evaluate the existing propositions and to pinpoint the areas requiring additional research.

Until the twentieth century, very little empirical information was published on the subject of black-white marriage. With the turn of the century, however, a few writers systematically reported the frequency of black-white marriages in a specific city or state for a particular number of years.

FREQUENCY OF BLACK-WHITE MARRIAGES

Table 1 is a listing of all empirical studies known to us that are based upon complete population information or a representative sample of a population. The total frequency of black-white marriages is presented along with the percentage of black-white marriages in relation to *all* marriages and in relation to all black marriages. The table illustrates the relatively few studies reported in the literature and their diversity in terms of populations and years studied.

As Table 1 indicates, Hoffman (14) published the earliest series of statistical data on black-white marriages. The percentages of black-white marriages of *all* marriages for Michigan, Rhode Island, and Connecticut are .03, .17, and .10 respectively. In comparing these early findings with studies dealing with intermarriages since 1948, we notice that there has been a slight increase over the last sixty years. The percentages of black-white marriages as related to all marriages are, however, all well below 1 percent. It should be noted that one reason for the low percentage of black-white marriages in Pavela's (19) study of Indiana (as well as Panunzio's [18] of Los Angeles) is that the state law barring black-white marriages was still in force when the data were collected. If one accepts Gordon's (11) data on Connecticut (he gives no formal source for his information), Table 1 shows that over the last sixty years black-white marriages in that state have increased from .10 to .23 percent of all marriages. There has also been an increase in the percent of black-white marriages as a percent of all black marriages.

As mentioned previously, Table 1 points out the inconsistency and unrelatedness of the existing empirical studies on black-white marriages—especially in terms of the populations investigated, the time period studied, and the type of data collected. It is therefore virtually impossible to document any definite trends or tendencies

TABLE 1

A Summary of Empirical Studies of
the Number of Rate of Black-White Marriages

Researcher	Population	Time Period Studied	Total Number of Black-White Marriages	% Black-White Marriages Of All Marriages	Of All Black Marriages
Hoffman	Michigan	1874–1893	111	.03*	
Hoffman	R.I.	1883–1893	58	.17*	
Hoffman	Connecticut	1883–1893	65	.10*	
Hoffman	Boston	1855–1887	600		
Stone	Mass.	1900	52		
Stone	Boston	1900–1904	143		13.6
Wright	Phila.	1900	6	.10*	1.0*
Stephenson	Boston	1900–1907	222		
Wright	Phila.	1901–1904	21		
Drachsler	N.Y. City	1908–1912	52		1.1
Deporte	N.Y. State	1919–1929	347		3.8
Wirth and Goldhamer	Boston	1914–1938	276		3.9
Wirth and Goldhamer	N.Y. State	1916–1937	569		2.9
Herbert	Wash., D.C.	1923–1932	61	.11*	
Panunzio	Los Angeles	1924–1933	5	.003*	.1*
Golden	Phila.	1922–1947‡	41	.04*	
A. Lynn	Wash., D.C.	1940–1947	26	.03*	
Burma	Los Angeles	1948–1959	1067	.28*	
Barnett	California	1955–1959	1173	.32*	4.6*
Pavela	Indiana	1958–1959	95	.12*	
Gordon	Connecticut	1953–1959	285	.23	
Heer	Michigan	1953–1963	1132*	.18*	2.0*
Heer	Hawaii	1956–1964	74*	.10*	16.9*
Heer	Nebraska	1961–1964	8*	.02*	.53*
	Wisconsin	1964	43	.16*	7.7*
Annella	Wash., D.C.	1931–1965	818	.77§	

*Computed by first author using data presented in original publication
†Exclusive of New York City
‡Represents totals from years 1922, 1927, 1932, 1937, 1942, 1947
§Represents years only from 1956 through 1965; data computed by first author

between 1874 and 1965, except to note the apparent upturn in black-white marriages in recent years.

SEX DIFFERENTIAL IN BLACK-WHITE MARRIAGES

Table 2 summarizes the available data on the sex differentials in the rate of black-white marriage. Ignoring the 1960 census data for a

TABLE 2

A Summary of Empirical Studies of
Black-White Marriages by Sex and Race of Marriage Partners

Researcher	Population	Time Period Studied	Black Groom White Bride Marriages Number	Percent	White Groom Black Bride Marriages Number	Percent
Hoffman	Michigan	1874–1893	93	84	18	16
Hoffman	R.I.	1883–1893	51	88	7	12
Stone	Mass.	1900	43	83	9	17
Stone	Boston	1900–1904	133	93	10	7
Stephenson	Boston	1900–1907	203	91	19	9
Drachsler	N.Y. City	1908–1912	41	79	11	21
Deporte	N.Y. State	1919–1929	262	75	85	25
Wirth and Goldhamer	Boston	1914–1938	227	82	49	17
Wirth and Goldhamer	N.Y. State	1916–1937	424	74	145	26
Golden	Phila.	1922–1947	24	59	17	41
Lynn	Wash., D.C.	1940–1947	19	73	7	27
Burma	Los Angeles	1948–1959	800	75	267	25
Barnett	California	1955–1959	921	78	252	22
Pavela	Indiana	1958–1959	72	69	19	71
U.S. Census	U.S.	1960	25,496	50	25,913	50
Heer	Michigan	1953–1963	862	76	267	24
Heer	Hawaii	1956–1964	59	80	15	20
Heer	Nebraska	1961–1964	6	75	2	25
	Wisconsin	1964	38	88	5	12
Annella	Wash., D.C.	1931–1965	523	62	295	38

moment, we see that black men intermarry more frequently than do black women, and white women intermarry more frequently than white men. On this point the data are nearly unanimous. But though the black male-white female percentage is higher, there has been a rising percentage of white male-black female marriages. Combining all the studies based on marriages that occurred between 1874 and 1904, we found that the mean percent of black groom-white bride marriages in relation to all black-white marriages was 87 percent.

For studies done after 1940, the figure had dropped to a mean of 75 percent.

The census figures for 1960 stand in sharp contrast to the more limited studies based upon marriage records in individual states or cities (26). The census figures show a 50–50 distribution in the two types of black-white marriage. Since these figures refer to all the existing marriages at that time, they do not represent a continuing shift in the direction of a more equal distribution of the two types of interracial marriage. Either the more limited studies are consistently biased, or some type of systematic bias has crept into the census data. The latter may occur if there are differentials between the two types of intermarriage based on whether or not the racial information is supplied by both partners, on whether or not the wife is home when the enumerator calls, or on the amount of "passing" that has taken place from the Negro to the white category. Census procedures led either the enumerator or the computer to assume that both partners were of the same race when racial information was not otherwise reported. There is therefore a real possibility that systematic bias may seriously distort the census information.

WHITE-NONWHITE MARRIAGES

Some studies have not confined themselves to reporting on black-white marriages, but have dealt more generally with white-nonwhite marriages.

TABLE 3

A Summary of White-Nonwhite Marriages
by Sex and Race of Marriage Partners

Researcher	Population	Years Studied	Total white-nonwhite marriages	Nonwhite Grooms White Brides		White Grooms Nonwhite Brides		Percent of all marriages
				Number	Percent	Number	Percent	
Jacobson	U.S.A.	1939	1142	559	49	583	51	.08
Lynn	Wash., D.C.	1940–1947	353	309	88	44	12	.30
Burma	Los Angeles	1948–1959	3079	1970	64	1109	36	.70
Barnett	Calif.	1955–1959*	4614	2857	62	1757	38	1.2
	Wisconsin	1964	160	93	58	67	42	.59
Annella	Wash., D.C.	1931–1965	2535	1757	67	778	33	

*Does not include data from 1956

Table 3 presents the numbers, percentages, and sex differentials for white-nonwhite marriages in specific populations. A striking finding, which once again raises the issue of the sexual distribution of these marriages, is presented by Jacobson (15). He reports that 51 percent of all white-nonwhite marriages in the United States in 1939 occurred between white grooms and nonwhite brides. Jacobson explains his discrepant findings by stating that all previous studies consisted of relatively small samples and were limited geographically. Further, he points out that black-white marriages are not uniformly distributed throughout the country. Jacobson therefore suggests that previous studies were only representative of the particular areas under investigation. Unfortunately, at the present time it is impossible to estimate the reliability of the figures to support either viewpoint.

Jacobson aside, the data in Tables 2 and 3 are perhaps indicative of a trend that will be further accentuated in future black-white and white-nonwhite marriages.

SURVEYS ON BLACK-WHITE MARRIAGES.

Table 4 is a summary of the data available from specific samples that are *not* representative of the given population. Rather, in each survey the researcher has studied only those interracial couples that it was possible to locate.

Baber's sample was made up of "mixed marriage cases personally known to his students" (2). Both samples studied by Golden were obtained in a similar manner (10). The fifty "interviewed families" were chosen from the black-white couples known to friends of Golden. In addition, the selection of the fifty couples was done by first making arrangements over the telephone, which would tend to eliminate lower-class families. The data on Golden's sample of ninety-one cases were obtained from other individuals who knew of the couple. Because of the small number of studies on black-white marriages, many findings from these surveys have been used as the basis for deriving propositions about interracial marriage. For example, Golden's findings are very frequently referred to when specific characteristics of black-white marriages are being described.

Both Roberts' (21) and Schuyler's (22) studies are good examples of how nonrepresentative samples, over time, come to be referred to in the literature as being complete surveys of specific populations.

TABLE 4

A Summary of Nonrepresentative
Studies of Black-White Marriages
by Sex and Race of Marriage Partners

Researcher	Population Period Studied	Total Black-White Marriages	Black Groom White Bride		White Groom Black Bride	
			Number	Percent	Number	Percent
Baber	N.Y. City 1930	25	18	72	7	28
Lynn	N.Y. City 1949	15	*		*	
Golden	Phila. 1949–1950	50	44	88	6	12
Golden	Phila. 1949–1950	91	72	69	19	31
Roberts	Chicago 1925–1938	188	147	78	41	22
Schuyler	Cleveland 1920's	1100		40		60
Schuyler	22 cities 1920's	3131		80		20
Smith	N.Y. City 1960	22	13	61	9	39

*Original source not available

Roberts' work does not include all black-white marriages in Chicago between 1925–1938, but only the number of couples he was able to locate; nevertheless, many secondary sources incorrectly refer to his study as a complete survey. Perhaps the most dramatic example of grasping at straws and transforming them into data relates to the reports made of Schuyler's work. Many studies that present these data treat them as being complete empirical surveys of black-white marriages for Cleveland and twenty-two other cities (Barron [5, p. 117], Drake and Cayton [9, p. 138], and Golden [10]). It turns out, however, that Schuyler's figures are based upon estimates made by Negro observers. There is no way of knowing anything about the accuracy of these estimates, and it seems far better to discount the figures than to transform them into population survey statistics.

The sex differentials reported by Schuyler for Cleveland show a higher percentage of white grooms and Negro brides. Each of the authors mentioned above notes these unique findings, and indicates, usually in a footnote, that Schuyler's original publication was not seen. The meaning of such a footnote cannot be appreciated until one attempts to obtain a copy of Schuyler's work. After a great deal of searching, we located a copy and discovered how slim the data really were. There is little point in placing any credence on Schuyler's figures on the sex differential.

As Table 4 indicates, except for Schuyler's data, these studies also support the finding that black groom and white bride marriages occur more frequently— at almost a 3:1 ratio. It should be noted, however, that there is a good deal of difference between Golden's samples. For purposes of generalization, it must be emphasized that these studies—based upon nonrepresentative samples and observer estimates—cannot be relied upon with any great degree of confidence.

AGE AT MARRIAGE

On the average, persons entering black-white marriages are slightly older at the time of marriage than others entering marriage.

TABLE 5

Black-White Marriages by Sex
and Median Age: A Summary of Studies

			Median Age at Marriage*			
Researcher	Population	Period Studied	Black Male	White Female	White Male	Black Female
Wright	Phila.	1900	33.7†	25.3†	27.7†	30.5†
Wirth and Goldhamer	Boston	1914–1938	29.1	26.0	31.6	23.9
Lynn	Wash., D.C.‡	1940–1947	(22.7)	(21.1)	(22.7)	(19.3)
			31.0	21.5	44.5	23.5
Burma	Los Angeles	1948–1958	(26.7)	(22.2)	(24.7)	(25)
			27	25	34.7	26
Pavela	Indiana	1958–1959	(27.3)	(20.4)	(23.7)	(23.7)
			27.4	22.2	25	21.5

*Figures in parentheses represent median age at marriage for total population
†Mean age instead of median
‡Data computed for all interracial marriages involving blacks

Table 5 is a summary of the figures available from specific studies on median age at marriage. The data in all studies are not comparable. For instance, Lynn provides age data on first marriages as well as later marriages (16). In the studies by Wirth and Goldhamer (27), Burma (6), and Pavela (19), however, it is not possible to ascertain whether they include the ages of those individuals who were marrying for a second or third time. The data are nevertheless complete enough to show that most of the individuals involved in a black-white marriage have been marrying later in life than individuals who were undertaking a racially homogamous marriage. In addition, Table 5 indicates that the grooms, both black and white, were on the average considerably older than the brides. In three of the studies, the median age of the white groom is at least eight years above that of the black bride. These differences may reflect a higher proportion of remarriages, or a longer period to establish economic stability, or perhaps other dynamics that enter into the decisions of contracting a racially mixed marriage.

SOME PROPOSITIONS ABOUT INTERMARRIAGE

A major theoretical contribution to the study of black-white marriages has been made by Robert K. Merton (17). Although Merton offered no data, he presented the following hypotheses concerning the relative frequencies of several types of intermarriage: (1) marriages of lower-class black females with lower-class white males have about the same frequency as marriages of lower-class white females with lower-class black males; (2) marriages of lower-class white females with upper-class black males are the most frequent type of intermarriage. Merton states that marriages involving lower-class white women and upper-class black men occur most frequently because such marriages involve "a reciprocal compensatory situation in which the Negro male 'exchanges' his higher economic position for the white female's higher caste status."

Some of the literature of the early 1900's does mention that economically inferior white females were marrying financially more stable black males (Reuter [20, p.40]; Baker [3]), even though no data were presented to support such statements.

In looking at the data from the empirical studies, we find that Merton's hypotheses are not borne out—perhaps because of social changes. Wirth and Goldhamer found that the two types of marriages mentioned by Merton (number 1 above) "do not occur with about the equal frequency but in a ratio of 1 to 3" and "that the type of marriage mentioned as being the most frequent [number 2 above] is, in fact, less frequent than several other types"(27).

The few studies published since 1950 are even more convincing in refuting Merton's original hypotheses. Working under the assumption that one of the most significant variables involved in assigning a class level to an individual is his occupation, both Golden (10) and Pavela (19) have come up with similar findings. Golden found that in both his samples "the majority of Negro husbands were either on an equal or a higher level than their white wives, and most of the white husbands outranked or equaled their Negro wives in occupational status." Golden concludes that in the black-white marriages of Philadelphia, there seemed to be a tendency toward homogamy in the occupational area. Similarly, Pavela found that persons involved in black-white marriages in Indiana during 1958–1959 were roughly equivalent in occupational status. These studies suggest that Merton's contention—prosperous black men will marry economically inferior white women—is now questionable. There is still considerable room for exploring the "exchange" hypothesis in interracial marriages, but at the very least, the data suggest that liberal attitudes may be coming to play a larger role in such marriages.

SUMMARY AND CONCLUSION

After reviewing the empirical literature on black-white marriages, we find it clear that there are a great many gaps in our knowledge. Additional study and analysis are required in all of the areas we have touched upon.

Despite the uncertainties, we can draw the following tentative conclusions:

1. In proportion to all marriages there is a very small number of black-white marriages occurring each year in the United States.

2. Although the data are incomplete, there appears to be a recent increase in the number of black-white marriages in relation to all marriages and in relation to all black marriages.

3. There is a higher proportion of black male-white female marriages than of white male-black female marriages. However, there are indications that an increasing number of white males and black females have been intermarrying in recent years.

4. The individuals entering black-white marriages are older at the time of marriage than the individuals entering racially homogamous marriages in the general population.

Finally, in view of the fact that state laws prohibiting interracial marriages were not declared unconstitutional until 1967, it is hardly surprising that such marriages occurred with low frequency. Further, because of the recency of most empirical attempts to study black-white marriages, it is difficult to present an accurate historical account of this social phenomenon. The contradictory findings and interpretations in the available studies call for further research efforts. For example, the variable of geographic location, suggested by Jacobson, should be investigated to determine what effect it has on the frequency of black-white marriages. Even more urgent is a careful review of the reliability of the census data on interracial marriage. Much more information is also needed on personal, social, and family background variables of the individuals involved in a black-white marriage.

The data from these studies have illustrated that time, place, and conditions have affected the incidence of black-white marriages. Although the data in this chapter give only slight indication that the rate of black-white marriages is increasing, there are several relevant social changes presently occurring that will undoubtedly have an impact upon the rate of interracial marriage. Will the increasing recognition of the educational and political rights of blacks affect the rate of black-white marriage? Will the growth of black pride and black power influence intermarriage? What about black separatism, white backlash, desegregation, and generally changing attitudes? In the short run the outlook is cloudy. In the long run it seems clear that altered conditions brought about by the changes in the 1960's will bring further changes in their wake, and will eventually lead to much higher rates of interracial marriage.

10

ARI KIEV, M.D.

The Psychiatric Implications of Interracial Marriage

This psychiatrist, strongly interested in the effects that social climate has on personality, writes of the psychodynamics of interracial marriage within the current context of social and cultural barriers. In his discussion based upon contemporary concepts of social psychiatry, the author emphasizes the inescapable need for all individuals to function within some personal reference framework. He believes that success in an interracial union rests upon individual capabilities, such as insight into one's own personality requirements, as well as into those of one's partner. Dr. Kiev's contribution emphasizes the role each is forced to play in a society riddled with cultural taboos, and which rewards acceptance of the majority's prejudices.

INTERMARRIAGE IN THE MODERN WORLD

Changes in marriage patterns and customs reflect the profound changes in the social, economic, and cultural spheres that characterize the modern world. Evidence of these changes is found in the increased incidence of divorce, sequential marriages, and novel living arrangements such as communal living and group marriages. Similarly, the increased contact of people from diverse backgrounds and the powerful social forces creating social change have led to an increasing incidence of marriage between people of different racial, religious, and ethnic groups. Brought together by common educational and occupational interests, international travel, and changing urban environments, many people enter into such marriages without sufficient preparation to handle some of the problem areas they are likely to encounter. This chapter examines some of the crucial psychosocial processes that may affect favorably or adversely such relationships. Particular emphasis is given to the mental health implications of the differing values and attitudes held by the husband and wife in such marriages.

The family may be viewed as a social organization whose basic functions concern mutual security, procreation, and the preparation of children for the particular needs of the larger social system. The family may serve emotional and cathartic needs as well as economic and religious ones. The particular norms governing these functions vary from culture to culture. To the extent that social norms are concerned with the maintenance and the stability of the family and of the social system, they tend to encourage resistance to change, favoring instead the perpetuation of custom and tradition. Where the family unit plays a critical role in the larger society—as, for example, in an agricultural society as compared to the modern post-industrial society—the community will be very much interested in the individual's choice of marriage partners since the family is serving many more purposes than simply fulfilling the emotional needs of its members.

By and large contemporary society is characterized by fewer constraints on behavior as compared to its traditional structure in the past. Also, the individual is more independent of the basic norms of society, being both less aware of and less concerned about group pressures and sanctions. Both these factors undoubtedly contribute to the greater incidence of interracial marriages in most modern societies.

CULTURAL TABOOS AGAINST INTERMARRIAGE

Social customs and taboos effectively serve as ethical prescriptions for living. Taboos pertain to prohibited behavior patterns which have a fair probability of occurring but which are viewed as potentially disruptive to the social group. Taboos are reinforced by shared beliefs that serve to strengthen the group and by sanctions imposed against taboo violations. Taboos against various forms of intermarriage are strongest in traditional agrarian societies where role relationships are fixed and well defined, and the family functions as an economic and territorial unit. Where such traditions abound, violators of the taboo are more likely to be influenced by individual psychopathological factors than by relatively healthy responses to changing social conditions.

The disappearance of traditional constraints in the modern world reduces the influence of taboos against intermarriage and the frequency with which sanctions are applied against taboo violators. Social change leads to increasing unfamiliarity with both the positive and negative social norms.

Today's increasing freedom from traditional constraints and the increasing personal role in determining one's choice of marriage partner are accompanied by a concomitant loss of the practical guidelines to behavior that traditional rules and taboos provided. The absence of constraints is associated with an increase in anxiety and uncertainty about making choices, as well as an increase in the chance for erroneous or impractical choices. This is particularly likely if the individual ignores significant racial, religious, or ethnic differences between himself and his prospective partner, or prejudicial community attitudes toward such marriages.

Differences in basic cultural values between husband and wife can contribute to conflict. To the extent that individuals understand these factors beforehand, they may be able to avoid considerable conflict and perturbation. Awareness of community prejudices, for example, may assist individuals in dealing with one of the major strains imposed on interracial marriages. Intermarriages that are perfectly acceptable in an overseas social setting may not fare well when the individual returns home or moves to a different geographical location within the same country. This is well demonstrated in the case of the GI's who return to America with Asian wives or in the case of the African in Europe who returns with a white wife to his native village. The same relationship that functions quite smoothly in one situation may prove to be the source of considerable conflict when and if the person encounters community opposition, prejudice, and nonacceptance of his foreign-born and racially distinct spouse. Conflict is especially likely to occur when an individual has incorrectly assumed that he is independent of his reference group and able to sustain himself in the face of group prejudices and social exclusion.

PROBLEMS RESULTING FROM INTERMARRIAGE

How readily the individual can cope with the social realities which oppose intermarriage obviously relates to the strength of his self-concept, or sense of identity. Social attitudes toward intermarriage, which are most explicitly expressed in emotion-laden taboos, set limits on individual behavior and serve to keep cognitive maps of the community intact. The greater an individual's sense of identity, the more capable will he be to act independent of the community. Often, though, what appears to be an act of independence is in fact rebellion against social pressure to conform. This reactive assertiveness may enable the individual to make the initial move, but it does not usually help him later on to sustain the relationship in the face of both external social pressures and internal marital pressures.

The extent of external pressure will depend on whether the

intermarriage taboos are rooted in every-day economic activities, or whether they pertain to widely held political, religious, or ideological beliefs. In traditional societies where roles are fixed, it is important for the proper functioning of the marriage and the larger extended family that the husband and wife accept their respective assigned roles. The more they share these basic attitudes and expectations, the more they will be able to avoid major interpersonal conflicts.

In modern industrial or postindustrial society, shared interests and attitudes which make for satisfactory relationships are influenced by personality factors and by all the experiences and social pressures that continually influence individual behavior. Relationships are less fixed and more subject to changes. These changes are in turn reinforced by an egalitarian ethic and a present-time orientation which stress individual choice and reduce awareness of the significance of racial, ethnic, or cultural factors in handling the problems and stresses of married life.

SOME PSYCHODYNAMIC FACTORS IN RACIAL DISCRIMINATION

There are numerous conflicts and problems generated by status discrepancy where the individual's performance is not commensurate with his educational level or social status because of racial discrimination. Such discrepancies may cause considerable frustration to the individual and his spouse.

Status discrepancy means that the individual is ranked differently from what one would ordinarily expect in terms of prestige and reward based on his social status. Those in positions of status discrepancy will behave differently from those in congruent statuses. Thus, behavioral patterns may in part differ from the norm when the person functions on inappropriate status levels. The head of an interracial family group may show greater deviation from the norms of the strata than his wife, and as a result he may be subjected to far greater strains in his relationship with others. A wife, for example, may share certain values with a lower-status individual to a greater extent than does her spouse, who may be superior educationally or occupationally.

Sensitivity in such a situation may be reflected in the tendency of the interracial couple to misinterpret the humor or remarks of others, to block out communications, and at times to react defensively or in a self-defeating way to avoid what they interpret to be the hostility of others. They may become defensive and guarded over their own hostile feeling and continually qualify their own communications. A reduction in communication, flexibility, and adaptive behavior may result.

Discrimination and status discrepancy may serve neurotic ends for some people. Oftentimes, individuals will unconsciously utilize various interpersonal strategies to maintain a disadvantaged position. This may be reinforced by the spouse's relatives, who may derive some gratification from the individual's status discrepancy or from his suffering, which affords them the chance to be condescending or feel martyred. Even where the individual has resolved the issue and has no negative self-image, he may be made terribly uncomfortable by condescending efforts to "make him feel at home," the price for which is often to play the role of the racially distinct individual. Kindness and hospitality make it difficult for the individual to assert his uniqueness as a person, which may require assertiveness and independence. Indeed, the more he responds to the cues of others out of concern for their positive estimate of him, the less likely will he be able to develop a secure self-view and patterns of life compatible with his own interests.

Various role distortions may occur, which can undermine the individual's self-image. Let's take the example of a man who is interracially married and who is in a position of status discrepancy because of his race. The parents of his wife may unwittingly conspire with her to alter her perception of and relationship with her racially distinct spouse. In addition to this intensification of dependency trends, social stigma or social discrimination may encourage the husband to turn to his wife's relatives and to others to check his own plans in order to avoid difficulty. This will reduce or inhibit much of his initiative, encourage dependency, and increase the likelihood of conflict. The crucial point occurs when the individual accepts the view of others about his social handicap or recognizes a need to "take it easy," and thereby ceases to fight the efforts of others to put him in the role of the scapegoat.

The more ambiguous and subtle the social discrimination, the greater will be the individual's discomfort. Whether he accepts the scapegoat role will depend on his strength, on the situation, and on the need of the relatives to foster dependency by reinforcing his handicap.

Feelings of anxiety or inadequacy can trigger the need to retreat into the role of the racially distinct outsider. Occasionally, an individual may exhibit signs of growth and increasing individuality, manifested by initiative, spontaneity, self-interest, and goal-directed behavior. It may take the form of job seeking, residential moves, or expressing publicly opinions which are contrary to those traditionally held by the family. For various reasons, his wife's family may be threatened by the individual's independent behavior and it may non-verbally communicate this discomfort to him, questioning his plans or concealing its anger by advising him to "do what he wants."

The spouse's family may communicate the idea that his initiative may put too much pressure on his wife. This may induce enough guilt in him to make him withdraw from the field of action. Accepting the majority view, he may attribute his individualistic strivings to misconduct or illness, a process that further inhibits the expression of his own personality.

Guilty for having offended others and frustrated by his own nonperformance, the individual may retreat into a negative non-threatening role allocated to racially distinct outsiders. Of course, one motivation for getting into this kind of situation may have to do with the deviant need of the individual to complement society's need to protect itself by finding a visible target on which to project its hostilities.

The likelihood that the outsider will experience difficulty in his relationships with the spouse's family will, of course, increase when there is family crisis, or if the family has an upwardly mobile orientation and is sensitive to its precarious social position, a position handicapped by the presence of the outsider.

THE EMOTIONS OF STRESS AND CONFLICT

In the early stages of marriage, the major problems of the interracial family pertain to the initial responses of the community to the spouse's racial difference. These may manifest themselves in interpersonal tension and conflict and realization of the individual's inability to function in certain areas of the society because of discrimination and/or because of his own inner anxieties. Problems frequently appear in the process of entering particular educational, occupational, or residential situations. This is especially likely if the culture is unfamiliar and the individual has not made adequate preparation. This is often the case when an individual hastily enters an interracial marriage without examining the potential problems that he may encounter. If problems develop, the individual should consider the possible connection between his difficulties and the racial issue, avoiding any inclination to ignore or deny the existence of this connection. Ignoring the psychological significance of racial factors can only lead to internal mental conflict and can seriously undermine the strength each spouse can give the other.

In later stages, the marriage may undergo the normal internal strains of married life. These strains may be intensified if the marriage is subjected to external social pressures.

Cultural differences may have a significant effect on basic unspoken assumptions about the character of the relationships between husband and wife, parents and children, extended family and the community. Here, issues of power, dependency, and mutuality will be important. Cultural differences will not only affect the handling of crisis situations but also the normal concerns of marriage pertaining to children, sex, food, money, and the extended family. These areas constitute the basic issues, or foci, of family life and include the relationship between spouses, the procreative activities, and the family's role in the larger social context.

Women from traditional cultures have special appeal for some modern men because of their willingness to support patriarchal values, their deference to male authority, and their basically supportive and nurturing approach toward men. In general, they are more home-oriented, less individualistic, and more concerned with meeting the traditional obligations of the wife. Few problems are encountered at first. These women find satisfaction in supporting the dependency needs of their spouses, who in turn may respond with paternalistic concern and protective attitudes. Indeed, the man may feel he has solved the problem encountered in the type of modern marriage in which relationships are more reciprocal and more egalitarian and do not permit the man the same opportunity to feel like the "lord of the manor."

When a child is born and the mother turns her attention to the child, thus fulfilling her culturally determined expectations about being a "good mother," she may provide less attention to her husband. The husband may or may not react to this with a sense of rejection, depending on the extent of his own dependency needs. Much depends on whether the child is a boy or a girl. It may be easier for the father to identify with a boy, seeing the attention given to the child as an indirect expression of attention to him. Jealousy toward the child may present little problem until much later, when the boy may be viewed as a real rival because of the greater involvement of the mother with the boy.

Obviously, we are dealing with very complex scenarios, the outcome of which will depend on a variety of factors, responses to such factors, and the presence or absence of other people in the lives of the couple.

One common response to the wife's overinvolvement with the child may be for the husband to stop viewing her as a sexual or love object, and to seek to bolster his threatened masculine ego through the pursuit of other women. In the traditional setting, where the wife may be supported in her attention to the maternal role by a large extended family, the husband's sexual exploits, which are serving adaptive ends, may not be very disruptive to the marriage. Indeed, they may perform a stabilizing role by enhancing the husband's self-image and by reinforcing his willingness to support the wife in the maternal role. However, in the industrial or postindustrial society, the wife does not have the support of the extended family and is very much in need of her husband's support. The absence of the husband's support may make it very difficult for her to adapt and to care for her children and home, and it is in such a setting that one begins to see the first signs of reactive depressions, hysterical disorders, and other psychological abnormalities of mood, thought, and behavior.

Crisis situations developing in this context are difficult to resolve, particularly because of the inability of the parties involved to see the basic unconscious values and attitudes which are contributing to the conflict. Without appropriate intervention there may ensue a number of years of conflict which only become resolved when the children have grown sufficiently for the woman to seek more personal supports and gratification from a job, or school, or periodic visits to her original home.

Other problems derived from basic value differences relate to the woman's feelings of rejection by her husband's family who may not be as supportive as she expects them to be. This may produce considerable conflict. She may also be affected by her husband's insensitivity, which may not be balanced by other sufficiently supportive relationships.

The scenario is different if the couple continues to live in the traditional society where the woman and the man can obtain great support from her extended family, so that she can devote more attention to her husband as well as her children.

A man from a traditional society married to a woman from a modern society may have considerable difficulties in the early stages of marriage. Attracted by her apparent independence on an intellectual level, he may not be aware of his own dependency needs or his need to be treated deferentially, and may have considerable conflict at first. Even the advent of children may not bring the much sought-after resolution of his conflict because of the wife's unwillingness to cater to the dependency needs of the children as much as he believes she should. She may even express an unwillingness to have children or a desire to limit their number, or she may express hostile feelings toward them—all of which may be foreign to him and at variance with his internalized value system. His wife may resent his overinvolvement with his family, especially if he still returns to his mother for emotional support and continues to defer to his father in making certain decisions which she may feel are his to make. He may have difficulty in contending with her sense of freedom and the relative ease she has in establishing relationships with people, men and women. Should they live in a modern society, he may feel less adequate in dealing with a variety of individuals from such society who act condescendingly toward him and communicate nonverbally with his wife in what to him may appear to be too familiar a manner.

CLINICAL EXPERIENCES

Additional culturally relevant issues which can become problems and which are seen only in crisis situations are suggested by a number of clinical experiences I have had. In one instance, problems developed from the failure of a self-oriented Eastern husband to respond with anger to the masochistic demands of a perfectionistic European wife. If he had openly expressed the anger he was feeling, he might have reduced the pressure of her own internalized sense of guilt. His continued supportiveness and passive compliance with her demands served only to heighten her anxiety, depression, guilt, and internalized anger, and they did not provide her with either a controlled limit on her demands or with a target for her hostility. The same passive supportiveness might be more useful in a situation of a schizophrenic individual in greater need of a tolerant, supportive, and undemanding setting. Indeed, helplessness in a woman is more acceptable in an interracial marriage because it gives the spouse the opportunity to play a supportive role and to feel important. Unfortunately, where both members of the marriage are helpless, the situation is less satisfactory since only with difficulty can they rely on culturally available prejudices to explain their common plight. Where the racial issue is raised in this situation, there is a risk that the spouse may reconsider the feasibility of continuing the relationship. Only if the healthy spouse is taking up the fight against the established prejudices as a way of being supportive can this particular ideological support be used to strengthen the relationship.

Conflict is less readily tolerated in interracial marriage since there is always the possibility that it will raise the specter of the racial issue. This issue is a potential weak spot in the relationship, depending, of course, on the extent to which there are other negative influences in the immediate environment conducive to the break up of the relationship.

The relative coolness and self-containment of a European woman in the presence of a depressive illness in her Asian husband, and her conscious effort to remain calm and controlled, were badly misinterpreted by him. He saw them not as signs of strength and levelheadedness, but as proof of his hypochondriacal delusions that he suffered from cancer. In this instance, the culturally patterned responses to stress contributed to an escalation of the tension, which finally was relieved by intensive psychiatric treatment. A more characteristic Oriental response to illness, and more supportive for this man, would have been a more maternal, nurturing, and concerned response. Oriental women would be more likely to handle the stress of illness in a husband with activity-oriented action; while stoicism and quiet strength are more characteristic of the Western European response, which in this situation did not meet the needs of this man.

That the supportive, action-oriented response is not always good is suggested by the experience of a young European woman who felt obligated to care for her mother despite the mother's protestations that she could care for herself in her own home. After her mother and father at her insistance moved in with her, the young woman soon found herself overwhelmed by an excessive work load, little free time, and the gradual alienation of her husband, an American teacher who felt none of her obligations and who was unwilling to relinquish his own freedom and limit his activities because of his wife's self-imposed obligations. This is an example of the tremendous force of the drive to help others, even at one's own expense, which can, as in this case, reach pathological proportions. Here, too, we see how certain traditional values can be in sharp conflict with the American emphasis on self-reliance and independence.

Similar instances, where obligations to the extended family take precedence over those to the nuclear family, can be found in Latin cultures, in Mexican-Americans, and in the Caribbeans. These and other cases illuminate some of the conflicts and problem areas liable to affect individuals in intermarriages. The significant point to emphasize is that there are basic value differences between people from different cultural backgrounds. Also, most problem areas that create conflict relate to decisions about various ostensibly mundane matters.

VALUE DIFFERENCES

As already noted, implicitly learned and usually inarticulated sentiments govern attitudes toward infants. These sentiments are the result of the individual's own experiences as a child, of his parents' attitudes, and in some instances of his own participation in the rearing of a younger sibling. Major conflicts in marriages may emerge as a result of differences in these values without the individuals being aware of the reasons for the conflict.

Arguments over breast-feeding are not uncommon between Western European and American women who are reluctant to breast-feed and men from traditional societies who interpret this as a rejection of the child and, indirectly, a rejection of themselves. That these differences are cultural and situational rather than racial is suggested by the fact that in England, West Indian women, confronted with the necessity to work full time, stop breast-feeding their babies, much to the chagrin of their husbands.

The role of the extended family, particularly that of the mother-in-law, is another area of frequent conflict because of differing views about and responses to her involvement with the management of a newborn baby. It acts as if she were an authority on the subject, and if she is motivated by her own neurotic needs to become in effect the baby's mother, to infantilize her daughter or daughter-in-law, and to escape her own marriage, she can have considerable impact on the marriage. The psychodynamic issues are less noticeable when she is bolstered by a set of cultural institutions.

Traditional societies define more rigidly the roles of men and women, place greater emphasis on age, preservation of the status quo, the inequality of the sexes, the prerogatives of men, the constraints on women, and the significance of inherited versus achieved status. Traditional societies delineate how money is to be handled, how relatives are to be treated, how children are to be trained, how social contacts are to be established or avoided, and other issues which play a significant part in the daily flux of marriage. Cultural differences expressed in the behavioral dimension of these values can create conflicts for the couple from different backgrounds. These values represent basic assumptions about life and interpersonal relationships learned early in life, and they influence behavior to a much greater extent than is ordinarily assumed.

RELEVANCE OF INTERMARRIAGE ISSUES TO PSYCHIATRIC
TREATMENT

It is important to understand the structure and function of marriage, its role and its significance for individuals and for society, in order to fully understand its significant dimensions and thus be able to assist people in coping with present and future problems. The study of family patterns, with particular emphasis on variations in marriage partners, brings to the fore certain crucial elements of marriage relationships. Since the role that the family plays in society is becoming quite different from its traditional one, these issues are particularly relevant to the future. Not only the role of the family has become less crucial, but the very approach to the concept of family is undergoing significant changes. The communes are one example of a new type of "family," quite different from anything we have known before. As these living arrangements based on certain shared political or religious or ideological interests become more common, cultural differences will assume greater significance as a possible cause of psychological problems. Cultural differences may contribute to blind spots in the recognition of emotional illness in others, in the identification of areas of emotional stress, in the acceptance of the need for treatment, and in the selection of the type of treatment required. The kinds of issues we have been considering are also highly relevant to premarital counseling, marriage counseling, and psychotherapy of people with different cultural backgrounds.

Intermarriage requires many adjustments on the part of the partners. As yet, there is little information to determine the extent of the difficulties that these intermarriages may involve. Much work remains to be done to ascertain which individuals can be successful in such marriages and in which communities, which marriages are not likely to succeed and will therefore result in crises that require therapy, or end up in divorce because of the basic incompatability of two individuals from different racial-cultural backgrounds. So far, it has been found that when the participants have insight and positive background experiences and are in a relatively open society, the marriage will prosper. Some individuals, however, cannot tolerate the stresses created by the differences in their basic values. It becomes important, therefore, to recognize that problems arise from social pressures, interpersonal differences, and value differences, as well as from ordinary psychological conflicts. To the extent that individuals entering into these situations are aware of such social pressures and basic personality and value differences, they may be better able to prevent the development of conflict or, at least, to understand the conflict and manage it when it develops.

Those who do well do so because they have defined the nature of their differences in advance and have been able to anticipate each other's expectations so that, in case of disagreement, they do not become overly anxious and insecure about mutual acceptance. Interpersonal conflict in intermarriage also occurs when the individual brings negative background experiences or conflicting feelings about his race into the family situation and thus makes additional demands on the family. This results in an abnormal state of tension and anxiety at home, which, in turn, contributes to the individual's anxieties and to his job adjustment problems.

Sensitivity to cultural values and attitudes is therefore crucial in the psychotherapy of individuals from other cultures who are members of interracial marriage, since it enables the therapist to get at less obvious causes of interpersonal or intrapsychic conflict. Ultimately, the aim of therapy and counseling is to assist the individual to understand value conflicts, to foster greater maturity, self-reliance, and self-respect, and to increase the process of individualization.

11
Interviews by the Editors
on Interracial Relations

What do young people think, and how do young people feel, about interracial marriage? To answer more fully such questions, the editors provide two interviews, reported as they were recorded, with young, urban adults. Both interviews were conducted in early 1971 in the New York City area.

In the first interview, in which nine college students participated, members of the group set forth some of their conceptions about the interracial marriage relationship. They speak freely and to the point, and, not surprisingly, they show a genuine awareness and understanding of both the problems and the opportunities. It is refreshing to have them share their thoughts, to let them expose their feelings. But the interview, we think, speaks for itself.

The second interview is with Judy, a white 22-year-old college student who has spent several years with Tony, a black 23-year-old medical student, now removed from the East Coast.

The questions are pertinent, the answers clear and searching. Judy is articulate, informed, and very much capable of exploring the range of her feelings as well as the difficulties the couple faced in the two years of their relationship. Again, we feel, the interview speaks for itself.

A. A Group of College Students Review Their Conceptions

Participants:

JIMMY, *30*, married, dark Puerto Rican
JEFF, *22*, single, white
NANCY, *19*, single, white
FRANCES, *19*, single, black
KENNY, *20*, single, white
LINDA, *19*, single, black (engaged to Nick)
NICK, *23*, single, white
RICHARD, *20*, single, white
DENISE, *28*, married, white

JEFF: I would like to approach this from the angle, "What would cause a person of a particular subsociety to cross racial grounds on face-to-face level, and marry outside of his or her group?

LINDA: Today an intercultural marriage is not considered as drastic as an interracial marriage for the simple reason that interracial marriage invites attack from society for some strange reason. We'll ask the question why later on. It seems to be that an interracial couple encourages people to dig up all their prejudices. They feel righteous enough to do something about it, like burn somebody's house or something like that. As for the question, "What motivates a person to come out of his subgroup and participate in an interracial experience?" I have to believe this is done for personal reasons. If you really like someone, you have to be able to rise above your subgroup, and you have to be strong enough not to care about what people think. A person who depends on what somebody else thinks would probably not be found in an interracial relationship.

JIMMY: We had agreed that there are several factors that are involved in a person's decision to have primary group relationships with persons of another racial group. This person is generally not really involved too deeply with any one group; he is on the periphery of several groups. He may be a student, but does not belong to any fraternities or sororities. He may be a "liberal," but does not get involved wholeheartedly in any particular cause. If a person who is entrenched in group values becomes involved with a person of another race, he would find himself cut off from both groups.

NANCY: Concerning what Jimmy said, being on the periphery would also have to deal with an interracial relationship as opposed to an intercultural relationship. In an intercultural relationship, a member of one culture can blend into another and become submerged if he chooses to do so. But if your skin is a different color, it's much more obvious and much more difficult to submerge into another person's group. So you would be on the periphery of either group.

DENISE: Regarding the point about the periphery, it would have to be such a person. First of all, an interracial relationship was probably exotic at one time. It would take a lot of guts. It's getting more common, and probably evolutionary-wise it's what should be. The way that we have blended cultures I think that we can blend races, and I think that eventually we won't know the difference. But now it would have to be someone from the periphery. What hard-core individualist would dare to make that scene? But then you're saying that's someone who wasn't really from any group—a "from nowhere" guy, and that's why he's making it. That's not so. I don't see it like that. There are some that can find it "exotic." I think that's now past. I think that now there's the understanding that we're the same people with the same feelings and go on from there. We're getting color-blind.

JEFF: Bunk. I say that because there's so much built-in racial stereotypes; to say cultures blend that's a lot of bunk. People really
don't want to blend. I want to close with one thing from *Assimilation in American Life* by Gordon. He says on marital assimilation: "Prejudice and discrimination are no longer a problem,
since eventually the descendents of the original minority groups
become indistinguishable and since primary group relationships
tend to build an in-group feeling which encloses all members of
the group." That's bunk.

DENISE: About one hundred years ago, all right, there was such a
big difference, but speaking from an evolutionary point of view
the difference doesn't exist any more.

JEFF: Of course it exists. Are you saying we have a mulatto race? We
don't.

DENISE: Sure, and we'll have it more.

JEFF: Let's be realistic.

NANCY: I have to agree with Jeff. In an interracial marriage a child
needs a sense of identity. You can't say to a child, "You're nothing, you're in-between." He has to feel "I'm black" or "I'm
white"—"I'm something."

JIMMY: We have just finished discussing intercultural marriage, and
we can see that one person here is a product of such a marriage
—a Catholic and a Jew. Big deal! You can pick up your roots and
establish new roots. You cannot change your color, though. I
cannot change my color, and not because I want to, but I am just
stating a reality. Right now that is not a big thing, thirty-five
years ago maybe. Not now, and we're speaking of now.

NICK: A person to be on the periphery must be an individualist. He
must not care to a great extent what other people have to say
simply because the majority of other people don't agree with
him, and I don't see a great mulatto breakthrough in the future;
I don't see that the races are going to intermingle. I do think that
children need an identity.

JEFF (to Linda):   If you do get married, what will your children be?
How are you going to combine them?

NICK: The children would have to be black. The children are black
because the people would say they are black. If we tell the child
he is not black, and he walked into school the first day, and he
is called nigger, he would say, "Why am I being called nigger?

Mommy and Daddy told me I'm not black." There is a law in this country, I don't know if it is written or not, which says that if you are one-sixteenth black you are black no matter what other blood you have. So, in order for our children to have an identity our children would have to be black.

LINDA: I think that anybody who is going to marry somebody of another race (black and white) and think that their children are going to be mulatto are only kidding themselves because, as Nick said, everybody in society will say that the children are black. They will be discriminated against like they were black. There is no way that they could possibly pass for white until they grow up and go out on their own. If they want to pass for white then, that is their business. A couple cannot be colorblind like Denise said because how can you be colorblind and then say to your kid, "You are a mulatto"—whatever that is. You are black because it is not good enough to be colorblind. To be colorblind means that you can't get your mind far enough to like the color that the other person really is. You would rather ignore the color and say, "Well, we are the same, you are not different." But what you are you are, and if you are going to marry somebody of another race, you should be able to really like what they are. What are you going to do when society condemns you for what you have done? If you have to ignore it, and if when somebody says to you, "Aren't you upset?" you say, "Well, I really don't care. I really don't see what color they are," if that is your attitude about it, well, you better think twice about it. About the question on how people of an interracial group will be accepted by primary and secondary groups, I think that most interracial couples will have to go to one family, either the wife's or husband's. Very few couples can go to both families, because usually one family will accept the situation and the other one says, "Forget it." Secondary groups—the question is that if a husband is going to make what in this country is called a comfortable living, then it is much easier for the couple to be accepted into the society because they can be economically equal to everyone else. They don't have to live in a lower-class environment. Most interracial couples are in the middle class because people in the middle class, as they go up the economic ladder, move into a neighborhood where they can live, where they are equal economically to everybody living there, and they won't have the problems you would have living in an area where your economic standards are different from those around you.

JIMMY (to Denise): That would also refer to the comment about being exotic. Now that's a liberal term, "exotic"—and that is a transitory stage anyway. It comes down to, "Would you marry a nigger?" and "No, you wouldn't." You might date one, but you wouldn't go and take him home to Mamma, that's the big thing. We are talking about the term "exotic," and that implies a transitory, not permanent, stage, and we are talking about permanent relationships.

FRANCES: I think that it would be easier to be accepted by primary groups because of different factors of dating. Chances are that friends and parents would become accustomed to the fact. Because you are getting married, they would face up to it. While secondary groups, people you work with, they may not be willing to have dinner with you. Only when your economic status is raised can you become less dependent on secondary groups.

JEFF: The more your needs are not satisfied, the more you are dependent upon the group you are going to have to mingle with on a face-to-face basis.

NICK: I just want to disagree with something that Frances said. The question of how someone will be accepted in primary versus secondary groups. I think that it is a lot easier for these couples to be accepted by a secondary group, by workers, etc. than by the people of primary groups (parents, friends, relatives) simply because it doesn't hurt the people of the secondary group to accept them. It is no skin off their nose. They don't have to make any commitments to accept them, whereas you do when the members of this marriage live in your home. The secondary groups are just not losing anything by accepting these couples, and there is no way that they can get hurt.

FRANCES: In what you have just said, they would not really be accepting them, they would just be ignoring the fact.

NICK: There is a difference, then. Do you mean accepting them and loving them as people, or merely accepting them and putting up with them? I took it as putting up with them, and it is a lot easier for fellow workers than for relatives.

JIMMY: There is also the question about the sexual relationships between a black man and a white woman, because that is usually the pair we think about. We don't think about a white man and a black woman. . . . One writer brings out that this emanated from the South, not the South itself but from the Old South, where the thinking was that a woman is supposed to be feministic, very pure. If the concept is that a woman is supposed to be very pure, you can't see yourself going to bed with a woman representing it, and I understand that. But you can see where this leaves a person like the white Southerner. He would more or less have to direct his sexual aggression towards a woman of another race. Since the black woman was the more readily available thing there, because she was a *thing* and she wasn't a person, he could direct his sexual aggression towards "it" and have mulatto children and house nigger's children, as many as he wanted. Meanwhile the black man had nothing else to do: his woman was being occupied, and here's this white woman up in the mansion doing nothing. So you can see that opposites attract each other. Is it due to history or whatever? I am not going to say it is due to this or that, we don't know. But it existed, let's accept it.

LINDA: I just want to clarify the point about the peripheral personality. A person who doesn't need to depend on the group to have his needs satisfied is more likely to be involved in an interracial relationship than one who has to depend upon the group and conform to its thinking. It's not bad to be a peripheral personality. It's not deviant nor abnormal. Some people need reinforcement from the group, and others don't.

NICK: Yesterday Richie was bringing up the point that you couldn't bring up someone and let him be totally ignorant of inequality, or something to that effect. You don't have to be either black or white to be equal. If a couple gets married, they can have equality between themselves and still retain their black or white identity. Equality does not melt the color.

JIMMY: An interracial marriage is individual. It's not group-sanctioned. If a person wishes to do so, he may at the expense of some of his friends and group relations. It's not for us to decide right here whether or not we agree with an interracial marriage.

LINDA: People who get involved in an interracial relationship seriously and get married are usually peripheral personalities. They are not so involved in their own particular racial group that they're hung up and cannot break away from it and do what they want.

JEFF: To sum it up. Man is a naked ape. If you take a bunch of people and strip them naked of society's conventions, people are going to be attracted to each other regardless of skin color. Realistically, we're not going to strip ourselves, thus this isn't possible.

RICHARD: If a family brings up a child within one social setting, not to like black people or Italians, their child will tend to grow up with the opinions that the family has. Now, if a young couple who went to college and has some insight and has been "liberalized" get married and bring up their children with their views, what is to prevent this child from marrying a black person, or from not wanting to marry a black person? He's not going to see black or white, he's going to see somebody that he really cares for. It's a matter of how a child has been brought up since birth. We're all speaking of prejudice because that's the way we were brought up. If our kids are brought up not to be hung up about black and white, they will not be hung up like we are about interracial marriages. I don't think we should stress "you're white, you're black." When we speak of other races, do we consider them different physically, are traits transmitted through the genes, etc? Do we have prestereotypes toward the races? I'm not asking to define race, but we should talk somewhere around this subject.

MODERATOR: Questions from the class. First question: Why does somebody marry outside his racial group in the present cultural-social situation?

JEFF: It has to do with the way you were brought up and your environment. Linda here is an example. She said yesterday that she grew up basically in an environment where she was in contact with white people. This does not necessarily make for an interracial situation, but it may increase the possibility because there are contacts. Also, a person may just have an individual need. For example, a white liberal girl may have this need to go out with a black guy to show how liberal she is.

NANCY: There is the idea of rejecting your parents' values. If you take two people with similar backgrounds, why would one be involved in an interracial relationship as opposed to the other? In order for a person to have such a relationship you would have to reject your parents' values. A comment was made before that people would have to be very strong and have guts. This is true. You would probably have to reject your parents' values and maybe even your parents. It would have to come down to that. It would also involve how much your parents' opinion of you means to you.

MODERATOR: Another question from the class: What are the present barriers to an interracial marriage? What obstacles may one expect to find and have to overcome in order for the marriage to be happy and productive?

LINDA: As long as you don't make any obstacles for yourself, a lot of them come from the outside. For example, if one person is marrying a black because he or she is a liberal and feels this is the thing to do, they would have to be two very unintelligent people not to get around to the real reasons why they're each marrying the other person. An intelligent couple knows that to be equal you don't have to get rid of the color you are, that being equal comes from yourself, then all the obstacles come from the outside. Like Nancy said, a lot depends on what your parents say.

MODERATOR: There is another question: How much of an obstacle are you presented with, and how much strength do you have to overcome this obstacle?

LINDA: It depends on the couple. Some people's parents might say, "If you marry that person, I'll kill you," and in that case you have a real problem. You can tell that the parents are really dead set against it.

MODERATOR: Would black parents be as likely to say the same thing as white parents?

LINDA: Of course, why not? But I can't answer this question and say that this is the real obstacle. It really depends on the individual couple. It depends on what kinds of problems they have. If the husband is going to have a job as a policeman, you are going to have different problems because the group of people that you are going to be associating with are going to be less likely to accept your marriage than if your husband is going to be an artist, or some occupation where (a) he is going to make a lot of money, or (b) he is going to be mixing with a so-called liberal circle of people who aren't hung up on this kind of thing.

KENNY: Where there is no prejudice, there is no real problem, but the fact is that this type of prejudice is widespread in this country. Problems connected with interracial marriage emphasize the fact that there is prejudice. That fact alone will make the decision about interracial marriage very hard because society won't allow it to exist peacefully because of the emotions involved.

MODERATOR: How many students in this class would think that they could seriously contemplate an interracial marriage if a situation occurred where the individual of another race were someone who as a person they felt they could love and respect?

NICK: I have the same question but I just want to phrase it in a different way. How many people in the class, who love somebody, would still love that person, would still be as willing to marry that person, if he were a different color? You love that person because of the person, I'm assuming. Now, if that person happened to be of a different color, would you still love that person as much, and if not, why not?

DENISE: You know, Nick, that's what I asked yesterday. In fact, I made no reference to them [Nick and Linda], I didn't know that they were connected in any way, but that's exactly what I asked yesterday, and yesterday it was said that realistically all you can see is color—you can't love and have color as a variable which doesn't exist for you.

NICK: I'm saying that when you love a person, you love *the* person —you don't love him or her because of the color, you don't look at the color.

JIMMY: You don't ignore the color.

DENISE: But you don't use it as a crutch either.

NICK: That's right, you can't ignore it. But you don't look and say, "Because she's that color I love her." I love the person.

MODERATOR: How many in the class in this racist society, under the current conditions, could conceive of actually leaving the family, and would leave it for the reasons that we pointed out—that the other loved individual is a human being with qualities which they find worthwhile and who satisfies their needs? [Counts and announces] Eight out of forty people here.

RICHARD: I don't think that's a question that can be asked and for

the simple reason that you don't know how you're going to feel
—you're going to have to think of the consequences. You don't
just get married because you're in love right away. Later on,
when you have to live under these pressures, there's going to be
a lot of conflict.

JIMMY: Are you going out with a young lady? Do you love her?

RICHARD: Yes.

JIMMY: Now, what I'm asking you is not to put yourself in my shoes,
but take the case that the same thing would have happened,
except now she is black. And you realize that all the while you
haven't received any kind of social condemnation because you
aren't legally married yet. But you are contemplating marriage,
and now you realize you're going to have to deal with certain
other things. We're asking, would you consider marrying?

RICHARD: Would I consider it, yes. But would I do it, is another
story. I don't know.

MODERATOR: This question is directed to Linda. If you do marry
outside of your race and your child has light skin, how would you
handle a situation where the child wants to pass as white so he
could live a "better" life?

LINDA: First of all, what's light skin, how light do you have to be to
pass for white? I'll assume by "light" skin you mean "white" skin
and by "child" you mean someone in college who's on his way
out of the house. If anybody here thinks that his life belongs to
his parents, or his kid's life belongs to him, then he's got it all
wrong. I would do the best I can in raising my kids. The children
that Nick and I have would be black, but if they wanted to pass
for white that is their business. If they said to me, "What do you
think of the idea?" I would not personally agree with it—it would
be a hard thing for me to understand because I could never pass
for white, and for that reason I would subjectively say, "Well, I
don't think I like the idea." But could I say, "Do it, and I'll kill
you or throw you out of the house and never love you again"?
I would never say that.

MODERATOR: As far as the families are concerned, which would be
more disturbed by such marriages, the black or the white?

JIMMY: I don't like that question anyway, because I interpret it as
assuming that the black parents wouldn't mind if their kids
turned white as much as the white parents would mind if their

kids turned black. I think it would be fair to say that when a child is due to marry, white, black, brown, whatever the color is, the parents are crying because they're losing him. They're losing some ties—sure the child is going to come back home to visit, but they're losing some ties, and parents tend to be reactive in this way. If you're a parent, you can appreciate this. I am, I'm a father.

LINDA: To the question that was directed to me, you notice that they didn't ask what Nick, my white fiancé, would say, because they assume that Nick would like it if the child decided to be white, he wouldn't mind at all.

JIMMY: And that Nick's parents would be more outraged than your parents.

MODERATOR: But the question is: Which family would you expect to be more outraged or disturbed?

JIMMY: I would expect both of them to be outraged.

MODERATOR: In other words, what you're saying is that the families themselves would have to be taken into consideration, and there's just as much possible acceptance or rejection by a black family as there would be by a white family. Don't you think it possible that a small percentage of interracial couples have been motivated to get together because it may be a source of approval by their peer group, i.e., among so-called "hip" types, much of whose behavior is a reaction or protest against anything which can be considered the Establishment? In other words, would this be a way of proving their nonconformity?

NICK: In any situation, when two people get married, there's always the possibility that they're doing it to conform or to show nonconformity. The direct answer to the question is yes. It's a possibility, it can always exist in any marriage, whether it's interracial or not.

JIMMY: I wish to add to that, that in such a group where there's a subculture of rejecting the Establishment, you'll find that a lot of kids believe themselves to be liberal. I know a few brothers that have taken advantage of white girls in such type groups, and these girls have been dying to be taken advantage of. What I'm saying is, it's not love, it's lust. I think that answers some of the undertones of that question.

FRANCES: Well, one of the main reasons for interracial dating, I think, would be rebellion. When it gets down to marriage, it's different, because once you're married you're expected to have children, and when it comes to having children (that is, a white woman and a black man) and she has this black child, then all of a sudden she realizes what she's been doing. It can't be put out of her mind any more. When she was dating it was "the style," when they were engaged everyone would look, but when she has his black child, it could have a real effect on her mind—it's just not "the style" any more, it's past the stage of rebellion, now she has an offspring.

NANCY: Anyone who would enter into an interracial marriage under those circumstances is being totally blind, and unaware of reality. It's just being "hip" and totally blind.

JIMMY: And it's destroying a life.

MODERATOR: The problem of the children of such marriages remains. The parents as adults will get along but the early experiences of these children seem to be of great importance. What would you expect the children of such racial situations in this society to undergo as far as their personalities are concerned?

JIMMY: I would like to touch on that, because I did not have the opportunity to explain further on the intercultural marriage— for instance, among Puerto Ricans, and in the Caribbean, and some South Americans specifically. Now there is a problem here as to whether it is interracial or intercultural. Now I believe, since I am basically Spanish, my last name is Spanish, and I identify myself as a Puerto Rican, that I do not recognize color so much. In other words, I can marry anyone in my culture group, Puerto Rican or Cuban or anything like that, and do not recognize color per se. In other words, I have no hesitation in marrying a very black Puerto Rican or a white Puerto Rican. But when you come to say "the American society" or "American culture," you have another thing. If you identify yourself as being a black Puerto Rican, it is synonymous with being a black man in this country. You all know the history of the black man in this country. And Puerto Ricans and Spanish people do not want to identify with such. Or, we don't identify ourselves racially as much as ethnically. Persons could be of Latin heritage or Spanish background, and they do not see themselves as being married interracially.

JEFF: I want to address you, Jimmy. You seem to be saying it is not interracial. There is just one human race. If you marry anyone outside of your culture (whatever that is), you are marrying another human being, you seem to be saying.

JIMMY: No, you see, it is a bit complex in the sense that Puerto Ricans are multicolored men, polka-dotted you know, either very black or very white. You would be surprised how white Puerto Ricans can be. But the point is that a black and a white Puerto Rican can get married, and it is not a question of race so much as social standing; money speaks and all that. Whereas if that same white Puerto Rican were to marry a black person in this country, it would be racial then because this black person has a different culture, and that white Puerto Rican has a different culture.

FRANCES: To me it seems that you are saying that outside of the United States, like in Puerto Rico or something like that, because of the same culture it would be easier for black and white to marry. But here, once a black Cuban comes, and he marries a white woman, well he is getting into this racial society while it doesn't exist in Puerto Rico.

JIMMY: Right. We do have prejudices—I should tell you about that —but it is along a tribal barrier, not along a racial barrier at all. It is socioeconomic, that is the best way to describe it.

FRANCES: Before all this, you asked about the identity of the children. Well, they would be black in a black-white marriage. The problem, I think, would arise if one child were dark-skinned and one were light-skinned. Maybe some would look like they were white and, as Linda said, if they wanted to pass for white what would they say, especially if they have a black brother?

MODERATOR: What problems would you anticipate in bringing up a white and black child in the same household? With whom would they identify, the white parent or the black parent?

FRANCES: I was speaking to a psychiatrist about it, and she has these interracial couples and in all instances, in all cases, it is a white mother and a black father. All the aggression seems to be taken out on the oldest child, who happened to be the son, and he is the darkest. Once the white mother gets married and sees she has a black child, she is really uptight, but she doesn't know what to do about it.

LINDA: We got into this when Richie said that Nick and I should be careful of this in order to bring up our children without prejudice and to overcome some of these problems. But the problem is that everyone else is going to bring up their children with prejudices. So it is not going to do us any good to bring up our children and tell them that everybody is the same, no matter what color they are. Because, as Jeff says, when the kid goes to school and someone says, "I don't care what color your parents are, you are still a nigger," then that is a problem. I said yesterday that all black children have to have some kind of protection. I don't think that it occurs to a white person what problems a small black child faces—being put into white society where he is supposed to be subhuman, to have no intellect, and to be a typical aggressive black animal. To survive in this situation is a fantastic problem.

MODERATOR: How would you handle the children's problem?

LINDA: I would handle them like any child; the question is how would I handle the people who discriminate against my children?

MODERATOR: Where would you live?

LINDA: I would live in the kind of house I now live in, in the suburbs, in a big house with all the things I always wanted to have and that I have had all my life. All I can say is that where we would live would depend on what kind of job Nick had— whether we had to live in the city or the suburbs. I would not go very far outside of the city.

FRANCES: Suppose your child came home and said, "Mommy, some little white boy called me nigger," that's what you really want to know how to handle.

LINDA: I would answer what my parents answered for me—that there are a lot of people in this world to whom your color really matters. It's really not important, but they're not intelligent enough to know that what color you are doesn't matter. You should just ignore them. But if the kid comes home with a black eye and said, "Somebody called me nigger and I beat him up," I wouldn't punish him.

DENISE: Before, you mentioned a white mother having a black child, Frances, and the reality of it probably being disturbing. But she has a black husband, and supposedly loves him. Isn't this

a reproduction of the person she loves, of her husband and herself?

FRANCES: Her husband, no matter how close she is to him, is not
her. When she sees this black being coming from her, then it's
a part of her and it's more realistic.

JIMMY: You have to remember that she didn't go into this relationship honestly.

DENISE: Oh, you're talking about something superficial.

JIMMY: Right.

FRANCES: Marriage because of rebellion, and then once you have
this child you realize . . .

DENISE: Yes, then the whole jig would be up.

NICK: We agree.

MODERATOR: How do contemporary attitudes affect dating and social life? What are some of the problems they can anticipate
meeting in the society in which they're moving?

FRANCES: It depends upon the effect subgroups have on them. If
the group that each of them belongs to finds it fashionable to
date interracially, I don't think they would have much of a problem. They would be aware of the fact that they'd probably be
stared at, but it wouldn't really matter.

B. An Individual Student Discusses Her Experience

INTERVIEWER: How long were you going out with Tony? [A black man 23 years of age.]

JUDY: [a white woman, 22 years of age]: About two years.

INTERVIEWER: Did your family know about your relationship with him?

JUDY: Not in the beginning, but they did around the end of it.

INTERVIEWER: What did they have to say?

JUDY: Well, they were very upset. They felt that a white woman should not go out with a black man. They preferred that I would have stayed with someone of my own race.

INTERVIEWER: When you were a child, do you remember any talk of interracial couples within the family?

JUDY: We never spoke about it, but if we should see one in the street, there was always a derogatory comment. "How disgusting!" or, "Why should a white woman lower herself to go out with a black man?"

INTERVIEWER: Was this more on the part of your mother or father, or both?

JUDY: Generally on the part of my mother.

INTERVIEWER: Did your father ever say anything?

JUDY: He never said anything, no.

INTERVIEWER: Were there ever any interracial marriages within your family?

JUDY: One, my cousin married a black woman.

INTERVIEWER: What was the attitude of the rest of the family?

JUDY: Well, he moved to Florida and, as far as the family is concerned, he is a nonexistent cousin.

INTERVIEWER: What were your plans with Tony? Were you planning to be married?

JUDY: Well, we were living together and marriage was in the far distant future, but Tony is in medical school now, so we really couldn't consider anything like that till he got out of school.

INTERVIEWER: What was the attitude of Tony's family towards your relationship?

JUDY: His family hated me. They were just overly upset that Tony could go out with a white woman, especially with the black situation, black consciousness, and the black woman becoming conscious of the fact that she's a woman, they felt that Tony should definitely go out only with a black woman.

INTERVIEWER: Do you know if this also stemmed from his childhood?

JUDY: That I don't know. I guess his family always assumed that he would only go out with a black woman.

INTERVIEWER Did you find any problems, as a couple, because you were of different races?

JUDY: Do you mean the effects of our family on the relationship?

INTERVIEWER: No, your own views and what you felt. Did you find any problems?

JUDY: No.

INTERVIEWER: What about Tony?

JUDY: Um, he was affected more by it than I was, I think, because he felt that he should be playing the game that people expected him to play, of a black man going out with a white woman. That the black man is showing his white woman off. That that's the epitome of being a real "stud"—going out with a white woman.

INTERVIEWER: Was he playing this game?

JUDY: No, he couldn't. He couldn't play the game, that's what upset him so much. He could use it as an escape if he could play that game.

INTERVIEWER: What was your peer group's attitude? Your friends and his friends.

JUDY: Most of my friends really didn't care. Most of my friends knew Tony and liked him. They sorta expected us eventually to live together.

INTERVIEWER: Did you associate more with your friends or his?

JUDY: Um, I don't know. Our friends were mostly of the same group. We met the same political group, and all our friends were basically the same.

INTERVIEWER: What, in general, were your peer group's attitudes towards interracial couples, not you and Tony, but in general?

JUDY: Well, some of them thought it was fine. Some of them thought it was a cop-out for the black man, nor should a black woman go out with a white man; they felt that was equally a cop-out. The same sort of gig, you know, black consciousness and black man becoming aware of his own power as a black man, the black woman becoming conscious of the fact that she's no longer secondary to the white woman. A lot of them felt that interracial couples are just politically devastating.

INTERVIEWER: What about on the emotional level? As people?

JUDY: How did they feel? Or how did we feel?

INTERVIEWER: How did they feel.

JUDY: Well, I guess emotionally they felt it was possible. Black or white, it doesn't much matter emotionally.

INTERVIEWER: Yes, but I think there is a certain amount of racism, even in young people today and, not talking politically but more on a social and emotional level, that people do have attitudes other than political towards interracial couples.

JUDY: You mean their gut-level reactions?

INTERVIEWER: Yes, that's more or less what I mean.

JUDY: That's sort of rough, it really is. I don't know if their gut-level reactions were against us. I just always thought they were fighting for us. It was never mentioned. In any sort of group situations, nobody ever talked about it or anything, it was just sort of an accepted thing I was living with Tony.

INTERVIEWER: What's your relationship with Tony?

JUDY: There is no relationship with Tony. We're not speaking to one another, we had a very big argument over nothing that had anything to do with race. He's in medical school in Utah, and I'm in New York.

INTERVIEWER: When you were living together, were there any thoughts of marriage, or having children?

JUDY: Marriage for either one of us would have been done just to facilitate getting apartments and living together. Marriage wasn't important. And as far as having children, I could just as soon have children out of marriage as married. It didn't affect us at all. I have no thoughts of having children now or for the next five years from now.

INTERVIEWER: Do you think that going with Tony was any kind of status symbol?

JUDY: In my own peer group?

INTERVIEWER: Being the one who is going to fight the Establishment and break the rules?

JUDY: Maybe for some, but not for most and not for my close friends, it wasn't. I never looked at my relationship in that way, and I hope that they didn't. I certainly wasn't fighting the Establishment; I was in love with the man.

INTERVIEWER: You were talking about the game and copping out, and the game sort of implies a status symbol for Tony and possibly for yourself. Do you think that, even though you say that Tony wasn't playing the game, it did have some effect?

JUDY: Oh, I think it did in the beginning of the relationship. I think that it was flattering for Tony to find a white woman who he considered his equal. That was one of the things Tony had— never finding a woman who was his equal intellectually, emotionally, never knowing any women who could really understand him.

INTERVIEWER: When you were living together, did you have any associations with the neighbors?

JUDY: The neighborhood we lived in was predominantly a black neighborhood. Most of the people just accepted it, and it was an odd way of acceptance. I was not accepted as a white woman, I was accepted as Tony's woman. There is a difference. Like they could come up to the apartment and sit and rap about the girls they were going out with, or the white woman one of their friends was going out with without any regard for the fact that I was white, it had nothing to do with it. I was just Tony's woman, like a piece of furniture, I was like a chair or a couch. After a while it was just accepted that I was going to be there.

INTERVIEWER: Do you think they would have reacted differently towards you if you had been a black woman?

JUDY: In the beginning they might have, when they first discovered that we were living together. I think their reactions would have been different in the beginning if I had been a black woman. In the beginning they were really shocked. Especially because of Tony's political work, they were shocked that he could live with a white woman. They never expected that. But after a while . . .

INTERVIEWER: At this point, when they reacted towards you with shock, what did they do and what were your feelings?

JUDY: Well, they were sort of fighting it. They would block me out of conversations or they were very careful about what they would say.

INTERVIEWER: How did that affect you?

JUDY: Well, it made me uncomfortable. I mean, there were times that I would just leave the apartment, go for a walk, or go into the bedroom and close the door.

INTERVIEWER: How did it affect Tony?

JUDY: He too was uncomfortable. In fact, in the beginning he just had less and less friends over until his friends just came one evening, and it was all right. It hit a peak, and then after that it was okay.

INTERVIEWER: How did this affect the relationship?

JUDY: It was strained, it certainly was.

INTERVIEWER: Did you ever talk about it?

JUDY: Sure. He couldn't understand his friends. Well, I guess he could understand them intellectually, their feeling toward me as a white woman. I don't think that emotionally he could understand it because love is love. Emotionally he was in love with me and to be blocked out because I have white skin, to Tony was absolutely incredible.

INTERVIEWER: What is the economic and social position of your family in relation to Tony's?

JUDY: My parents aren't poor, but they certainly aren't as wealthy as Tony's family. Tony's family is very wealthy. His father has a tremendous amount of money, and his paternal grandmother also has a tremendous amount of money. But his parents are divorced. I don't know his mother's position; I've never met his mother.

INTERVIEWER: Upon the initial encounter you had with Tony's father, what exactly happened?

JUDY: Well, when I went to Tony's house, he had just called and told his father that he was in love, and he was bringing the girl home to meet him. We walked into the house together, his father shook my hand, and said, "How do you do," and sat down in the living room to wait for the girl that Tony was in love with. It never occurred to his father, since I was white, that I could be the girl that Tony was in love with. So we all sat down for about half an hour waiting for this fantastic black woman to come into the house, so his father could greet her with open arms. It was really funny when his grandmother realized that I was the one. Her face fell, there was a dead silence in the room, she excused herself, and that was the last I saw of her.

INTERVIEWER: Did you and Tony talk about this reaction?

JUDY: We spoke about it only in the respect that my parents would have reacted the same way, except they probably would have thrown us both out of the house.

INTERVIEWER: How did it affect you and Tony that both your families were so violently against the relationship?

JUDY: It was rough. It was hard because both Tony and I are very close to our parents. He's very close to his father and his grandmother, and I'm close to my parents. It's a very hard thing to disregard all your parents' wishes when you really love them. To do something that you think is right, the fact that it is right, doesn't make it any easier. It makes it just as hard, if not harder. Like to prove to them that it's right and to prove it to yourselves; I mean there's always that doubt in your mind—am I doing it because it's the status thing to do? There's always that doubt in your mind, especially when you get your parents' reactions, people's reactions in the street.

INTERVIEWER: What kind of things happened in the street?

JUDY: Well, after Jeffrey Miller's funeral, Tony and I went to Columbia. We were sitting on the lawn having lunch, and he had his arms around me, and this photographer came over. He was white, and he started taking pictures of us. So Tony and I sort of ignored him. It was all right ignoring him until he asked us to pose, would Tony put his arms around me a little tighter, lean a little closer, or perhaps would he kiss me. Tony sort of looked up and said, "Would you please go away?" And the man sort of completely ignored it, just as if Tony had said absolutely nothing. So Tony started getting angry, and he said to the man, "Would you please take your fucking camera and go away?" And the man still didn't go. So Tony, with this fantastic smile on his face, said to the guy, "If you don't take your fucking camera and go away, I'm going to take your fucking camera and shove it up your goddammed ass." The guy, because Tony was smiling, wasn't absolutely sure that Tony was really angry. Maybe the man was about five-two and Tony was about six-one. And Tony started getting up. I think the man thought Tony was endless, just would never stop rising. Until Tony took off after the man, and the two of them went running across one of the lawns at Columbia University. That was the end of that. What happened to the pictures, I don't know. What the man did with them, I don't know.

INTERVIEWER: Were there any other experiences on the street? Did you get strange looks?

JUDY: Strange looks, of course. I mean, people would sort of turn around and stare after us. And a lot of black women would have these really bad reactions toward us.

INTERVIEWER: Did anybody ever say anything?

JUDY: Well, one woman asked Tony if he thought he was white going out with a white woman, where was his head at, doesn't he know what the Panthers are trying to do, and Cleaver's in exile. I mean, she just went through the whole rap.

INTERVIEWER: And what did Tony say?

JUDY: He said, "Yeah," he just nodded his head and yessed her right along through. And at the end he just said, "And what happens if I love her?" And she said, "Well, you can love a black woman, too. What makes that so different?" Which is true, but you can't control meeting someone and falling in love. That's something you can't control at all.

INTERVIEWER: How did those encounters affect you and Tony?

JUDY: In the beginning it hurt, it really hurt. Because it was just something that I accepted that I was in love with this man, and it hurt me that people had this reaction. Why couldn't they sort of leave us alone? We weren't bothering anyone. And after a while, I mean, you just sort of block it out, you don't see it, you don't see the looks, you don't even hear the comments. It just, I guess, becomes a part of you. It's like wearing the same perfume over and over again, you just become so used to the smell that you don't notice it any more.

INTERVIEWER: Did you at this time have any interracial friends?

JUDY: You mean, any interracial couples as friends?

INTERVIEWER: Yes.

JUDY: My friend married a black man who is now becoming a black nationalist, he's becoming a Muslim. She has two children, and their relationship is almost completely at an end. They can't live together, because all of his friends are Muslim, and they will have nothing to do at all with white people. The fact that she's his wife has nothing to do with it—she's white first. He teaches at an all-black college.

INTERVIEWER: Did you and Tony ever talk about their experiences? And relate them to your own?

JUDY: Not too often, other than the fact that Tony couldn't really understand why he was becoming a Muslim. I mean, politically was the only way he viewed why he was becoming a Muslim.

INTERVIEWER: What do you think your relationship would have been to your parents and Tony's family if you had gotten married?

JUDY: Well, I don't think that my parents would have ever accepted it. I think they would have blocked me out as a child. But Tony's father and grandmother would have accepted it. They were a lot more open-minded, I think, than my parents.

INTERVIEWER: Do you think this put a strain on your relationship with Tony?

JUDY: Yeah, it definitely would have. In fact, I couldn't even see living with him for ten years without it affecting our relationship adversely, divorce or separation or something.

INTERVIEWER: You mean, you would be going into the relationship knowing the strain of giving up your family ties.

JUDY: Well, you never go into a relationship that way. I would go in always hoping. I mean, this is like 20/20 hindsight. It's like looking back and seeing that it may not have worked. I would have never gone into a relationship like that. You always fight to keep it going.

INTERVIEWER: Do you think that you would have any animosity toward his family for resenting you, or that he would have any animosity towards yours for resenting him?

JUDY: No, I mean it was expected. His father and grandmother are both very old, and their views are just expected.

INTERVIEWER: Do you have any sisters or brothers?

JUDY: Yes, I have one sister who is married.

INTERVIEWER: Did she ever meet Tony?

JUDY: She never did, but my brother-in-law did. He liked him, but he couldn't understand why a black man would go out with a white woman. He really couldn't understand it. I guess he agreed with most of the black women that Tony and I encountered—that a black man should only go out with a black woman. He could understand the love, but he couldn't understand the politics behind it.

INTERVIEWER: Does Tony have any siblings?

JUDY: He has one sister and one brother, and they're his step-sister and step-brother.

INTERVIEWER: Do you know their views?

JUDY: No, I never met them, and Tony didn't talk about them. He had very little contact with them.

INTERVIEWER: Throughout the interview you keep mentioning that it is politically wrong for a black man to go out with a white woman. What about you? You're a white woman going out with a black man. Is that as wrong at this time?

JUDY: I can only view it from the black viewpoint; it's as draining emotionally on both parties. It's as draining emotionally for a white woman to go out with a black man. But with the new politics . . . is sort of how I'm viewing it.

INTERVIEWER: Yes, but you keep talking about politics when actually what is transpiring here is a love relationship, not a political relationship.

JUDY: No, that's not true. An interracial couple is a political relationship. It's an emotional one, too, but it's certainly a political one, especially with black consciousness and racism; that's what makes it political; that's what makes it so hard to have — because of all the political implications of it. That's what makes the relationship so hard to keep going, you can't block it out. It's not like a normal love relationship, where you have hassles about fighting and dating and stuff like that; there are just too many implications in an interracial relationship to block out—to talk about only the love aspect, that wouldn't be the true relationship.

INTERVIEWER: Then, as I see it, you view your relationship as a political arrangement.

JUDY: No, both. Both, you can't block out the politics, and you can't block out the emotions.

INTERVIEWER: You mentioned before that both you and Tony were politically active. Do you think this affected your seeing your relationship in a political light?

JUDY: Well, I'm not even sure that I really understand the question. It had to affect the relationship. I mean, a lot of Tony's friends were members of the Panthers. Both of us were politically active. It would be hard for us to block it out. Maybe if you're not politically involved, it's easier to block out the political aspects of the relationship.

INTERVIEWER: What about the social aspects? It's more a social problem or a political one?

JUDY: It's both. I mean, interracial relationships are so many things combined, that if you're politically active, then politics also enter into it. You're not socially sterile, so you're always aware of people's reactions to it and your family's reaction to it. And you're also aware of your emotions and your feelings for one another. But that's what comes under doubt the most, your feelings. You're sure of the love, but you're not really sure that you're not doing it to buck the system, to prove that it can work for everyone else. That always comes into question.

INTERVIEWER: What about the myth, the sexual myth associated with the black man. Did that have any effect?

JUDY: I don't think it had an effect, but I don't think it's something that can be blocked out. I mean, it's amusing to me this fantastic black myth about the black "stud," the guy who knows his way around the streets of Harlem and dresses up in really fancy outfits, and drives a Cadillac, and it's really a status symbol to go out with a white woman. Also that myth that the black man is really powerful in bed; they think every white woman wants to

lie back on her back, stretch out, and be taken by a black man.
I mean, really have him sock it to her, you know, and then plead
that she didn't love it. I mean, it's this fantastic black myth, that
the black man is such a fantastic lover, fantastic, so sexually
potent.

INTERVIEWER: And how did this affect your relationship?

JUDY: I don't think it did. I mean, I didn't expect Tony to perform
like a circus seal when we were in bed together. I don't think it
affected our relationship at all. I didn't view Tony as a stud. I
mean, what can I say about our relationship?

INTERVIEWER: Well, since this myth does exist, did you have any
experiences where people asked you personal questions?

JUDY: No one ever asks. It's like the interview itself, no one ever
asks what's really on their mind; but the looks, or when they used
to go to the apartment, and they would check the size of the bed
with their eyes, people always used to do that. Or they'd look at
us and sort of eye Tony's crotch, or look at his arms to see how
big they were. I mean, it's people's attitudes like that, nothing's
ever said, people are much too polite for that.

INTERVIEWER: How did you notice that? Do you think possibly it
was in your mind and people weren't really doing that?

JUDY: Oh, sure, anything can be in your mind. I could have been
projecting any number of thoughts, I could have been projecting
that people were turning around on the street to stare at us, but
I don't think that's totally true. Certainly it was projection, that's
something I'm totally aware of, but I don't think it was all projection. Certainly some of it was, but some of it wasn't. Some of it
had to happen, just because of people. People are always curious
about things like that.

INTERVIEWER: Yes, but what I'm trying to point out is that you say
this myth didn't affect your relationship, but just on the point
that you say you projected these attitudes, didn't it thereby
affect your relationship?

JUDY: Yes, but that happens in any relationship. I don't think it
mattered because Tony was black. Projection happens in any
relationship. It certainly had to affect our relationship. It happens with any couple, whether they're interracial or not. One
woman is always going to notice another woman staring at her
boy friend and feel it as a threat; that affects their relationship,

too. The fact that Tony was black and I was white didn't affect it any more than was natural.

INTERVIEWER: Do you think you would ever get into an interracial arrangement again?

JUDY: Yeah, I think I would. But not because the man was black, but just if I met a man who happened to be black and I loved him, I wouldn't have any qualms. I think I would go in better equipped this time to handle it, the problems. The first time is always the hardest, for anything. You're a novice, as you go along you get to know the tricks of the game, so to speak, which is a poor way of putting it. You get to know what to expect, it doesn't hurt the second time around as much as the first.

INTERVIEWER: Do you have any final comments to make about the interview or on your relationship with Tony?

JUDY: Nothing really about the interview, except some of the questions themselves just really put you on the spot, you can never really give complete satisfactory answers to them. Should I hear the tape again, I'm sure I would regret some of the things I said, or wish I'd said them in another way, and I'd like to take them back. That's all I have to say about the interview.

Comparative and Cultural Aspects of Interracial Marriage

INTRODUCTION

Most of the readers of this book know something about, and have many feelings toward, the racial situation in the United States. Readers know that although the United States is considered by many to be a racist society, feelings and practices vary widely from one area of the country to another. People's attitudes and feelings toward interracial marriage have been shaped since the very earliest years of their lives through experiences in their nuclear families, in their neighborhoods, and in the communities and areas of the country in which they matured.

Interracial marriage is not, of course, a peculiarly American experience: it has existed for long time, is worldwide, and its practices differ from one part of the world to another. Part II makes us more aware of its aspects elsewhere. The chapters that form this section of the book offer us a perspective on, and contribute to, a deeper understanding of interracial marriages in societies that may be vastly different from our own. Some are older, others involve different political and social traditions, and still others have value systems that may well be very dissimilar from our own. In spite of great individual differences, however, people are more nearly alike than different; and what each human being, wherever he may be, brings to his relationships with others is very much an expression of his experiences, of his difficulties, and of his hopes. In order to understand interracial marriage as a social phenomenon in other parts of the world, we must understand some of these experiences and feelings.

The chapters that constitute Part II are designed to provide us with the background we need in order to reach this understanding.

Chapter 12 examines interracial marriage among Puerto Ricans both in Puerto Rico and on the United States mainland. Of particular interest is the analysis of the transformation that a majority group undergoes when, by migration to the mainland, it becomes a minority group in an ethnically and racially heterogeneous society.

Chapter 13 is a novel and in-depth investigation of interracial marriage in Brazil, a country widely hailed as a genuine racial "melting pot" in which presumably there is little or no perception of color. On the basis of numerous interviews that he conducted in Rio de Janeiro, Dr. Aroldo Rodrigues casts doubt on the "color blindness" of the residents of that city and, inferentially, of Brazilians at large.

Chapter 14 offers a surprisingly perceptive and informative look at biracial marriage among the Japanese, and at the situation of "mixed-blood" children in a homogeneous and traditional society.

Interracial marriage in a multiracial society is the subject of Chapter 15. The author looks at Trinidad as a "natural laboratory" in which to observe interracial marriage, and examines the forces that are transforming the traditional values of the island and are having a profound influence on racial relations.

The oldest minority group in our midst is that of the American Indian. And yet very little is known about the intimate relations between the Indians and their non-Indian neighbors and about the Indians' attitudes toward interracial marriage. Chapter 16 provides some of the answers that have been missing until now.

Chapter 17 takes us to Cuba and to the effects that the revolution has had on the island's social order and on its racial climate.

The final chapter in Part II deals with Hawaii where not just two or three, but many racial groups have been thrown together. Furthermore, the historical background in Hawaii differs from other locales, where one race invaded and conquered another. The Hawaiians were long politically and economically independent. The diversity and complexity of changing attitudes towards interracial marriage in these islands of idyllic reputation is enlightening.

Taken together, the seven chapters that constitute this section of *Interracial Marriage* are full of useful material that cannot fail to deepen our perception of and provide the basis for a more informed knowledge about biracial marriage practices in other parts of the world. Against such a background, we are likely to understand more fully and to feel more deeply about our own American experience with interracial marriage.

12

ANTHONY LA RUFFA, Ph.D.

"Interracial Marriage" Among Puerto Ricans

In this chapter, Dr. La Ruffa investigates interracial marriage among Puerto Ricans in two very different settings: on the island of Puerto Rico, where the culture is fairly homogeneous and the racial backgrounds rather heterogeneous, and in New York City, where the Puerto Ricans represent one of the area's many minority groups.

In order to put interracial marriage in its proper perspective, the author examines in depth the social scene of both settings, with special attention to the problems of the Puerto Ricans as an emerging minority group in the continental United States.

The author studies the social mobility and the accessibility to power of the Puerto Ricans in the United States, and he comes to the conclusion that with respect to political and economic strength the Puerto Ricans have experienced the smallest amount of structural assimilation of the major ethnic and racial groups. This lack of standing has an important bearing on the interracial unions of Puerto Ricans with members of other groups.

RACE AND RACIAL CONSCIOUSNESS AMONG PUERTO RICANS

Puerto Ricans are a particularly interesting group for the study of what, in social science parlance, is generally being referred to as "interracial marriage." There are a number of reasons for this. Puerto Ricans in the island share a common culture and can be viewed more or less as ethnically homogeneous. Yet, racially speaking, they are a rather heterogeneous group that combines a variety of biological traits, including West African, European, and, to a lesser degree, Arawak Indian. Puerto Ricans in the United States, as represented to a large extent by migrants and their offspring in the New York City area, continue to be relatively ethnically homogeneous and racially heterogeneous in the context of a larger society whose members constitute a variety of ethnic and racial groups. We have, then, two settings in which to discuss the implications of "interracial marriage" as practiced by a group which shares a common history: within an ethnically homogeneous but racially diverse context, the island; and against a background of ethnic and racial heterogeneity, in the United States. This raises a number of basic questions concerning racial groupings, ethnic groupings, and the assimilation process. It would seem important, therefore, to discuss these concepts in order to clarify the issue of "interracial marriage" as it takes place in two Puerto Rican populations.

ETHNICITY

The term "ethnic group" has been used primarily by sociologists to encompass a wide spectrum of collectivities in American society. Milton Gordon, for example, views an ethnic group as ". . . a type of group contained within the national boundaries of America . . . [and] . . . which is defined or set off by race, religion, or national origin, or some combination of these categories." Although he acknowledges that race, religion, and national origin are somewhat different concepts, nevertheless they share

> . . . a common social-psychological referent, in that all of them serve to create, through historical circumstances, a sense of peoplehood for groups within the United States, and this common referent of peoplehood is recognized in the American public's usage of these three terms, frequently in interchangeable fashion. [5, pp. 27–28]

Others use the term ethnic group in a more restricted sense, equating ethnic groups with national origin groups.

Both usages, it would seem, are quite ambiguous. The former confounds cultural and racial criteria in the ascription of group status —a position, incidentally, that could be extremely confusing in light of the Puerto Rican experience. The latter definition, although more acceptable, tends to stress a collective historical-identity approach to ethnic groups. More, I think, is needed. In my view, an "ideal" (in the Weberian sense) ethnic group consists of individuals who speak a common language, share similar behavioral characteristics, tend to maximize their intragroup interactions—interactions which are predominantly personal, informal, and face to face—and usually minimize their intergroup interactions—which tend to be more formalized and impersonal—and finally, have a sense of collective identity.

The degree of group ethnicity, of course, varies. Italian-Americans are less clearly identifiable as a distinctive ethnic group as compared to Hopi Indians, Puerto Ricans, or Mexican-Americans. Further, Italian-Americans exhibit substantial internal ethnic variation. Some speak the language, share a traditional cuisine, have similar value orientations, and tend to restrict interpersonal relationships to within the group. Others just recognize a historical relationship and may have some sort of emotional commitment to the "Italian heritage." Puerto Ricans in American society, however, show less internal variation as an ethnic group, and, to a much greater extent than Italian-Americans, display their ethnicity in language, behavior patterns, quality and quantity of intragroup interactions, through a minimization of intergroup interactions, and in a consciousness of kind.

In short, then, Puerto Ricans come closer to the "ideal" delineation of an ethnic group within the context of American society than the Italian-Americans. In the island setting, ethnicity as a concept is of limited value in that one is dealing with a relatively homogeneous culture, and variability is more apparent in the structural dimension (i.e., class-caste and interpersonal relationships) than in the behavioral dimension. It should be noted, however, that other ethnic groups besides the Puerto Ricans do exist in the island. Two prominent examples are Cubans and Americans. The latter group occupy the more lucrative and prestigious positions, live in relatively expensive residential enclaves, and, in general, manage or control a considerable portion of the financial resources of the island. Despite some degree of ethnic variation within the context of Puerto Rican society, ethnic homogeneity is much more prevalent in the Island as compared to continental United States.

RACE

The question of race has been an incubus plaguing the anthropologist for more than a century. Today many physical anthropologists disagree as often as they agree regarding a generally acceptable definition of race. Yet, there appears to be some measure of consensus among specialists about viewing races as "breeding populations," or genetically distinguishable populations (4, p. 7; 6, p. 150) Few nonspecialists, however, view race in a strictly biological sense. Most individuals hold to a social and cultural definition of the term that is a "layman's understanding" of what constitutes a race. Very often this means classifying individuals on the basis of skin color, hair texture, and facial features—the most visible phenotypic characteristics. Puerto Ricans, for example, stress color and hair texture. Individuals are *moreno* (black) *trigueño* (mulatto), or *blanco* (white). In addition, they have either *pelo bueno* (straight hair) or *pelo malo* (kinky hair). Although color distinctions are quite important, hair texture appears to play a more significant role in the Puerto Rican racial classification system. Swarthy individuals with *pelo bueno* are often said to display American Indian characteristics. *Parece como un indio* (he resembles an Indian) is an expression that I frequently hear when individuals with light complexions refer to their darker-skinned kinsmen. To be Indian-like carries less of a stigma than to be labeled black.

Puerto Ricans are extremely race conscious (in the social and cultural sense of the word) despite a kaleidoscope of shades and hues especially in the *trigueño* range. Or, perhaps, to phrase it more precisely: Puerto Ricans are race conscious *because* of large numbers of *trigueños* in the population. The two poles of the color spectrum —black and white—are clear enough to most Puerto Ricans, who react negatively to the former category and somewhat proudly, or at least positively, to the latter. The majority of the population, the *trigueños*, aspire to be white, and this is manifested in a sensitivity to differences in hair texture. Even a rather dark *trigueño*, as long as he has *pelo bueno*, will identify much more readily with the higher-status racial grouping—*los blancos*—than with *los morenos*.

And, as I have indicated earlier, *morenos* with *pelo bueno* are frequently classified as Indian-like by friends and kinsmen.

Race consciousness among Puerto Ricans has been reinforced considerably by the island's socioeconomic and political ties with the United States, a relationship nurtured by more than seven decades of American dominance. Writing in the late 1940's, Sereno noted:

> The presence in the island of many Americans belonging to a middle [and upper] socioeconomic level[s] has reproduced, within the influence of the people, the same pattern of discrimination prevailing in the continental United States.
>
> A "realistic" approach to good relations between "metropolis" and "colony" has established a pattern of accepted discrimination in those political and social circles which are in close contact with the Americans. [9, p. 264]

For many male Islanders whose contact with Americans in Puerto Rico was minimal, the shock of institutionalized racial discrimination became quite evident when they were drafted into the U.S. Army (beginning with World War II) and shipped to the southern United States for basic and advanced training. Very often black Puerto Ricans and dark *trigueños* were separated from white Puerto Ricans and given basic training with black Americans. Many islanders remained in the training camp on weekends rather than go into town and risk experiencing the humiliation of being separated from lighter- or darker-skinned buddies. One's ethnic identity as a Puerto Rican was seriously undermined by certain visible phenotypic characteristics.

A comparable situation, though somewhat less overt, faced Puerto Ricans who migrated from the island to urban centers of the northeastern and midwestern United States. Since dark Puerto Ricans are frequently classified as black Americans, first- and second-generation Puerto Ricans in the mainland frequently become quite confused about who they are. Piri Thomas graphically dramatizes this dilemma in his autobiography, *Down These Mean Streets* (11). Piri Thomas and his father are dark Puerto Ricans, unlike the other members of his nuclear family. I should like to quote parts of a conversation between Piri and his brother José who is rather disturbed by his older brother's plans to travel "down South."

> "I'm a Negro."
> "You ain't no nigger," José said.
> "I ain't?"
> "No. You're a Puerto Rican."
> "I am, huh?" I looked at José and said, "Course, you gotta say that. 'Cause if I'm a Negro, then you and James is one too. And that ain't leavin' out Sis and Poppa. Only Momma's an exception. She don't care what she is."
> ... "So whatta you got to find out, eh?" he [José] said. "You're crazy, stone loco. We're Puerto Ricans, and that's different from being *moyetos.*" [blacks] ...
> "That's what I've been wanting to believe all along, José," I said. "I've been hanging on to that idea when I knew it wasn't so. But only pure white Puerto Ricans are white, and you wouldn't believe that if you ever dug what the paddy said."
> "I don't give a good shit what you say, Piri. We're Puerto Ricans and that makes us different from black people." [11, pp. 143–144]

Piri's odyssey through parts of the American South with a black companion was an attempt to share a collective experience with black Americans, an experience which, hopefully, would sustain his identification with this ethnic group rather than with his own natal ethnic group. He was desperately trying to resolve his dilemma, a dilemma he shares with tens of thousands of other first- and second-generation Puerto Ricans in the United States.

What becomes clear, I think, in this rather lengthy discussion of race and racial consciousness among Puerto Ricans is that we are dealing with one ethnic group comprised of several racial categories. This makes it very difficult in the context of Puerto Rican society to view interracial marriage as it is generally understood in the social-science literature. Moreover, equating race with ethnic group or minority group further blurs any efforts to come to grips with the problem. Gordon's statement that ". . . there is a common social-psychological core to the categories 'race,' 'religion,' and 'national origin'—*the sense of peoplehood* . . ."* (5, p. 28) applies least in the areas of race as far as the Puerto Rican is concerned. In fact, race consciousness, intensified considerably by Puerto Rico's association with the United States, has been an extremely divisive force. It has turned Puerto Rican against Puerto Rican and seriously undermined a "sense of peoplehood."

ASSIMILATION

Discussion of interracial marriage very often involves the question of assimilation. It is not at all unusual for some social scientists to view marriages between racial or ethnic groupings as evidence of assimilation. Fitzpatrick, for example, argues that there are significant numbers of second-generation Puerto Ricans in New York City marrying out, and this denotes a degree of cultural assimilation, or, as he phrases it, "acceptance of mainland American ways" (3, p. 406). Berry, in his general text, *Race and Ethnic Relations*, writes: "Many investigations of intermarriage, however, have clearly shown that assimilation and intermarriage are closely related . . ." (1, p. 265).

Assimilation, like interracial marriage, is one of those hydra-like concepts that generate more confusion than clarity. In combination, they make rather strange bedfellows. I think it is important for us to know what assimilation means and what, if any, relationship obtains between assimilation and interracial marriage.

A passage from a paper I presented at the 39th International Congress of Americanists in Lima, Peru, on August 6, 1970, will clarify for the reader my ideas on assimilation.

> Departing from the more traditional anthropological approaches to assimilation and following somewhat the lead of Milton Gordon,

*Emphasis added.

> . . . I view assimilation in both a cultural and structural sense. Conceptually speaking, cultural assimilation implies that the group takes on behavioral characteristics of the "core" or "dominant" society. (Members of the United States' "dominant" society, for example, share a "core culture," that is, patterns of behavior which are commonly associated with a middle-class, white, Protestant, Anglo-Saxon orientation. In Puerto Rico, the "core culture" may be identified with the emergent middle sector, a sector which has expanded dramatically in recent years and the members of which share an ideology molded by U.S. values and attitudes.) Structural assimilation occurs if (a) members of the group interact with individuals in higher strata positions on a primary relationship basis and (b) members of the group have complete mobility in the society and equal access to power positions. [7, p. 2]

Any discussion of assimilation must focus on groups rather than particular individuals. Whether any one individual marries in or out has very little bearing on the overall structural assimilation of the group. Large numbers marrying out, however, may very well erode the political potential of the group, thereby retarding structural assimilation of its members.

"INTERRACIAL MARRIAGE" AMONG PUERTO RICANS

As noted earlier, the Puerto Rican "case" raises a number of serious questions about the issue of interracial marriage as commonly understood by social scientists. I should like to deal with the issue in terms of ethnicity, race, and assimilation—the three concepts that I have previously discussed.

INTERETHNIC MARRIAGE

To what extent do Puerto Ricans marry individuals of other ethnic groups? Very little statistical information is available on interethnic marriages of Puerto Ricans in the New York City area. I personally know of a number of instances involving such ethnic groups as Italian, Jewish, Negro, Chinese, Irish, and Dominican (Santo Domingo), to name some. Most cases involve females marrying out. In an article published in *The American Catholic Sociological Review*, Fitzpatrick noted some evidence of interethnic marriages in six parishes of New York City. These parishes were selected ". . . because they represented six different situations and would offer evidence of types of marriage in widely different circumstances" (2, p. 10). In the various interethnic marriages cited by the author, Puerto Rican women rather than men were involved in most instances (2, p. 14).

Since the data are scanty, one can make only provisional statements at this time. My feeling is that marriages between Puerto Ricans and members of other ethnic groups in the New York area are not too common. I suspect this to be true, as well, in other urban centers to which Puerto Ricans have migrated and in which they have settled in significant numbers.

In the Island, where ethnic heterogeneity is less prevalent than in the United States, the question of the extensiveness of interethnic marriages would appear secondary to a consideration of marriages which cut across racial groupings. Yet, as stated earlier, there is a rather large, influential American "colony" in Puerto Rico. Furthermore, substantial numbers of Cuban refugees have emigrated to the Island in recent years. Today these groups constitute the two most important nonindigenous ethnic populations in Puerto Rico. The actual number of Puerto Ricans marrying Americans or Cubans is not known, though I would guess that the frequency of Puerto Rican-Cuban marriages exceeds the figure for Puerto Rican-American unions. I personally know of cases of Puerto Rican-American marriages, and in most instances these marriages united continentals with islanders of either the middle or upper strata. Other ethnic groups are, of course, represented in Puerto Rico, but in considerably smaller numbers. Marrying a Spaniard, for example, is thought to be especially prestigious and usually involves individuals in high-status positions. This appears to be true as well for Puerto Rican-Latin American (i.e., Colombian, Venezuelan, Mexican, etc.) types of marriages.

INTERRACIAL MARRIAGE

The term "race" is here used to identify groups of individuals in terms of generally accepted phenotypic characteristics. Islanders, as already noted, utilize skin color and hair texture as major identifying traits. In terms of the former criterion, individuals are grouped as *moreno*, or *de color* (black); *trigueño* (mulatto); and *blanco* (white). Hair texture types fall into two categories: *pelo bueno* ("good," or straight hair) and *pelo malo* ("bad," or kinky hair).

Marriages with *un(a) blanco(a) con pelo bueno* (a white person with straight hair) are rated high. The lowest rating is given to marriages with *morenos(as) con pelo malo* (blacks with kinky hair). We have, then, six individual types, and if we pair these types, the possibilities amount to 36.* Although I cannot state unequivocally that I have observed all 36 types of marriages, and I include here consensual unions as well,† I feel safe in saying that I have seen most, if not all, possible combinations. Unions involving *blancos con pelo bueno* with *morenos con pelo malo* are not too common and rarely occur across class-caste lines, a point that Scheele (in Steward, *et al.* [10, p. 442]) corroborates in his study of the upper stratum of Puerto Rican society. If a man from a prominent family does marry "interracially," it is very often to a "wealthy light-mulatto woman" (8, p. 81). Both Scheele and Rogler reported their observations more than two decades ago, but the situation has changed little, especially in regard to "interracial marriages" involving upper stratum individuals. If anything, the frequency of "interracial marriage" has probably decreased, not only in the upper stratum but for a growing number of individuals in the middle sector. Apparently, as Puerto Ricans become more affluent, they become more race conscious, and this is manifested in color and hair sensitivity in the choice of one's mate. Affluency and a greater awareness of racial differences are, in my judgment, consequences of Puerto Rico's economic, political, and ideological ties with the United States.

A great deal of what has been said so far about "interracial marriage" indicates that there is some correlation between the phenotypic characteristics of one's mate and one's position in the social hierarchy. This became quite evident to me in my field experience in a Puerto Rican community six years ago. The community, which I will call San Cipriano,* is located on the northeastern coast of the island, approximately fifteen miles east of San Juan. Phenotypically, Ciprianeros are predominantly black and are usually singled

---

*The total number of possibilities would be much greater if one were to consider the degree of *pelo malo* or the combinations of skin color and hair color of different texture. See Mintz (in Steward, *et al.* [10]). I have singled out criteria on which there appears to be widespread consensus. I suspect, however, that there is some degree of local variation in number and emphasis of criteria.

†Marriages may be either formal or consensual (or common-law). A formal marriage is one which is legally sanctioned by the state. A consensual marriage is one which is recognized and sanctioned by the community.

*This is a fictitious name for the real community. Initial research in San Cipriano was made possible through a grant provided by the Research Institute for the Study of Man, New York City.

out by Puerto Ricans throughout the Island as *Africanos,* an epithet which, incidentally, discloses a great deal about the racial attitudes of the Islanders. I should like to comment briefly on social status and "interracial marriages" within the community itself. The most successful merchant in San Cipriano, a dark-skinned man, left his common-law wife—a *trigueña*—for a white bride. The man has since died, and the woman's social contacts have been predominantly with people outside the community. At the time of my field work, the daughter of the second wife (a *blanca*) married an outsider, a *blanco* with a college degree. With few exceptions, Ciprianeros were conspicuously absent from the wedding reception.

Among members of the middle stratum, I noted a number of households where one or both parties were light. In one particular case, a phenotypically dark owner of a relatively successful local clothing shop brought in a light woman from a small town in the interior of the island. Although the man had fathered a number of dark children from other women, he was particularly proud of his *blanca* daughter, singling her out for special treatment. Even in a predominantly black community, the "ideal of whiteness" is evidenced somewhat in the greater frequency of black-white and white-white marriages in the middle and upper strata. Mintz makes a similar observation in his study of Cañamelar, a sugar-producing community on the southeastern coast of Puerto Rico.* He writes:

> Speaking very generally, it might be said that "white" men may marry "Negro" women in special cases, but that the reverse is much more common—a "white" woman with little to offer but her "whiteness" may be able to marry a very successful "Negro" husband. As one moves out of the rural proletariat and into higher socioeconomic groupings, there is undocumented evidence that a successful "Negro" family will seek to find acceptable "white" husbands for the daughters. Among the rural proletariat "Negro," "white," and "mixed" alike—there obtains an ideal of whiteness. [10, p. 411]

It would appear, therefore, that "interracial marriages," though relatively frequent in Puerto Rico, in no way suggest that race is not an important factor in the sociocultural life of the people. Race con-

---

*Although Cañamelar does not have as large a phenotypically black population as San Cipriano, there are substantial numbers of people evidencing a West African genotypic component living there.

sciousness, expressed in an "ideal of whiteness," discloses itself in the form and extent of "interracial marriage" characteristic of the middle and upper strata. Although race has always played a notable role in the history of Puerto Rico, it is my impression that its influence has grown perceptibly in recent years, paralleling to a great extent the industrialization of the island. As Puerto Ricans become more middle class, they become more race conscious; as they become more race conscious, individuals seek "whiter" mates. All of this suggests to me that racial polarization is developing in the island: *blancos-trigueños* vs. *morenos.*

The sparse data available on the form and extent of "interracial marriage" among Puerto Ricans in New York City suggest that an "ideal of whiteness" is equally important to migrants and their descendants. As in the island, *trigueños* represent the majority of the Puerto Rican population of New York, but identify more readily with white rather than black Puerto Ricans. Statistical data cited by Fitzpatrick on interracial marriage seem to support this (2, p. 12). The author divides the Puerto Rican population into three racial groupings: *trigueños(as)* (mulatto), "colored" (black), and white. *Trigueños (as)* are involved in 72 of the marriages listed by Fitzpatrick: 37 *trigueño-trigueña* marriages; 7 "col-ored"-*trigueño(a)* marriages; and 28 *trigueño(a)*-white marriages. It is important to note here that the number of *trigueño(a)*-white marriages is four times that of "colored"-*trigueño(as)* marriages, which indicates that a *trigueño(a)* would much more likely choose a white over a black Puerto Rican as a marriage partner.

In addition, the data provided by Fitzpatrick intimate a polarization of racial groupings in the Puerto Rican population—black vs. white and *trigueño*—despite the author's contention to the contrary. Fitzpatrick writes:

> I think the evidence here is sufficient to indicate that the widespread acceptance of marriage of people of noticeably different color is continuing in the New York situation and there is no reason, as of the present moment, to expect it to stop. It does not support, to any great extent, the theory that the Puerto Rican community will gradually split into two different groups, one white, the other identified with the American Negroes. [2, p. 13]

I read the evidence differently. Less than 8 percent of the marriages mentioned by the author involve a "colored" (black) person in an interracial union. If one were to add this to a figure of roughly 15 percent, which represents the number of *trigueño(a)*-white marriages, the total number of interracial marriages according to Fitzpatrick's statistical data amounts to 23 percent, a rather low proportion among a group where, reputedly, there is "the widespread acceptance of marriage of people of noticeably different color." Moreover, Fitzpatrick has not given proper consideration to the large number of *trigueños(as)* in the Puerto Rican population, a failure which, incidentally, is reflected in the underrepresentation of this particular racial grouping in his sample.* Less than 40 percent of the individuals cited are *trigueños(as)*. It would be interesting to speculate on the kinds of statistical data on marriages that Pentecostal ministers could provide. My impression is that the number of *trigueño-trigueña*, "colored"-*trigueño(a)*, and "colored"-"colored" marriages would increase somewhat. And what about consensual unions? There is a significant number of Puerto Rican common-law marriages.

The reality of racial polarization, as vividly described by Piri Thomas in his book, has become apparent to me in my own experiences with Puerto Ricans in the New York City area. I personally know of two cases of individuals who face the dilemma, "Do I identify with my natal ethnic group (Puerto Rican), or with an adopted one (black American)?" One case is that of two persons married interethnically (Puerto Rican-black) without crossing color lines; another is that of two people married "interracially" (black-white) but intraethnically (Puerto Rican-Puerto Rican). The enigma of identity, aggravated by the racist attitudes and practices of non-Puerto Rican whites, and equally so by white and *trigueño(a)* Puerto Ricans toward individuals of their own ethnic group, has caused many Puerto Ricans to view themselves as black Americans. Racial polarization has split families, undermined the collective strength in ethnicity, and pitted ethnic group against ethnic group.

ASSIMILATION

Assimilation has been, more or less, implicit in a good deal of the discussion so far. However, I should like to consider briefly the implications of "interracial" and interethnic marriage among Puerto

---

*Fitzpatrick quotes the 1950 census report figure of 8 percent as the number of non-white Puerto Ricans (2, p. 8). This, of course, is meaningless since the greater proportion of the 92 percent classified as white are *trigueños(as)*.

Ricans as evidence of their assimilation into the "mainstream of American life." I intend, therefore, to restrict my comments to Puerto Ricans in the New York City area.

Earlier I stated that interethnic or, for that matter, interracial marriage, is not a good index of assimilation. The crucial variables in understanding assimilation are, in my opinion, structural rather than cultural, and the collectivity, not the individual, is the significant focus for discerning the extent of assimilation. Ideally, from a *structural* point of view, complete assimilation implies: (1) "that members of the group interact with individuals of the dominant society on a primary relationship basis," and (2) "that the group has complete mobility in the dominant society and equal access to power positions" (7, p. 2). Although both structural factors are significant, the latter appears to be the more important in gauging the degree of assimilation. Recent evidence on family income and occupational mobility indicates that Puerto Ricans continue to earn the lowest yearly median income and have the highest unemployment rate of all major ethnic groups in New York City (7, pp. 6–8). As far as political power is concerned, the Puerto Rican ranks far below the other larger ethnic collectivities. Whatever interethnic and "interracial marriages" have taken place in recent years have had very little impact on the structural assimilation of the Puerto Rican.

CONCLUSIONS

Puerto Ricans are an interesting population for a discussion of "interracial marriage" for two principal reasons. First, one has an opportunity to view the phenomenon in two dissimilar sociocultural contexts: in the Island, with its relatively homogeneous culture; and in the New York area, with its multiple ethnic groups. Secondly, Puerto Ricans are relatively heterogeneous as a racial group. This type of situation makes it difficult, if not impossible, to follow the more traditional thinking about "interracial marriage." The concept has been frequently used to designate marriages between ethnic groups as well as racial groups. In other words, a Puerto Rican-German marriage and a black Puerto Rican-white Puerto Rican marriage would both be labeled "interracial" despite the fact that the former is clearly interethnic (and may be "interracial" as well) and the latter intraethnic yet "interracial." The Puerto Rican case clearly demonstrates the need for a careful rethinking of the term, especially in view of the fact that ethnic groups and racial groups are analytically separable collectivities, each distinguishable by different sets of criteria. Specific sociocultural characteristics—i.e., language, behavior patterns, interpersonal relations, and a "we feeling"— define the former, whereas phenotypic, i.e., commonly accepted biologically visible criteria, identify the latter.

Furthermore, a discussion of the Puerto Rican case raises a number of vital and relevant issues regarding race relations and assimilation. I pointed out earlier that Puerto Ricans are very race conscious, and one can expect this feeling to become more intense in the years ahead. Islanders and Puerto Ricans in the United States will show increasing racial discrimination both intraethnically and interethnically. Although race consciousness in the Island dates back to Spanish times, it has grown dramatically in recent decades. Racism and affluency seem to go hand in hand. Puerto Rican migrants in the United States, finding a racially hostile environment, are especially sensitized to physical differences, and wittingly or unwittingly transfer these feelings and attitudes to their offspring, many of whom later experience a serious identity crisis.

Finally, interracial marriage is often used as evidence of assimilation. Measuring the extent of assimilation on the basis of the frequency of interracial and interethnic marriages is patently misleading. Assimilation can only be properly assessed in terms of structural variables, the two most important being the degree of social mobility and the accessibility of power positions. Data on interethnic and interracial marriages focus on individuals marrying out, the majority of whom are generally females. This type of information tells us hardly anything about male "assimilation" and consequently can be extremely misleading. What is needed is an approach which recognizes that structural assimilation can and must occur in a society like ours with its diverse ethnic and racial groups, and yet that each group has the option to maintain as best it can its own cultural and biological identity. My own observations of Puerto Ricans in New York City have convinced me that in areas where it counts—i.e., economic and political power—they have experienced the least amount of structural assimilation of the major ethnic and racial groups. As the situation stands, it seems unlikely that there will be any really significant change in this pattern in the years ahead.

13

AROLDO RODRIGUES, Ph.D.

Interracial Marriage in Brazil

In the chapter that follows, Dr. Aroldo Rodrigues of the Catholic University of Rio de Janeiro provides us with information about biracial marriages in that former capital city of Brazil. This information was gathered by the author in the course of an investigation that he conducted himself. In this respect his observations are quite unique, because so many statements about Brazilian interracial marriages are based largely on impressionistic notions, often made by travelers from other areas during a brief visit to Brazil.

Professor Rodrigues is careful to point out that his findings apply only to Rio de Janeiro and that therefore they are not representative of the country as a whole. This, however, does not limit the value of his contribution to our knowledge of interracial marriage and of the broader areas of race relations in what is perhaps the most dynamic country in the Southern Hemisphere.

THIS CHAPTER will focus primarily upon the responses of a sample of Brazilians, residents of the city of Rio de Janeiro, to a variety of aspects of marriage between black and white persons. Interracial marriage is, therefore, defined in this chapter as marriage between representatives of these two ethnic groups. The small number of persons with distinct Indian traces and, more importantly, their complete assimilation into the white and black segments of the Brazilian population, rendered irrelevant the study of marriages between Indians and members of these other ethnic groups. The first of these two reasons justified the exclusion of Orientals too, although in other parts of Brazil (São Paulo, for example) this would not hold. It is important that the reader keep in mind this narrow definition of interracial marriage during the entire chapter.

Besides the above reasons for not considering other ethnic groups in this study of interracial marriage, there are other justifications for singling out marriage between blacks and whites. Brazil is well known as a country in which blacks and whites live in great harmony, and also as a country that shows perhaps the highest rate of miscegenation as far as these two groups are concerned. In the

The author wishes to acknowledge his indebtedness to Mrs. Marília Moura Campos for her invaluable help in all phases of this work; to Mr. Ivan Moura Campos for computer programming; to the Rio Data Centro of the Catholic University of Rio de Janeiro for facilitating access to its IBM computer; to Miss Raquel Wjuniski, Miss Elizabeth Belchior, Miss May L. Medeiros, and Miss Vera Bockhor for helpful comments in the initial phases of the questionnaire construction; and last, but not least, to the American Psychology Foundation which facilitated this work through a Post-Doctoral Research Grant for Foreign Students awarded to the writer. To all, the author expresses his deep gratitude.

influential book *Bandeirantes and Pioneers*, Vianna Moog asserts
that

> In fact, if Brazilians were asked what the highest, most edifying
> and significant aspect of Brazilian civilization is, they would have
> not the slightest hesitation in pointing to the almost complete
> absence of insoluble racial problems. Not that these are entirely
> nonexistent or that the institution of slavery has not also be-
> queathed, in terms of discrimination and segregation, the heavy
> burden of its odious heritage, or that the psychological passivity
> resulting from it has already been fully overcome or is even on the
> way to being fully overcome. . . . But at least its most aggressive
> and menacing branch—pure race conflict—is tending to disap-
> pear. And when at times it attempts to revive, it no longer appears
> under the open and prickly form of the racial issue, properly speak-
> ing, but as a function of class conflict, contrary to what occurs in
> the United States, where race conflicts exceed those of class, the
> latter tending to disappear. Brazilians are against racial prejudice,
> not only because they do not believe in ethnic purity in absolute
> terms, but also because they refuse to accept racial superiority or
> inferiority as the exclusive or even preponderant explanation of
> the differences between civilizations. [5, p. 34]

The evidence for miscegenation is overwhelming. Marvin Harris
refers to this aspect when he says that in Brazil "there are, to be sure,
Negroids and Caucasoids, as well as all of the intervening grades
resulting from widespread miscegenation, but neither the Negroes
nor the mixed or mulatto types nor the whites may be said to constitute by themselves separately identifiable, significant social segments" (2, p. 54). Moreover, data from the 1960 census of the
Brazilian population revealed the existence of a fair amount of mixed
or mulattoes in one region (the exact figure for the entire country
could not be obtained). This becomes even more significant if we
take into account the fact that Brazilians are not too strict in defining
Caucasians. People that, in most other countries, would be considered mixed, are listed as Caucasians in Brazil. If miscegenation is
clearly recognized and easy to verify in Brazil, the evidence for lack
of interracial conflict and prejudice is based primarily on the existence of such miscegenation, and on the minute incidence of overt
conflict between blacks and whites in this country. The lack of cogent
empirical evidence on this subject, however, led people (e.g., the
above-mentioned Marvin Harris) to wonder about the existence of

the so-called racial paradise of Brazil. Based on his observations in the state of Bahía (one of Brazil's twenty-two states), Harris has this to say:

> Let these who regard Brazil as a "racial paradise" remember that this paradise is occupied only by fictional creatures. The real men and women of Bahía are not members of "races," except insofar as any collection of human beings may be said to have an objective racial identity. As far as actual behavior is concerned, "races" do not exist for the Brazilians. But classes exist both for the observer and for the Brazilians. This is the first fact to be digested if one is curious about why racial identity per se is a mild and wavering thing in Brazil, while in the United States it is for millions of people a passport to hell. [2, p. 64]

The impressionistic overtones of this quotation serve the purpose of showing that the lack of concrete data on the smooth relations between blacks and whites in Brazil affords the utterance of opinions contrary to this otherwise generally accepted state of affairs. Moreover, it brings back Vianna Moog's previous assertion that the race situation in Brazil presents itself more clearly in terms of a class struggle, rather than a conflict generated by race differences.

We have, then, on the one hand people who would team up with Vianna Moog, Gilberto Freyre, and many more; on the other, people like Marvin Harris, and certainly others, who question the existence of good relationships in Brazil between the two races we are considering here, either by simply denying such good relationships, or by offering alternative interpretations for the absence of overt conflict (e.g., absence of competition between the races owing to the low economic level of most blacks, confounding of race with class prejudice, etc.). Furthermore, we have seen in both quotations a distinct concern with the role performed by social class differences in the context of racial relations in Brazil. Linking these aspects of the issue of race relations to the topic of this book, we felt it worthwhile to inquire further into the topic of interracial marriage in Brazil. Specifically, we wanted to gather some data on the attitudes and opinions toward interracial marriage, as well as on some of its specific aspects—expectations for the future; successes and failures of this type of marriage (in itself and as compared with marriages between people of different social classes); frequency of interracial marriages; perceived reaction to them; possible influence of age, religion, social class, sex, and other variables on the aspects listed above; etc. The results we arrived at are discussed in the section of this chapter that deals with attitudes and opinions toward interracial marriage in Brazil. For a better understanding of the racial situation in Brazil, however, a quick look at the historical background and the present state of affairs related to the subject seems in order.

A BRIEF OVERVIEW OF RACE RELATIONS IN BRAZIL

Before 1888, the blacks in Brazil lived as slaves, working for the whites in the large farms owned by the latter. Miscegenation was already under way, so that the 1890 census showed that the population was composed of 45 percent whites, 42 percent mixed, and 13 percent blacks. Differences in status based exclusively upon the color of one's skin were clear at that time. As Lamounier points out, "Color was above all a mark of position in the social scales"(4). And, quoting Florestan Fernandes, he adds: "The form of organization . . . established a relationship among the White, the Mulatto, and the Negro, such that the latter was to the former as the slave to his master. Gradations of color were not, by themselves, imposing enough to attenuate the social determinations involved in the relationship of interracial subordination and domination" (4, p. 4).

It is interesting to note that, despite the clear social discrimination based on race during the slave period, the number of people of mixed blood kept increasing. Perhaps the best account of how that happened can be found in Vianna Moog's *Bandeirantes and Pioneers.* Moog calls attention to the fact that for many centuries the Portuguese—the settlers of Brazil—had been used to people of fairly dark skin. During eight centuries, says Moog, the Moors occupied the Iberian Penninsula, which led the Portuguese to become accustomed to be ruled by people of dark skin, contrary to other peoples of Europe who always lived under white domination (5). This may very well account for the prompt miscegenation that occurred in Brazil even during the slave period. After the abolition of slavery, a period of transition was initiated. The blacks were freed then, but they faced a variety of problems. As highlighted by C. Furtade (1), the former slaves, by virtue of their own experience as slaves, hated work and loved leisure. For them, work was something evil, and only the minimum necessary for keeping alive was sought. They would

rather "buy" leisure than keep working when the minimum necessary for a poor living had been attained. Furthermore, the slaves
after abolition faced two very difficult problems: first, their own
limitations (e.g., illiteracy, lack of skills, lack of achievement motivation, etc.); second, competition by European immigrants. When the
signs of abolition of slavery became clearer, many land owners began
to turn their attention to immigrants who, at that time, were coming
in large numbers to Brazil. The competition between ex-slaves and
skilled Europeans was, obviously, extremely disadvantageous to the
former.

The problems faced by the slaves after 1888 made it quite difficult for them to improve their social condition. Until recently, the
number of public schools in Brazil was extremely small, and only
those who could afford a private school could get an education. This
situation has changed, and now anybody, in most states of the Union,
can go to public schools. This significant improvement will soon
make possible an increase in the number of educated and skilled
blacks who, because of the situation that confronted them after their
freedom from slavery, were prevented from leaving the bottom of
the socioeconomic hierarchy.

The situation sketched here explains the limited contacts, at the
upper socioeconomic and educational levels, between blacks and
whites in Brazil. Nevertheless, at the lower strata of these levels,
people of both races interact quite frequently, with, apparently, no
signs of friction at all. Also at the upper strata of the socioeconomic
and educational hierarchy, blacks and whites interact cordially, although, as stated earlier, such situations arise very seldom owing to
the lack of opportunities for improvement on the part of most blacks.
This situation led M. Harris to make the pertinent remark that "in
Brazil one can pass to another racial category regardless of how dark
one may be without changing one's residence. The passing is accomplished by achieving economic success or high educational status.
Brazilians say 'Money whitens,' meaning that the richer a dark man
gets, the lighter will be the racial category to which he will be assigned by his friends, relatives, and business associates. Similarly,
light-skinned individuals who rank extremely low in terms of educational and occupational criteria are frequently regarded as actually
being darker in color than they really are" (2, p. 59).

Here lies the crux of the race argument as far as Brazil is concerned. Specifically, is the lack of overt conflict between blacks and whites due to a genuine absence of racial prejudice, or is it merely an illusion created by the existence of a *class prejudice* that masks *racial prejudice?* In other words, one can wonder what will happen in Brazil when the blacks reach the level of socioeconomic and educational status that many whites have reached. Will there be then an overt reaction against the blacks? Will the supposed "hidden prejudice" manifest itself openly?

It is our hope that the empirical results reported in the next section may throw some light on these questions, with particular attention to the main topic of marriage between whites and blacks.

ATTITUDES AND OPINIONS TOWARD INTERRACIAL MARRIAGE IN BRAZIL

The results reported in this section were obtained through person-to-person interviews of 248 adults living in the city of Rio de Janeiro. Limitations of time and financial resources prevented the drawing of a truly representative sample. Care was taken, nevertheless, to have the sample consist of people of both sexes, ranging in age from 18 to 69 years, of all social classes and all levels of schooling (from no schooling to college graduates). *Only whites* (88 percent) *and very light mulattoes* (12 percent, normally taken in Brazil as whites) *were interviewed.* Although not representative for broad generalizations, the sample includes a large spectrum of relevant variables. Each interviewer was given a quota of people characterized by certain patterns of the above-mentioned variables and was free to choose the interviewee, once the specifications were met.

Throughout this section the data gathered from white and light mulatto respondents will be treated together, inasmuch as no significant differences between the two groups of respondents were found. We deliberately gathered data from light mulattoes because they are supposed to be more intolerant toward blacks than the pure whites themselves. Incidentally, the results did not bear this hypothesis out.

ATTITUDES TOWARD INTERRACIAL MARRIAGE

An attitude scale of the Likert type was constructed. Of sixty attitude items submitted to testing, seven were retained as the most discriminating between high and low scorers. Each of these seven items could be answered "agree completely," "agree in part," "no opinion," "disagree in part," and "disagree completely." Five levels of intensity of agreement were then made up, the *higher* the score, the *less* favorable the attitude toward interracial marriage. The results showed a clear predominance of favorable attitudes toward the issue: 73 percent of those interviewed fell in the two most favorable levels of attitude intensity toward interracial marriage, 14 percent were found in the mid category, and the remaining 13 percent showed unfavorable attitudes. This trend of results holds true for both sexes, all levels of schooling, all types of religious affiliation, marital status, and social class. Only when the variable *age* is singled out for analysis do we find that the younger the people, the more favorable their attitude toward interracial marriage.

In addition to the attitude scale prepared *ad hoc*, there were two other questions that tapped directly the respondents' attitudes toward interracial marriage. These two questions were: (1) If a person whom you like very much told you that he wanted to marry a black, would you consider it good, bad, or would you be indifferent to it? (2) If a campaign were to be initiated to ban possible restrictions on marriages between whites and blacks, would you support such a campaign?

Twenty-four percent of the respondents answered "good," 21 percent "bad," and 55 percent "indifferent" to the first of these two questions. As to the second, 74 percent indicated they would support the campaign, and 26 percent that they would not. Here again *age* showed some influence on the distribution of the responses: older people gave more "bad" answers to the first question than younger ones, and a greater percentage of the latter said they would give support to the campaign than the former did. *Schooling* revealed interesting results: for the first question, people with little or no education gave greater percentages of "good" responses than people with high education; however, in regard to the second question, schooling had no bearing on frequency of support—the overwhelming majority in all educational brackets showed ample support to the campaign. This may be interpreted as a recognition of the right of people to choose whomever they please as a partner in marriage, regardless of color, even though one might not like to have a friend marry a black. The difference between personal preference and recognition of right is, in our opinion, an important one, and may be regarded as one of the differences between Brazil and other countries as far as race relations are concerned. It seems that Brazilians do not question the right people have to what any human being is entitled to, regardless of the color of his skin. Segregationist countries, on the other hand, seem to have a large percentage of people who claim that human beings of different skin colors are entitled to different treatments as far as civil rights are concerned.

OPINIONS ABOUT INTERRACIAL MARRIAGE

In this chapter we distinguish between attitudes and opinions on the grounds of a clearer *affective* component in the former, and a more distinct *cognitive* component in the latter. In other words, the questions considered *attitudinal* involved answers with clear emotional overtones, whereas those considered *opinionative* required answers reflecting a certain knowledge about interracial marriage, without necessarily requiring emotional involvement. One of such *opinion* questions was: In your opinion, the general reaction of Brazilians to the marriage of a white person to a black or mulatto is favorable, unfavorable, or indifferent?

Twenty percent answered "favorable," 51 percent "unfavorable," and 29 percent "indifferent." Taken as a whole, the sample interviewed perceives other Brazilians, in general, as being against interracial marriage. It will be recalled that the attitudinal questions previously examined deal with the way the respondents actually feel toward the issue; this question refers to the manner they *perceive* Brazilians in general to feel about the matter. There is, therefore, no inconsistency in the results obtained. It is worth mentioning that 20 percent of the respondents under twenty years of age perceive Brazilians as being favorable to interracial marriage, and 56 percent perceive them as being unfavorable; on the other hand, among the people over sixty years of age, 62 percent perceive Brazilians in general as favorable, and only 23 percent as unfavorable to interracial marriage. As we saw in the previous section, younger people showed more favorable attitudes toward the issue than older ones. It may very well be that their own attitudes influenced the way they perceive others. The young ones see the others as too conservative on the matter; the older ones, on the contrary, see them as too liberal.

A second opinion item on the questionnaire was: In your opinion, who is more opposed to interracial marriage, the whites or the blacks?

Eighty-one percent answered "whites," 7 percent "blacks," and 11 percent reported no difference. This lends support to the position laid out in the previous section of this chapter, which implied that there was a direct relationship between "whiteness" and high social status. This apparently is still seen as true.

The last opinion question was: In your opinion, would you say that, in general, interracial marriages give good results?

Thirty-four percent answered yes, 18 percent answered no, and 48 percent said that they didn't know. When social class is taken into consideration, we find that 46 percent of the poor answered yes to this question, against only 20 percent of the upper class.

IS THERE A RACIAL PREJUDICE OR A CLASS PREJUDICE AGAINST
INTERRACIAL MARRIAGE IN BRAZIL?

As mentioned earlier in the chapter, several observers of race relations in Brazil postulate that there may very well be a strong class prejudice confounded, to some extent, with race prejudice. Owing to the general low economic level of most blacks in Brazil, it would be interesting to verify whether there is a race prejudice hidden in the noticeable class prejudice, or if there is instead a simple class prejudice which, of course, would not reveal itself whenever blacks of high economic level are concerned. Moreover, if there is only a class prejudice, discrimination against low-class whites should also be currently found. Let us see what our survey revealed in this respect, when the issue of interracial marriage was taken up for closer scrutiny.

The respondents to our questionnaire were asked to indicate which of three types of marriage—namely, marriage between black and white, marriage between people of different religious creeds, and marriage between people of different social classes—would bring the greatest number of problems, and which would bring the smallest. Interclass marriage was indicated by 58 percent of the sample as the type of marriage that causes most problems; interracial marriage was pointed out by 19 percent, and interreligious marriage by 16 percent; 7 percent said they could not single any one out. As to the type of marriage that causes the least number of problems, 56 percent indicated interreligious marriage, 24 percent interracial marriage, and 10 percent interclass marriage; the remaining 10 percent could not single one out. These data clearly indicate greater class prejudice than race prejudice. Furthermore, when asked whether there would be a greater number of interracial marriages if blacks were of higher economic level, 65 percent answered yes, 15 percent no, and 20 percent found it hard to tell. Still further corroboration of the existence of class prejudice, and also of its predominance over race prejudice, at least as far as marriage is concerned, is given by two other questions the respondents were asked. One was: What would you say if your white maid wanted to marry a black young man and asked for your opinion on the matter? Seventy-five percent answered they would approve of it, 9 percent indicated they had no opinion, and only 16 percent said they would be against the marriage. Finally, another question bearing on race and class prejudice in connection with marriage also revealed the same pattern encountered so far. Respondents were asked to explain why there are few interracial marriages among upper-class people. They could choose among four possible answers: because whites do not want to mix with blacks; because whites do not want to mix with people of another class; because of both these reasons; for other reasons. Twenty-two percent picked the first alternative, 42 percent chose the second one, and 29 percent chose the third answer. The remaining 7 percent said "for other reasons."

In every case in which there was a choice between an answer indicative of race prejudice and one indicating class prejudice, the results indicated a stronger preference for the option indicative of class prejudice rather than race prejudice. When we analyze these questions, taking into account age, social class, religion, degree of schooling, marital status, and sex, we find the same pattern with the following specific characteristics: (1) the higher the educational level and the socioeconomic position, the clearer the dominance of class prejudice; (2) the younger the respondent, the less color is indicated as an explanatory factor for the small number of interracial marriages among upper-class people.

Probably the most definite finding in regard to the topic of this section is the following. When asked if the color of one's skin is an important factor in marriage, 60 percent said that they agreed either totally or in part, 4 percent had no clear position, and 46 percent stated that they disagreed either totally or in part. When a similar question was asked for class rather than color, 76 percent answered they agreed completely or in part, 3 percent were undecided, and only 21 percent said they disagreed either completely or in part. This trend was confirmed when those interviewed were asked, whether it is more important for people who want to marry be of the same class or of the same color. Sixty-eight percent of them answered that it is more important that they be of the same class, and only 22 percent answered that race is more important. The same age factor noticed in regard to the other answers holds in regard to these data.

It seems that in the light of the evidence presented thus far we can conclude that class prejudice is stronger than race prejudice as far as marriage is concerned.

IS THERE RACIAL PREJUDICE IN BRAZIL?

As pointed out at the beginning of this chapter, generalizations for the entire country of Brazil based on the data gathered for this study are unwarranted. At any rate, the inferences afforded by these data are more justified than some common generalizations made by tourists who visit the country during the Carnival, and which are therefore based on sporadic observations. The present inferences are also more soundly grounded than generalizations drawn out of research of questionable quality made by observers in that choice spot for research on race relations that is the Brazilian state of Bahia. After this word of caution, let us see how the sample of 248 Brazilians responded to questions bearing upon the problem of racial prejudice.

Four questions in our survey dealt with this point. The most general question asked was: Many people feel that there is no racial prejudice in Brazil; do you consider this to be true, false, or neither true nor false? Fifteen percent of the sample judged the statement true, 44 percent found it false, and 41 percent considered it neither true nor false. In other words, if we exclude the undecided, a significant majority thinks that to consider Brazil as free from racial prejudice is *not* true.

Let us consider the other three questions relating to this subject. This set of questions deals with racial prejudice in the context of interracial marriage. The first of these three questions reads: In your opinion, are the whites or the blacks the ones who are most against interracial marriage? An overwhelming majority of 81 percent answered "whites," revealing not only an existence of prejudice, but also the direction of it. In other words, as perceived by whites and light mulattoes (the sample, it will be recalled, was composed only of these two groups), the whites are the ones who are most against mixed marriages.

The other two questions were: (1) In general, would you say that interracial couples (black and white) feel at ease in Brazil? (2) How would most people react if a mixed couple became their next-door neighbors in an expensive neighborhood?

Eleven percent answered the first question by saying that married people of different races (black and white) would feel at ease; 27 percent said they would find *many* problems; and 62 percent said they would find *some* problems. As to the second question, 29 percent said most people would react favorably and 54 percent said they would react unfavorably; 17 percent said they had no opinion.

In an attempt to attain an overall view of frequency of occurrence of interracial marriage, the interviewees were asked to indicate whether or not they knew any married couple in which one partner was black or dark mulatto and the other one white. The responses showed that 70 percent knew such couples. These 70 percent were then asked if in comparison with other couples, the mixed couples they knew were happier, unhappier, or as happy as most other couples they knew. Six percent answered "happier," 10 percent "unhappier," and 83 percent "as happy as." The other 1 percent either did not answer the question or the interviewer did not record it.

Is there racial prejudice in Brazil? To give a definite answer to this question is not an easy task. On the one hand, we have the data provided through the questions, some of which would indicate the existence of racial prejudice among Brazilians; on the other hand, we have seen that a good deal of evidence supports the opposite conclusion (e.g., the great number of people who knew marriages between people of different color, the dominant perception that these marriages are as happy or unhappy as any other type, the willingness of people to give support to a campaign in favor of eliminating restrictions to interracial marriage, etc.). Based on the evidence available, no conclusive answer can be offered. It is surprising, therefore, that one can come across statements like this: "Even Donald Pierson, the first North American to make a detailed study of Brazilian race relations, was somewhat carried away by his enthusiasm for Bahian inter-racial democracy, and tended to underestimate the amount of racial prejudice which actually existed, and which every Brazilian knows full well exists, except when talking to United States citizens" (2, p. 60). For this investigator the evidence of racial prejudice is abundant. Quite unfortunately, he presents no proof for his definite assertion. His evidence is based upon uncontrolled observation or, perhaps, unique intuitive powers. The writer of this chapter believes more in empirical data than in intuition. In the light of the data presented here, I am more inclined toward the position that there exists some sort of racial prejudice in Brazil, but much has yet to be unravelled before we can make a more precise and clear statement. The main difficulty lies in the confusing of black color and low socioeconomic status. To argue that *de facto* discrimination exists in Brazil, because of the high proportion of blacks who are prevented from going to luxurious hotels, restaurants, and clubs is grossly misleading, inas-much as low-class whites are equally discriminated against in these places. Moreover, many black politicians in Brazil have been con-stantly elected, and the color of their skin has never constituted a campaign issue. One of the most outstanding and most respected Supreme Court judges Brazil has ever had was a dark mulatto. He was accepted everywhere with deep respect and courtesy. What really seems to happen is that once the black has overcome the common handicaps of education and social status, the color of his skin is no longer a burden for him in Brazilian society. The anecdotal evidence here briefly presented, plus the controversial trends of the data obtained, justifies the previous assertion that it is not an easy task to answer conclusively the question about racial prejudice in Brazil.

Kersner and Lowndes (3) conducted a study in which fifty peo-ple—twenty-five of high socioeconomic status and twenty-five of low socioeconomic status—were asked to provide answers to a test based on Bogardus' social distance scale. Specifically, each respondent in-dicated to what degree he would accept blacks and whites of upper and lower classes. The results disclosed that, in general, (1) respond-ents of lower socioeconomic status show a higher degree of accep-tance of people, regardless of race and social class, than respondents of higher socioeconomic status; (2) all respondents show greater ac-ceptance of whites than of blacks; (3) they all show a higher degree of acceptance toward people of upper than of lower socioeconomic status; and (4) upper-class respondents show greater degree of acceptance toward people of higher socioeconomic status than for those of lower status, whereas lower-class respondents accept both without discrimination. These results confirm what has been stated previously: that is, there seem to be both a racial and a class prejudice, but the latter is stronger than the former; moreover, this seems to hold true more among people of higher socioeconomic status. Still further research is needed, not only to clarify the peculiarities of racial prejudice in Brazil, but also to control carefully the variables of race and social class. It would be necessary to see empirically what the pattern of race relations among people of different color and of the *same socioeconomic class* is, and also the pattern of relations among people of the *same race* and of *different socioeconomic status*. Only then a definite and truly enlightening answer can be obtained in regard to the issue considered in this section.

A FINAL WORD

This chapter was *not* intended to be a comprehensive account of the problem of race relations in Brazil. Rather, it focused upon a specific aspect of such relations, namely, interracial marriage of blacks and whites. It tried to reduce to a minimum the impressionistic evidence about the patterns of race relations in Brazil, on which literally dozens of thick books have been written. We chose an empirical approach to the problem, and designed a questionnaire for that effect which, despite its limitations and those of the sample, does add some empirical knowledge to this controversial topic.

In the light of the evidence presented in this chapter, the writer is persuaded of four things. First, as far as interracial marriage in Brazil is concerned, the negative reactions to it are much more clearly derived from the difference in socioeconomic status that exists between blacks and whites than from the differences in skin color; second, interracial marriage in Brazil is fairly well accepted, particularly when no class differences exist between the partners; third, the amount of racial prejudice in Brazil, although existing, seems much more attenuated than in other parts of the world where race conflicts break out frequently; and fourth, only when research is done, keeping constant the variable of race and varying that of socioeconomic status and, conversely, keeping constant the socioeconomic status and varying race, will we have a clear picture of the pattern of race relations in Brazil.

In his chapter on "The Brazilian Pattern" of race relations, Marvin Harris makes a point worth quoting. He says:

> Thus, although the pattern of 'race' relations in Brazil contrasts markedly with that of the United States, especially with that of the South, once Brazil's lower class is accorded its proper structural significance as the equivalent of the 'Negroes' in the United States, the stratification systems of the two countries actually bear a very close resemblance to each other. In both cases, the fundamental heritage of the slave plantation was the creation of severely handicapped minorities, darker in color than the rest of the population. [2, 64]

Based on the evidence reviewed in this chapter, one must agree that Harris correctly notes the difference in quality of race relationships in the United States and Brazil, but his account of the difference in complexity of the race issue in each country is oversimplified and misleading. After all, it should be readily recognized that it is much easier (at least conceptually) to change one's socioeconomic status than to change the color of one's skin.

14

HIROSHI WAGATSUMA, Ph.D.

Some Problems of Interracial Marriage for the Japanese

Uniquely qualified as an observer by personal experience and by his scientific training as an anthropologist and sociologist, Dr. Wagatsuma analyzes Japanese attitudes toward interracial marriage and toward "mixed-blood" children for an America increasingly concerned with Japan. His first-hand account of intermarriages of Japanese men and women with both black and white Americans provides for the first time information on how the people of the East view the other racial groups of the West.

His discussion is bolstered by data and facts gathered through professional interview studies of Japanese attitudes, as well as by the outlook expressed in contemporary Japanese literature, which often deals with interracial relationships and marriage.

INTERRACIAL marriages in Japan can be classified into two categories: marriages between Japanese women and non-Japanese men, and marriages between Japanese men and non-Japanese women. The incidence of marriages in the first category has been much greater than that in the second category. During the period of Japan's colonization of Taiwan (1895–1945) and Korea (1910–1945), a considerable number of Japanese women became the wives of Taiwanese and Korean men in the colonies and in Japan as well, but not many Japanese men married Taiwanese or Korean women. (It is likely that they took these women as prostitutes, and perhaps as concubines, but rarely as wives.) During and after World War II, some Japanese servicemen in Indonesia, Burma, and Thailand married native women and fathered children. The number of such marriages is unknown, but could not have been very large, and many of them were broken when the Japanese husbands were repatriated. Before World War II, a sprinkling of Japanese men—aristocrats, scholars, and diplomats—had European or American wives, but they were certainly exceptional cases. After the war, marriage with Western women seems to have increased somewhat among some scholars, foreign correspondents, and diplomats. These men either return and live in Japan or become "expatriates" in the land of their wives. In either case, the number is insignificant. On the other hand, since the end of World War II, a large number of Japanese women, estimated between 50,000 and 60,000, have married white or black Americans and moved to the United States.

We cannot examine all kinds of interracial marriages—between

Japanese men and white, black, or Asian women, and between Japanese women and white, black, or Asian men—because our space is limited and, more importantly, because there is a dearth of empirical data. Interracial marriages among the Japanese are a subject as yet scarcely explored, and studies are badly needed. We hope that this chapter will serve as an invitation to, and an initial preparation for, such studies.

Given these limitations, we will focus our attention on three subjects: (1) Japanese attitudes toward Caucasian and Negro racial traits, that might be an important factor in the understanding of the problems of interracial marriages; (2) marriages between American servicemen and Japanese women; and (3) some of the problems of "mixed-blood" children, the offspring of liaisons between Japanese women and white and black American soldiers.

JAPANESE ATTITUDES TOWARD NONORIENTAL RACIAL TRAITS

Among Japanese, particularly intellectuals, there is a more or less unconscious ambivalence toward the world of white people. Such an attitude is understandable if one takes even a brief glance at the recent history of Japan. Overwhelmed at first by its fear of the great power of the Western world, Japan caught up with the West in an amazingly short time, became the self-appointed champion of non-white Asians, and in this role boldly tried to win a place in the coterie of white imperialists. Failing disastrously after all, the Japanese found themselves receiving a "democratic education" at the hands of American teachers toward whom they felt great rivalry mixed with admiration. Such ambivalence, or "inferiority-superiority complex," is reflected in the Japanese attitudes toward the skin color and other physical characteristics of the Caucasians. As has been shown elsewhere in detail (6), interviews with contemporary Japanese men and women, both in the United States and in Japan, indicate that their attitudes toward Caucasian skin and other physical features are divided into opposites of likes and dislikes, depending, it appears, upon the degree of an individual's receptivity to Western culture and the extent of his identification with it.

More than half of the men and women interviewed considered Caucasian skin to be inferior to Japanese skin in terms of both texture and appearance. They claimed that Caucasian skin was rough, covered with wrinkles and marked by spots and speckles. Here are examples from some of the interviews. A middle-aged company employee said: "If you look at the neck of an old white woman, with all those furrows and bristles it reminds you of that of a pig." The comment of 42-year-old woman newspaper reporter was: "When I try to visualize a Caucasian woman, she is associated in my mind with skin of rough texture and unsmooth surface. The pores of her skin are larger than ours. Young women may have smoother skin, but older women have bad skin."

The idea that Caucasian skin is "ugly" is also expressed in a number of passages in contemporary literature. The following is an example taken from a book by Sawako Ariyoshi: "When a kissing couple was projected on a large [movie] screen in a close-up, then the ugliness unique to Caucasian female skin was magnified. The freckles covering the woman's cheek and throat became visible. . . . On the fingers of a man caressing a women, gold hairs were seen shining like an animal's bristles" (1).

Some of those who favored Japanese "white" skin suggested that Caucasian skin is not white but transparent. A male graduate student said: "This may be completely unscientific, but I feel that when I look at the skin of a Japanese woman I see the whiteness of her skin. When I observe Caucasian skin, what I see is the whiteness of the fat underneath the skin, not the whiteness of the skin itself. Sometimes instead of white fat I see the redness of blood under the transparent skin. Then it does not appear white but red." A college student said: "The Caucasian skin is something like the surface of a pork sausage, while the white skin of a Japanese resembles the outside of *kamaboko* [a white, spongy fish cake]." We may remind the reader here that before any sustained contact with the Caucasoid Europeans, the Japanese valued *their* "white" skin as beautiful and depreciated *their* "black" (actually, suntanned) skin as ugly. Throughout Japan's history, men and especially women have taken care not only to keep their skin "unsuntanned," but also to increase its smoothness by a variety of means.

While disparaging the quality of Caucasian skin, most Japanese admit that Caucasian facial and body structure is more attractive than the "flat face" and "less shapely body" of the Japanese. This view, combining the assertion of Japanese "skin supremacy" with the admission of the greater appeal of the refined Caucasian facial and body structure, is exemplified by a widely held notion that a Eurasian child will be very attractive if it inherits its Japanese parent's skin and its Caucasian parent's bone structure, but that the result of the opposite combination is likely to be disastrous.

For most of those Japanese without much personal contact with Westerners, skin is only one of several characteristics making up their body-image of a Caucasian. Other components of this image are the shape and color of eyes, the texture and color of hair, height, size, body weight, and overall hairiness. The image of a Caucasian with white skin, deep-set eyes, wavy hair of a color other than black, with a tall, stout, hairy body and large hands and feet, evoke in many Japanese associations with qualities of "vitality," "superior energy," "strong sexuality" or "animality," and the feeling that Caucasians are basically "disharmonious" as compared with Asians.

Positive attitudes toward Caucasian skin center on its being whiter than the so-called white skin of the Japanese and, therefore, more attractive. Many Japanese men, especially those who have sustained contact with Westerners, confess to the beauty of the white skin of Caucasian women. At the same time, however, they define these women as "inaccessible." This is largely because, in spite of such contacts, the feeling still persists, although in a weakened form, that the Westerners are in some sense totally "others" and remote. For example, a 35-year-old university professor, who had lived in the United States for seven years, had this to say: "Looking at the white skin, I feel somehow that it belongs to a different world. People understand each other a great deal but there is something which people of different races cannot quite share. It sounds foolish and irrational, I know, but somehow this is the feeling I have, looking at the white skin of a Caucasian woman." A 27-year-old graduate student, who had lived in the United States for four years, said: "Sometimes I feel that the white skin of the Caucasian tells me that after all I am an Oriental and cannot acquire everything Western, however Westernized I might be. It is like the last border I cannot go across and it is symbolized by the white skin. Is this my inferiority feeling toward the white people? I often wonder."

An extreme expression of inferiority feelings about the Japanese skin color compared with that of the Caucasian is found in *Up to Aden*, a short story by a French-educated author, Shusaku Endo (4).

In it the author emphasizes the basic difference between European tradition and Japanese culture, focusing symbolically upon the hero's somewhat exaggerated feelings about physical differences between a white French woman and himself. The hero, a Japanese student on his way home from France, recalls his painful love for a French girl. The following are a few quotations, in English translation, from the story:

> "Race does not make any difference!" the [French] girl said impatiently. "The whites, the yellows or the blacks, they are all the same!" That was what she said. Race does not make any difference. Later she fell in love with me and I did not refuse her love. Because there was this illusion that race does not make any difference. In the beginning, in love, we did not at all take into consideration that her body was white and my skin was yellow. When we kissed for the first time—it was in the evening on our way home from Mabyon where we had gone dancing—I shouted almost unintentionally to the girl who was leaning against the wall with her eyes closed, "Are you sure? Are you sure you don't mind its being me?" But she simply answered, "Stop talking and hold me in your arms." If race did not make any difference, why on earth did I have to utter such a miserable question, like a groan, at that time? If love had no frontiers and race did not matter, I should not have felt insecure even for a moment. In reality, however, I had to try instinctively not to envisage a certain truth hidden beneath my groan. I was afraid of it.
>
> Less than two months after that evening, the day finally came when I had to see the truth. It was in the last winter, when the two of us made a trip together from Paris to Lyon. It was in the evening when for the first time we showed our skin to each other. . . . Breathlessly, we remained long in each other's arms. Golden hair had never looked to me more beautiful. Her naked body was of spotless, pure whiteness, and her golden hair smoothly flowed down from her shoulders. She was facing toward a door. I was facing toward curtained windows. As the light was on, our naked bodies were visible in a mirror on an *armoire*. In the beginning I could not believe that what I had seen in the mirror was really my body. My naked body had been well proportioned for a Japanese. I was as tall as a European and I was full in chest and limbs. Speaking of the body form, I would not look inharmonious when holding a white woman in my arms. But what I saw reflected in the mirror was something else. Beside the gleaming whiteness of her shoulders and breasts in the lighted room, my body looked dull in a lifeless, dark-yellow color. My chest and stomach did not look too bad, but around the neck and shoulders turbid yellow color in-

creased its dullness. The two different colors of our bodies in embrace did not show even a bit of beauty or harmony. It was ugly. I suddenly thought of a worm of a yellow muddy color, clinging to a pure white flower. The color of my body suggested a human secretion, like bile. I wished I could cover my face and body with my hands. Cowardly, I turned off the light to lose my body in darkness . . .

"Hold me tight. We are in love and that is enough," she said to me once when we kissed at a street corner in the dusk. But it was not enough that we were in love. By love only, she could not become a yellow woman and I could not become a white man. Love, logic and ideology could not erase differences in skin color. . . . White men had allowed me to enter their world as long as their pride was not hurt. They allowed me to wear their clothes, drink their wine and love a white woman. They could not accept that a white woman loved me. They could not accept it because white people's skin is white and beautiful and because I am yellow and ugly. They could not stand a white woman falling in love with a man of such lifeless, muddy yellow color. Foolishly enough, I had not known or thought of it at all until this day [when the girl had announced her engagement to a Japanese man only to invite frightened blame and anger from her friends].

The characteristics of this widespread ambivalence may well be personified and symbolized by the Japanese image of a hairy giant (ketō). This image evokes in the Japanese a composite of feelings which include not only a sense of being overwhelmed or threatened, and fear or disgust, but also the admiration and envy for great vigor and strong sexuality that can easily satisfy an equally energetic and glamorous creature.

When Japanese men feel a vague sense of discomfort at the sight or notion of a Japanese woman marrying a white man, especially an American, the feeling may be related to their unconscious understanding that a Japanese woman, by choosing a white man, is challenging their worth as men and their virility. Consequently, actual sexual experience with a white woman may help some Japanese to overcome such feelings of inferiority toward Caucasians. One of the persons interviewed remarked that his uncle once told him that during Japan's control over Manchuria many Japanese men enjoyed sleeping with white Russian prostitutes: "My uncle said, having relations with a white woman made these men feel different, more masculine or something. The feeling is different from that one has after having had relations with an Asian woman." Generally, however, Japanese men seem rather overwhelmed and discouraged by the large physique of a white woman.

In contrast to this complex of attitudes about Caucasoid racial traits, the Japanese attitude toward the black skin and facial characteristics of American Negroes are generally clearly negative, although a number of Japanese women did marry black Americans after the war. The intellectual Japanese may show their awareness of recent racial issues in statements such as, "I know people should not feel different about Negroes, and I have no negative feelings about them," or, "I have nothing against them. I don't think I have any prejudice against them." These comments are generally followed by a "but" and by various expressions, unanimously negative: "I feel resistance to coming closer to them." "It's almost a physical reaction and has nothing to do with my thinking. It's almost like a biological repulsion." "It is a feeling of uneasiness and something uncanny."

Several Japanese have expressed the opinion that black skin is something novel to the Japanese and only for that reason a source of problems. "It is a matter of getting used to it," said a chemist in Berkeley, California. "We Japanese had little chance in Japan to come close to the Negroes. It is only natural, I think, that in the beginning we feel strange about their skin. Not only the skin color, but many things about their physical features are so different from what we are accustomed to. In the beginning, I felt kind of uneasy, if not uncomfortable, when I was close to my Negro friends. But you get used to it. I no longer feel anything special about them." The same idea was voiced by a Japanese woman married to an American Negro. "Frankly, I felt uneasy about it [his black skin] in the beginning, but you see it every day, from morning to evening; there is nothing else you can do except to get used to it. I did get used to it. Especially since he was very nice and kind all the time. Once you get used to it, you no longer see it."

Other Japanese believe that the Japanese attitude toward black skin is more than just a simple reaction to something novel. According to this view, black skin is associated in the Japanese mind with many undesirable traits. Other Negroid features are also the opposite of what Japanese have long valued as desirable physical characteristics. "Blackness is often associated with death, vice, despair, and other kinds of negative things." "A black-bellied man is wicked and black mood is depression" (female graduate student). "When something becomes dirty and smeared, it gets black. White skin in our minds symbolizes purity and cleanliness. Then, by an association, black skin is the opposite of purity and cleanliness. . . . Black skin after all suggests something unclean. It is not the natural state of things" (45-year-old housewife). A male university student had this to say: "Speaking of Japanese faces, we do not appreciate such features as a pug nose, snub nose, goggle eyes, thick lips, kinky hair. They are despised and often laughed at. What we prefer is just the opposite of these. But just think. Aren't they what the Negroes usually have?"

Whatever the reason may be, blacks—Americans or Africans—are undifferentiatedly seen by the majority of the Japanese as "black men, with inhumanly black skin, goggle eyes, thick lips, kinky hair, strong body odor, and animal-like sexuality and energy." Such an image invariably evokes negative feelings. Many said they felt indignation toward the white-American discrimination against Negroes. Some were fond of Negro musicians. Negro baseball players were well liked. And yet, as one said, their "basic feelings are repulsion and disgust toward Negro features." These feelings are frequently justified as a "physiological reaction, that one's reasoning cannot control." Many Japanese associate Negroes with "animality." This association appears in a number of contemporary novels written by noted Japanese authors. Many Japanese associate Negroes with the primitive tribes of the African jungle. This image leads to a widely held notion that contemporary black people, whose ancestors once danced to the sound of drums, possess an excellent inherent sense of rhythm, and are, therefore, likely to be successful in a musical career. Also, Japanese share with many Southern white Americans the notion that Negroes are sexually indefatigable.

Many Japanese believe that Caucasians, and particularly Negroes, have a strong body odor that is totally lacking in the Japanese. Many also believe that close physical contact, and certainly sexual contact, with whites and especially with blacks leaves its trace on a Japanese in the form of real or imagined body odor. In a recent novel, the Japanese mother of a mixed-blood girl fathered by a Negro soldier says: "Would it be possible that my body acquired and retains the body odor of this girl's father? Do I display some sort of trace of my life with a Negro man? . . . Something has permeated my body, and those people [Negroes] can sense that something as their own . . ."

This preoccupation with the "contagious" nature of such contacts can be seen in the following report by a Japanese graduate student at an American university, who had had sexual relations with a Negro woman: "I was not in love with her, nor was she with me. It was a game. To say the truth, I was curious about Negroes, after hearing so much about them. When it was over, however, I had to take a shower. The idea shocked me because it was ridiculous, but I was caught by an urge. It was almost a sudden compulsion to wash my body off, and I did." Possibly, in this particular case, guilt feeling over sexuality became focused on the blackness of skin, conceived as dirty. The idea of the "contagious" nature of skin contacts seems to exist, however, even without guilt feelings. When interviewed, three lower-class Japanese with less than six years of primary education independently voiced the notion that if a Japanese woman gave birth to the black baby of a Negro man, her next baby, and probably the third one also, by a Japanese father, would show some black tinge on the body. In other words, in the mind of these men, impregnation of a Japanese woman by a Negro man was associated with "blackening" of her womb as though by ink, so that the second and even the third baby generated in it would become "stained."

In short, Japanese attitudes toward black skin are almost uniformly negative, whereas they are basically ambivalent toward the physical characteristics of Caucasians. What are the implications of such attitudes for the interracial marriage? It will certainly be a very important research subject to see if and how the Japanese wives of Negro men overcame their initial negative feelings toward the blacks, and if not, what are the psychological implications of being married to a man whose physical appearance is so negatively conceived. One might also find out if and how Japanese men married to white women are free from the "inferiority-superiority complex" toward the Westerners that seems so prevalent among Japanese men. It should also be interesting to know if these basic "racial" feelings complicate actual or potential conflicts between Japanese husbands and their white wives, or Japanese wives and their Caucasian husbands.

In addition to these issues concerning differences in physical features, there are other factors vitally important for the understanding of the problems of interracial marriages. One such factor is the differences in the definition and anticipation of roles of husband and wife. And it is to this matter that we now turn, with special attention to the marital lives of Japanese women and their American husbands.

MARRIAGES BETWEEN AMERICAN SERVICEMEN AND JAPANESE WOMEN

Since the end of World War II, between 50,000 and 60,000 Japanese women are reported to have married American servicemen and moved to the United States. For example, from 1956 to 1957, at the height of frequency, one hundred such interracial marriages took place every week. During 1964, about thirty American servicemen were marrying Japanese women every week. Between April 1, 1969 and March 31, 1970, the number of American-Japanese marriages registered at the American Embassy in Tokyo was 1,380, and 80 percent of the men were American soldiers. In other words, every week during this one year, more than twenty American servicemen were marrying Japanese women.

How have these marriages been working out? Unfortunately, there is no systematic empirical data available in sufficient quantity to answer this question, but according to a Japanese reporter, Fujisaki, who interviewed social workers and Japanese war brides in Los Angeles, a large number of these marriages seem to have ended in either divorce or serious conflicts (5). According to Fujisaki, many of these husbands, once out of the military life and back in their home country, show very little sense of responsibility, do not support their family, drink heavily, and are unfaithful and even physically abusive to their Japanese wives. After these marital failures, many Japanese women look for jobs in Japanese restaurants and shops. In spite of their bitterness and loneliness, they do not return to Japan because of financial reasons or because they are afraid of the discrimination their mixed-blood children will experience in Japanese society. In addition, they think they will not be accepted by their relatives, having often married their American husbands in the face of family opposition and disapproval. Why do so many of these marriages fail? One cannot generalize, but a study of a small sample of such marriages suggests some possible causes (3).

This study was based upon interview materials and psychological test responses from thirty Japanese war-brides and their white American husbands in the San Francisco Bay area. At the time of the interviews (1958–59), the length of their marriages varied from one and a half years to ten years, but almost half of the couples had been married for less than two and a half years. In terms of their educational background and the socioeconomic status of their parents, there did not seem to be significant differences between husbands and wives. But there were certain personality characteristics common to most of the husbands and to most of the wives. The husbands showed marked feelings of insecurity and inadequacy, and lack of confidence in their masculine ego. They had a strong need for dependency, expressed in the need to be babied by their wives. Some of them showed rather strong unresolved feelings of ambivalence toward their mothers whom they conceived as domineering figures. Some of them were unable to control their aggressive impulses and were given to wild outbursts of temper. Most of them voiced definitely negative feelings toward American women, describing them as aggressive toward, and competitive with, men, wanting their own careers, or being very demanding. In marked contrast, they described Japanese women in positive terms, and saw them as passive, dependent upon men, and home-oriented. Among the wives there was a varying but marked degree of depression, sense of isolation, and profound feeling of inadequacy. Many of them felt that they had totally failed in their lives and could not satisfactorily cope with their present situation. They had been nurturant and warm in the initial stage of their relationship with the husbands, but they soon revealed a tendency to be controlling, aggressive, challenging, or castigating toward men. They were also concerned with their husbands' violence and aggression, a feeling that seemed justified by their actual experiences. They said that American women were much luckier than Japanese women having more leisure time and enjoying better education, a professional career, and personal freedom. In their view, American women were much more likely to have understanding husbands. Probably this was what these Japanese wives themselves had once dreamed of enjoying upon coming to live in the United States. They described American men positively, as kind, helpful, generous and yet manly to their wives, while stating that Japanese men totally lacked such virtues and were domineering and belittling toward their wives.

In spite of the apparent mutual appreciation, these thirty Japanese-American couples did not seem to be happy. There was little communication between the husbands and wives, and in many cases marital quarrels resulted in violent behavior on the part of the husbands. /

The picture that seems to emerge from the above study may be described as follows: a certain type of American man, because of lack of confidence in his masculinity and general feelings of inadequacy, may find it difficult to cope with self-assertive and often challenging American women. He may be attracted by the legendary image of the Japanese woman, portrayed as graceful, delicate and quiet, and prepared to sacrifice herself through dedicated subservience to her husband and parents-in-law. Such an image seems to be based largely on the customarily prescribed role for the Japanese woman and not upon her personality. On the other side, there is a certain type of Japanese woman who rejects the role of the selfless and subservient wife of a despotic Japanese husband. (In reality, Japanese husbands are not necessarily despotic nor their wives subservient, but such a stereotype does exist.) These women may be attracted by the image of a strong, masculine, and yet very chivalrous, American male. Neither of these two types fits into the role defined for them by their respective cultures. When they marry each other, the outcome may be the result of an unfortunate discrepancy in expectations: the American man, expecting an "Oriental doll," finds himself married to a "tough cookie" (if not openly so, at least covertly), whose sheer presence may constitute an added threat to his already shaky masculine ego (hence his violent reaction to her); and the Japanese woman, expecting a Western knight, finds herself tied to a weakling whose dependency needs disappoint and bother her. If she expresses her disappointment by nagging her husband, he may feel even more threatened, and react violently—thus creating a vicious circle.

We do not know the lot of the children of these unfortunate marriages in the United States, but we know something about the children of similar marriages in Japan. To these "mixed-blood" children we now turn.

THE "MIXED-BLOOD" CHILDREN

There are good reasons to believe that those who legalized their liaisons with Japanese women and took them to the United States were only a portion of the American servicemen who had sexual relations with Japanese women. Of the remainder, many lived with their women—and often with their children—for a considerable length of time as if married, until they left Japan for their homes. These liaisons produced "fatherless" children, black and white, who were to grow up in Japan; the more fortunate ones with their mothers and grandparents, the unfortunate ones in orphanages.

No one really knows for sure how many of these "offspring of the occupation" are in Japan now, partly because of the Japanese government's "hush-hush policy" and partly because these children are registered as Japanese (although mostly illegitimate), and their mixed racial background appears nowhere in official records. In August, 1952, the Japanese Ministry of Welfare mailed out questionnaires to hospitals, maternity clinics, doctors, and registered midwives, asking about the mixed-blood children born under their care. In December of the same year, the Ministry estimated that the total number of fatherless children of mixed parentage was 5,013 (2,635 boys and 2,378 girls—of these, 4,205 were whites, 714 blacks, and 94 of unknown racial background). This estimate is probably much too low for the specified time period (1945–1952), and it certainly does not reflect the current situation, as many more children have been born since 1952. The present estimate is that there are between 20,000 and 25,000 fatherless children of mixed parentage, of which probably one-sixth are black-Japanese *(Mainichi News*, January 16, 1968). Over a thousand mixed-blood orphans are believed to have been adopted into American families.

In recent years, because of their "exotic" look and singing and dancing talents, a few of the mixed-blood white children have been drawn into the limelight through appearances on stage and screen. Indeed, there has been a so-called "mixed-blood boom" *(konketsu būmu)* in the world of show business and fashion modeling. Weekly magazines have published photographs of these mixed-blood "talents"—movie stars, singers, dancers, fashion models, and some male athletes—and written gossip columns about them. Altogether, however, the celebrated ones are only a handful.

Notwithstanding the exotic careers enjoyed by the "élite," a great many more youngsters, particularly those of Negro parentage, are harassed by racial prejudice and social discrimination by the Japanese people at large. Most of the mixed-bloods have grown up in poverty, have received minimum education and, even in the absence of discrimination, are ill-prepared for lucrative employment. Many have grown up without much love, as their mothers worked or rejected or even deserted them. Added to these early experiences of deprivation were the pain and humiliation of being laughed at, stoned or beaten by the neighborhood children. Given all this, it is not surprising that most of these children are emotionally insecure, immature, dependent, passive or even apathetic, and often harboring hatred. Delinquency is not uncommon in this group.

They are stigmatized in more ways than one. Most of these children are illegitimate (which often prevents them from getting jobs and entering higher schools), and they are the "children of prostitutes." Whether or not their mothers actually were street walkers makes little difference in the mind of the Japanese—preferring a foreign victor to a Japanese man was no better than prostitution. Most importantly, they are "physically different." It is not hard to understand how the Japanese extend their negative feelings toward African and American Negroes (discussed above) to the Japanese children of black American fathers. And given Japanese attitudes toward the Caucasian physical features, it is not surprising that the Japanese children of white American fathers are also not favorably viewed.

The mixed-blood youngsters often become the object of sexual curiosity to the Japanese. In their minds a chain of associations seems to form in the following way: white men are sexually more passionate and stronger than the Japanese; these mixed-bloods must have inherited that quality from their fathers; their Japanese mothers must have been unusual women if they preferred and could cope with sexually powerful white men; these mixed-bloods must have inherited that quality from their mothers; *ergo*, they are sexually precocious, energetic, and enjoyable. A number of mixed-blood girls have been raped, boys sexually attacked. Probably the easiest form of employment a white mixed-blood girl can secure is a position as bar or cabaret hostess, and often she enjoys better wages than her pure-blood Japanese counterpart. Black Japanese girls do not have even this opportunity.

Even for those few fortunate ones who can secure employment, there remain further obstacles. The most formidable of them is the limitation of choice of marital partner. Almost unanimously, they want to marry Japanese. "I am a Japanese, fully inside," they all say.

Indeed they are, culturally—that is, in terms of their knowledge of language, their food habits, thinking patterns, etc., seen objectively. However, they are definitely not Japanese physically, and this is a considerable problem in a society of highly homogeneous and prejudiced people. Only a few successful white-Japanese fashion models and movie stars have been able to marry Japanese men. Even when Japanese are willing to marry a mixed-blood girl or boy, it is very likely that their parents and relatives will oppose it. In Japanese society—given the stress on interdependence among family members and relatives—it is difficult to have a happy marriage in the face of family opposition. And yet, it does not seem to occur to these mixed-blood youngsters to think of marrying one another.

Scattered all over Japan, the mixed-blood offspring of the occupation constitute a social problem. And yet only two individuals have made concerted efforts to help them. One is Mrs. Miki Sawada, the daughter of a noble family, married to a former Ambassador to the United Nations. She has dedicated her property and life to establishing and running an orphanage, the Elizabeth Saunders Home, where about 1,300 mixed-blood children have been raised. Of these about 800 have been adopted by American couples and now live in the United States. With the aid of the Pearl Buck Foundation in Philadelphia, Mrs. Sawada bought land in the Amazon area of Brazil and established the St. Stephen Farm as a place to which her "boys" could emigrate. About fifteen boys have already gone there. Mrs. Sawada's basic policy is to send the mixed-bloods out of Japan either through adoption into American families or emigration to Brazil. Unfortunately, only a small number of them can be helped in such ways. For those adolescents who still live in Japan, adoption is no solution. They are too old for it.

The other person is Mr. Imao Hirano, 67-year-old author, himself the son of a French-American father and a Japanese mother. As he has suffered prejudice and discrimination since his childhood, Mr. Hirano is determined to help children of the same fate. He has organized an association of the mixed-bloods, named it *"Remi no Kai"* (or Remi Club, after the hero of Hector Malot's juvenile novel *Sans Famille*) and opened his home to the youngsters. He has found jobs for many of them and has adopted several of them in order to eliminate at least one stigma—their illegitimacy. More recently, he has been trying to open a branch of the Remi Club in Okinawa, where at least 3,000 mixed-blood children are said to be leading difficult lives. Because Mr. Hirano's efforts are solely based on his personal income and individual activities, they are likely to have only a limited impact. The majority of the harassed youngsters of mixed parentage are left on their own in little corners of Japanese society.

CONCLUSIONS

The picture painted in this chapter is admittedly a gloomy one. This is certainly not the total picture of interracial marriage in Japan. There are American scholars, engineers, businessmen, correspondents, and ordinary citizens, happily married to Japanese women and living in the United States or in Japan. There are a number of relatively young Japanese husbands living in Japan happily with their Western wives, although, according to one reporter, many of these wives seem to be suffering from loneliness, lack of sufficient social contact, language problems, and financial difficulties (2). Their mixed-blood children, reared in the context of a stable family life, good education, social standing, and international contacts, certainly do not share, even in Japan, the lot of the illegitimate offspring of mixed parentage. These happy cases of interracial marriages have not been sufficiently reported anywhere and therefore have not entered the picture presented here. Presumably, however, they are still small in number compared with the many more numerous marriages between American servicemen and Japanese women, for many of whom, certainly not all, the picture might likely be somewhat similar to what we have seen here.

15

RUSSELL A. MCNEILLY, M.A.

Aspects of Interracial Marriage in a Multiracial Society— Trinidad, W. I.

It is logical to expect that on an island inhabited by several races the opportunity for intimate relations is ample. Professor McNeilly analyzes the attitudes toward interracial marriage in Trinidad, with particular attention to the often conflicting forces of religion, culture, economics, and educational levels. In the process, he reveals both the negative and the positive factors that currently affect young people contemplating such intimate relations, and contrasts them with the attitudes that prevailed in what he believes to be a rapidly disappearing past.

I NTERRACIAL marriage in Trinidad has been influenced by different social, psychological, and economic conditions. The society is highly mixed, with peoples of a number of races. Marriage therefore takes place between a host of races in novel and unique combinations. A few words about some of the factors contributing to these combinations may explain their uniqueness to which many inhabitants have grown accustomed.

One factor is represented by the social perception approach. Impressions and judgments of others are formed on the basis of the amount of information available. In recent years much more information has been gained about other races, and this helps to strengthen interest in and regard for the person of another racial background. A higher level of education and a more tolerant approach have had an effect in increasing interaction among the races. Rejection by the young of the historical opposition to marriage out of one's race has also contributed to the acceptance of people of different races. This factor has had a vital role in shaping the current attitude of Trinidad s society toward interracial marriage.

This society is a small one of approximately one million inhabitants confined to an area of 1,864 square miles. There is great mobility, and it is easy to know many people and be aware of the movements, customs, and culture of many others. The general breakdown that has occurred through nationalism and pressures from youth on various barriers, including social class, bigoted racial biases, caste, and color, has given greater opportunity for further mobility.

The youth have moved away from parental racial ideas and have stimulated a faster process of socialization beyond race. This strengthens perception on a large scale. As a result, marriage occurs in a number of cases without reference to the individual's racial characteristics.

Another factor is that of reinforcement. The more you meet, the more you tend to accept others, whatever their racial background. In Trinidad, however, where the races are still separated to a certain extent in clusters or pockets, this factor is not so relevant.

The third factor is the genetic consideration. Some people in the society, who are the offspring of mixed marriages, see nothing wrong in mixed marriages since they themselves are the product of it, and find it acceptable. Their view is that couples may not resemble each other phenotypically—i.e., in skin color, texture of hair, and facial features, but genotypically, they may be alike in certain ways, and thus may represent a good match for each other.

TRINIDAD—A MELTING POT OF RACES, CULTURES, CLASSES, CASTES

Mixed marriage is a complex phenomenon in Trinidad since the island is inhabited by a number of races. The society is like a natural laboratory in which the effects of interracial marriages can be observed and broad conclusions reached since some of the races found in this "laboratory" exist in many other parts of the world. We shall examine the racial picture with its related characteristics of skin color, class, and caste, which are relevant to interracial marriage.

First of all, it is important to keep in mind that greater tolerance of interracial marriage was already apparent in the years just before the second World War, and that during the fifties this attitude became increasingly common.

In the past, interracial marriage was affected by the ethnic stratification of the society. This society was characterized more by a caste system than by a class system. The races were frozen in their respective categories and it was difficult to break out of one's social stratum. Since mixed marriages were certain to disrupt this stratification, they were strongly discouraged. The white group was regarded as the upper-class; the colored people, both light and brown-skinned, and which would generally include the offspring of interracial marriages, were categorized in the middle-class, and the black people formed the lower-class. Whiteness, therefore, tended to put people automatically at the top of the social class scale, and blackness tended to place them at the lower end of the scale. Economic means assisted in breaking down the barriers of the scale.

Before the second World War, it was not so easy to disturb the order of this scale by interracial marriage. However, this pattern was broken when a non-white who went overseas for further education returned with a white wife.

With the establishment of self-government and nationhood in the fifties and sixties, the artificial barriers of race and prejudice-laden values received a great blow. The outlook on social class, skin color, and race changed with the greater educational opportunities and higher standards of living for all peoples in various walks of life, and with a new pride in nationhood. The young, moreover, played a great part in breaking down these barriers.

An examination of the population chart shows that, in spite of opposition from many sides and particularly from parents, there has been a considerable number of interracial marriages. This is reflected in the category designated "mixed." These figures are based on the answers given by individuals in response to the census question as to which race they felt they belonged to. In many cases in which the individual is mixed but has predominant characteristics of a particular racial group, he invariably claims the latter racial group as his own. It may further be assumed that the census figure for the mixed group should be larger than shown, since the mixed group should probably include a number from the group headed Negro and a fair number from the group headed East Indian. The contention is simply that a large part of the population is mixed, and this indicates the high degree of interracial marriage in Trinidad.

Table 1
POPULATION OF TRINIDAD AND TOBAGO BY RACE

Race	Male	Female	Total	Percent
Negro	176,380	182,208	358,588	43.3
White	7,873	7,845	15,718	1.8
East Indian	153,043	148,903	301,946	36.5
Chinese	4,709	3,652	8,361	1.0
Mixed	65,178	69,571	134,749	16.3
Lebanese, Syrian	824	766	1,590	0.2
Other	3,573	3,432	7,005	0.9
	411,580	416,377	827,957	100.0

Source: Census, 1968, *Annual Statistical Digest*, No. 18, Central Statistical Office, Trinidad and Tobago.

In such a combination of races it is inevitable that a fair incidence of interracial marriage should occur. Suspicions and doubts about the desirability of interracial marriage do exist within the family circle, but are not critical. As we have said, the pattern in recent times has changed radically, and it appears that the adult who was opposed to this practice, in the last decade has given up trying to prevent it. In the open, interracial marriage seems to be generally accepted even beyond being merely tolerated.

OBSERVATIONS ON INTERRACIAL MARRIAGE

The youth of the country display a new and profound appreciation for the basic dignity of the human being, irrespective of his race or color. Therefore, they don't see anything objectionable in dating on an interracial basis. This is especially true among children of broad-minded and outgoing families. Interracial marriage in such circumstances is not only respected but even encouraged. For example, in an East Indian family of my acquaintance, one of the children is married to another East Indian, one to a Canadian, one to a Negro, and another to a Chinese. A Negro family shows a similar interracial marriage pattern. One child is married to an Englishman, one to an East Indian, two to mixed people, one to a Spaniard, and another to a white North American. And there are quite a few families like these.

Interracial marriages have characteristic patterns. There are those in which local people of one race or mixed group get married with local people of another race. In this case both parties are Trinidadian, possess a common heritage, and have the same nationality. The parties may also be both Trinidadian, but with different religious backgrounds, which could create more problems than the racial factor. Or the parties may have different ethnic backgrounds, which may also pose greater problems than the racial factor.

Another pattern is seen in the Trinidadian who goes overseas to study or live and marries a person of a different race. In a number of cases the Negro or East Indian takes a white mate from Europe or America. In some cases both parties are school graduates and equal in education. In the past, the pattern of interracial marriage was almost exlusively that of a Trinidad man and an overseas white woman. Trinidad women were hardly ever involved in marriage with overseas white men. But recently there have been instances where a Trinidad woman has contracted mixed marriage with a white man from Europe or America. The earlier pattern was for the native to marry an overseas person who was white, probably to move up the social ladder, a factor which unconsciously affected the average Trinidadian.

In recent times, however, this pattern has been varied in that some Trinidadians have entered into interracial marriages with third-world peoples from other developing countries. Some nationals have married people from India, Africa, and the East Indies. In most of these cases the couples met while studying in institutions in England, Canada, or the United States.

Interracial marriage takes place to fulfill a freely expressed need to have the desired person—a particular human being—as a partner. In Trinidad, with its mixture of peoples, one tends to see no barriers between persons of different races and to feel that people are one and the same. One does not look for differences in race, customs, and the like, for these are characteristics that are imposed and fictitious. The individual looks for that which satisfies him and not for that which satisfies the group, for it is he who must make the decision to marry, and must live by this decision.

In an amorphous society such as Trinidad, it seems pointless to attempt to oppose interracial marriages since, in essence, they do not seem to be any different from other forms of marriage, and the evidence for their success or failure is as strong as the evidence for any other form of marriage. It is not interracial marriage that is objectionable; rather, it is the narrowly biased thinking of people whose tastes may be different or whose prejudices have been acquired by upbringing or association.

MINORITY GROUP VIEWS ON INTERRACIAL MARRIAGE

Various subgroups look upon interracial marriage in terms of the beliefs and outlooks with which they are familiar. It is important to examine a few of these since they play a significant part in making the pattern more intricate. We shall examine first of all the religious component of this pattern.

Table 2

RELIGIONS OF TRINIDAD AND TOBAGO

Religion	Number	Percent
Roman Catholic	299,649	36.2
Hindu	190,403	23.0
Anglican	175,042	21.1
Other Christian	108,520	13.1
Other or None	4,607	.6
Total	827,957	100.0

Source: Census, 1968, *Annual Statistical Digest*, No. 18, Central Statistical Office, Trinidad and Tobago.

In Trinidad, religious faiths place no prohibitions or even restrictions on interracial marriage per se, although they can and do express a certain degree of disapproval. Let us look briefly at their views.

The Roman Catholic Church today bases its position about marriage on the traditional view of the Church. Interreligious marriage has moved from its position of unacceptability to one of compromise, with meticulous care to keep the essential principles of the Church intact, namely:

(1) That the Catholic be permitted and assured free exercise of his religion;

(2) That all children born of the union, both boys and girls, be brought up as Catholics;

(3) That there be no other form of marriage before or after;

(4) That there will be obedience to the laws of the Church;

(5) That the Catholic promises to do "all that is possible to convert the non-Catholic."

Nor do the Protestant religions in Trinidad and Tobago prohibit interracial marriages on religious grounds, except perhaps for the fact that ideally they hope for Christian marriages. However, the couple and their children are free to select a denomination for themselves and for the upbringing of their children.

Hindus and Muslims also prefer marriages among people of the same faith, especially where it concerns their own faiths.

Like other universalistic ideologies, religions demand priority over racial or ethnic considerations. When romance is queen and religion the obstacle to interracial marriage, one of several alternatives is chosen. The couple may select to live in "common law," without the sacraments of a church. In other words, each partner maintains his or her religious identity. A second alternative is that of conversion to one common faith which the children will also follow. A third alternative is to have a civil ceremony without the religious sacraments with a resulting adherence or non-adherence to a faith.

It may be important to note that the welfare of the child does not depend very much on the religious beliefs of the parents, though religion may be a contributing factor. Emotional, mental, and physical welfare depend on the security and stability of the home. Difference of religion may be used as the reason for marital breakdown, which may actually be the result of other problems—infidelity, boredom, interference, ignorance, and lack of respect for each other.

A considerable section of the population is aware of the increasing trend toward interracial marriage over the past few years. In individual behavior there is greater tolerance for a practice that in the past was openly disapproved of, and a similar trend can be noticed in the political and economic fields. Attitudes vary with such individual characteristics as age, sex, intelligence, and personality traits, and very much with the economic status of the individual and the group with which he associates.

Marriage partners are chosen for various reasons. The ratings assigned by parents and the unmarried child to prospective partners are a kind of crude preliminary grading process. (The term rating refers to the relative desirability with which the unmarried and the parents, in a given situation, regard the available members of the opposite sex.)

In rating a potential mate for their children, parents seem to prefer mates of the same race, religion, and education; also, somebody who has a good job, is serious minded and reliable. It is often difficult to find all these attributes in a single person, so that there develops a scale of values with varying degrees of priority. The scales of values, and consequently the ratings by parents and by the unmarried child, may differ considerably at times, and then conflict arises.

There is an exaggerated tendency to think in terms of ethnocentric attitudes, which are susceptible to modification under social pressures. Racial groups seem to maintain a stereotyped concept of other races, and attempt to rationalize behavior in terms of these stereotypes. These stereotypes are a gross simplification, and sometimes distortion, of the whole spectrum of traits found in a culture. The greater the social distances, the more unfavorable the stereotype. As a result, stereotypes vary according to the "social interaction" and economic position of the groups.

The East Indians have been culturally and socially isolated through the island's political-economic structure dating back to the indenture system in the nineteenth century. As a result, they tend to be more conservative—a conservatism which is reinforced by their religion (predominantly Hindu), their peasant-agricultural economy, and their rural orientation.

The Chinese, Syrian, and Lebanese tend to live as closed groups, and many observers attribute this to their solid economic position in society. In these groups interracial marriage tends to pose a threat since it may undermine their economic security. The Negroes in Trinidad seem to be most open-minded when it comes to interracial marriage. There is a minority, though, especially among the females, who believe that the more advanced males should attempt to uplift their less fortunate "sisters" by marrying within their own racial group.

A characteristic of the lower and middle classes in Trinidad is a tendency to seek mates in the upper strata; yet, paradoxically, these same people are angered by the sight of "interracial" couples. They become especially vociferous during the Carnival Festival when many such couples are seen hugging and dancing to the rhythm of steel band music.

Few parents actively encourage, and few, at least overtly, forbid, interracial marriage. In spite of the fact that in the process of socialization they are taught pride in their culture—a culture that has no racial bias—when actual interracial unions are contemplated, parents try to dissuade their children, using rationalizations that are obviously based on prejudice. They fear shame and scandal, and the loss of their cultural identity. Parents are willing to allow social interaction, but not that which leads to marriage.

The unmarried and the teenager subscribe to the Romantic Love Ideal which involves meeting the "right person." The trance-like state that accompanies this type of encounter overrides racial and ethnic barriers. These barriers are also reduced by several other factors, such as increasing freedom to choose friends, groups, and mates; little social struggle and community pressure; increasing contacts with diverse racial groups in the community, at work, in schools, and in social and occupational pursuits; increased mobility of individuals through education and business; and greater individualism in urban areas. Comfort and solace are sought and found in persons of different racial origin. All these factors contribute to reducing the prejudice formerly held by individuals.

Ironically, interracial marriage is encouraged by social ostracism of girls known or alleged to have been going with a man of a different race. The girl is no longer accepted by the males of her race, and this forces her to keep associating with men of other races or to face the consequences of the ostracism. Provided the financial and educational means afford it, she may venture abroad, where she will probably develop associations with people of another racial group.

Girls, especially in the rural areas, are often confronted with authoritarian parents, a factor which leads to frustration and boredom, and often to eloping, as both an escape and an act of defiance. The majority of girls elope with a man of the same race, but in the absence of one, somebody of another race will do.

Education reduces the stereotypes, so that there seem to be more interracial marriages among the relatively educated. They also have a greater chance of coming together because of the opportunities provided by in schools, universities, and other similar settings.

RESERVATIONS

In spite of the tolerant attitude toward interracial marriage in Trinidad and Tobago, among the adult population there are reservations about the chances for success of interracial marriages. These reservations concern a number of areas, some very important, others perhaps, in the eyes of the outside observer, quite trivial. And yet, a factor such as eating habits may contribute substantially to uneasiness in an interracial marriage. Because of their differing upbringings, the races acquire tastes for different diets. A couple attracted to each other in a number of ways may find that their eating practices are radically different, and this may cause psychological and practical problems. However, through practice and association, this difference is sometimes overcome.

Different races generally observe different religious practices. The East Indian is usually Hindu or Moslem or Presbyterian. The Negro is mainly Roman Catholic, Anglican, Baptist, or Seventh Day

Adventist. When two people of different races come together, they are probably of different religious backgrounds. If objections are voiced, they are ostensibly based on religion, covering up what might be the true protest based on the interracial aspect of the marriage.

The races follow different customs in dancing, music, approach to courtship, and living practices in general. The Negro, for instance, is quite outgoing, and the East Indian is more reserved. When marriage takes place between members of these two groups, there must be adjustment of one or both if success is to be achieved. With young couples of these races the situation is somewhat better, because the young have acquired a West Indian outlook and are not so imbued with the mores that were imported by their immigrant forefathers.

Occasionally, the politician plays on racial differences to gain political advantage. This practice develops a certain antagonism and subtle intolerance among the less thoughtful members of the population and interferes with racial harmony. Couples linked in interracial marriages may suffer embarrassment and a feeling of displacement when race is played upon in this way.

Many critics of interracial marriage in Trinidad and elsewhere hold that while they see no problem in the marriage itself, they are concerned about the adjustment of the children to society. This is obviously a concealed way of expressing discriminatory tendencies. In fact, as far as Trinidad is concerned, children born of an interracial marriage are no more mixed or out of place than everybody else in the island who is of mixed blood. This criticism only seems to express an abstract feeling that has no practical justification in Trinidad.

CONCLUSIONS

In Trinidad and Tobago interracial marriage is tolerated because the population is multiracial, and because there are a number of unique mixtures in various combinations. On the whole, in these islands a number of races live together in relative peace and harmony.

There are instances where interracial marriage is not encouraged, but these objections are not stated in the open. Prejudice was based upon customs, religion, politics, and castes. In recent times this prejudice is disappearing particularly because the younger generation tends to rise above the narrowness of race and creed. If people are to live together as a West Indian community, they cannot perpetuate isolated clans and hamlets. They must be able to interact, and this inevitably leads to marriage beyond the boundaries of their own narrow racial grouping.

The love for the country and its people and the development of a humanistic approach in education have done a great deal to break down barriers and to develop toleration and acceptance of interracial marriages. This has further caused a reduction in prejudice, discrimination, bigotry, and old taboos that stood in the path of social growth. A great number of our international problems could be solved if through a process of pure socialization, unhampered by biased parents and teachers, people were to develop a free attitude towards other human beings and a respect for man, whatever his race, creed, and appearance. It is believed that the approach to interracial marriage in Trinidad can serve as a lesson to many countries. A truly humanistic education that is not merely "knowledge," may serve to develop tolerance toward and understanding of interracial marriage generally.

16

MARK NAGLER, M.A.

North American Indians and Intermarriage

Little has been written about the problems of the American Indian in his intimate relations with his Caucasian neighbors since the scurrilous novels of the 19th century. This does not ignore the numerous studies by anthropologists which have provided much information on mores, folkways, and kinship relationships within Indian tribal structures. However, serious studies of the effects of marriage between Indians and members of other races have been missing from the literature. Mr. Nagler uses the few contemporary professional studies available to describe the attitudes of Indians, economically as well as legally bound to the reserve, towards their white and black fellow citizens "outside." After a brief survey of the early contacts between Indians and their racial and cultural invaders, Mr. Nagler examines the patterns of intermarital relationships between the two groups and the effects that the Indians' unique status as wards of the government and their identity problems have had on such patterns.

ANTHROPOLOGICAL and sociological studies of the United States are replete with investigations of assimilation and acculturation, possibly because American society is composed of immigrants who live in cultural islands. Indians are considered as a "minority" in North American society, like the various immigrant groups. Sociological literature since 1900 has been concerned mainly with European immigration into the New World, and anthropological literature generally deals with the impact of white culture upon the American Indian or upon African and Asian cultures. Indians are increasing their realm of contacts with the white man, and as a result, the rate of intermarriage between them and non-Indians is increasing.

Intermarriage between Indians and Europeans began as white settlements developed in North America, and proceeded as a consequence of contacts with the settlers. These contacts, though, were structured by sex, racial differentials, legal and social pressures, and/or cultural prescriptions that defined various levels of "appropriate behavior." Sociologists, anthropologists, and ethnologists, among others, have noted with keen interest the effects of these contact situations; and they are now beginning to investigate the patterns of intermarriage between these groups. Indians, unlike other minorities in North American society, have been confined for legal and quasi-legal reasons to reserves,* and have only in recent

* "Reserves" and "reservations" will be used in this chapter as equivalent terms. "Reservation" is the American definition of the legal area which Indians may inhabit.

years begun to drift away from these "traditional habitats." This chapter attempts to shed light on the patterns of contact that bring about outmarriage among Indians and the attitudes concerning these "liaisons."

The Anglo-American race-caste system in North America is exceptional for its rigidity and for the fervor that underlies it, especially in those sections of the country where groups are in close contact. Indians, like blacks and Orientals in certain areas of the country, are socially and physically segregated in such a way that each group contains in large measure within itself the entire range of occupational and social statuses. North American Indians, like blacks, may rise occupationally or socially to the top of their own group. They rarely enter the dominant white group, and by virtue of their social status are inhibited from competing with them except in token measures. The Indians, unlike other minorities in North America, have been largely isolated by virtue of physical confinement on reserves, and this, according to Steward, "usually . . . averts the necessity of pigeonholing them socially" (11, p. 293). Where the Indians participate to a significant degree in local economic affairs, they are generally confined to the level of a laboring group, although they may rank above the blacks, whom they in turn may regard as being inferior. By and large, in the early days of North American colonial occupation, wherever Indians were conquered, they were treated merely as primitive populations who furnished the labor force needed by the settlers. Many Indians still earn their living by unskilled pursuits, which is in part an effect of their cultural background. "None the less," as Steward points out, "if anyone has exceptional ability and is favored by circumstances, he may realize his aspirations within the national culture. Consequently, many Indians and blacks have attained the highest professional, social, and political positions. They have become prominent artists, writers, lawyers, doctors, and legislators; many have even become the presidents of their republics" (11, p. 294). Preliminary data, although of questionable merit because of their limited coverage, indicate that the majority of those who succeed in the above occupations or professions are married to non-Indians. Traditionally, minorities in American society have regarded marriage with elements of the majority as a status acquisition and a measure of their acceptance in society.

In Canada, as in the United States, North American Indians rank at the lowest level of the hierarchy, and American studies indicate that in most instances Indians rank even below the blacks.

PRESENT CONDITIONS

Attitudes toward the Indians and the ability of these natives to function in North America are in part determined by their particular geographical location within the country. The majority of the North Americans have seldom, if ever, experienced contact with American natives, and hence the relationships between the two groups are caught up in the mythology of what the Indians actually represent. An exception is constituted by those areas of North America where large concentrations of Indians are found. In these areas, such as North Dakota, California, the South West, and Kenora, Ontario, Indians are at the bottom of the socioeconomic ladder and are regarded as the lowest mark on any scale of evaluation. Against this background have evolved various types and patterns of contact between North American Indians and other representatives of North American society, and marital patterns have been established, legal and nonlegal, as a consequence of such contacts.

INDIAN STATUS

In the United States as well as in Canada, Indians are legally defined as the descendants of the original inhabitants of America and are "banded" by specific terms under the law. Indians may lose their legal status for a number of situations and/or conditions. As a result, they are forced to relinquish the benefits that the government has traditionally awarded them by virtue of their official Indian status. One way of losing this status is through intermarriage. When intermarriage involves non-Indian males and Indian females, the Indian females lose their official status as Indians and whatever benefits they are entitled to by virtue of such legal status. They may no longer live on the reserve and are no longer entitled to the rights and privileges accorded to those of Indian status. On the other hand, when Indian males marry non-Indians (a rare occurrence), their wives receive legal Indian status, provided that their Indian mates choose to maintain Indian status. In Canada, Indians may officially relinquish their status and in return for doing so, they receive an amount of money that may range from fifty to a few hundred dollars.

Harold S. Jacoby, in an article entitled "A Half Century Appraisal of the East Indians in the U.S.," made a statement that can easily be applied to Indians although it concerned immigrant groups.

> When an immigrant group . . . enters a territory occupied by another, and usually larger, body of people, the two groups are separated from one another in three different ways. First they are culturally separate. Each has his own language, manners, beliefs, food preferences and clothing style. Secondly, they tend to be separate in the more durable social relationships . . . separate families, separate friendship groups, separate religious groups, separate clubs and organizations. And thirdly, the family lines will be biologically separate where family exists, and physical lines will remain wholly within one of the other populations, as summarized by Prodipto Roy in an article entitled "The Measurement of Assimilation: The Spokane Indians" [5, p. 2].

Assimilation can be broken down into three processes: (1) acculturation, (2) social integration, and (3) amalgamation. In his study, Roy points out that the smaller American Indian society will be assimilated into the larger white American society with practically no perceptible impact on the culture of the latter (8).

At first the Indians were regarded as a menace. After the breaking down of Indian military power in the United States and the formation of reserves in Canada, in some instances the Indians came to be idealized as "a noble red man." Liaisons between non-Indians and Indians were common, and in certain areas of North America, like Southern Manitoba, relatively large numbers of intermarriages took place, which created a group called the Metis (of French-Canadian and Indian descent). The whites' image of the Indians was for the most part a negative one. They were generally seen as occupying a low position on the so-called socioeconomic ladder, and, as a result, their social integration was inhibited by their position in society. This social position was in turn weakened by their separation from the other elements of North American society, and by the abject poverty in which the Indians found themselves in many areas of Canada and the United States.

In most instances, marriages between non-Indians and Indians took place as a result of social and environmental situations. These specific environmental situations brought Indians and non-Indians into direct contact with each other, and occurred mostly in areas where there was a shortage of European women. In the years following the arrival of Europeans in North America, liaisons between Indians and non-Indians followed the pattern of non-Indian males marrying Indian females. In spite of these special circumstances, marriages between Europeans and Indians were limited because of the prevailing negative attitude by North Americans toward interracial marriage.

The purpose of the foregoing introductory paragraphs is to describe the social environment within which contacts between Indians and non-Indians occur today. Indians, unlike most other "minority groups," do not have a common culture, a common religion, a common language, and a common attitude; in most instances, they also lack an organizational structure similar in strength and direction to that of other ethnic, racial, or social groups. For the majority of Indians, especially those residing within reservation situations, "Indianness" or commonality is acknowledged towards other Indians with whom they have contact. The attitudes that Indians exhibit toward fellow Indians and toward whites appear to be a consequence of the social environment in which they were raised. Indians who live in isolated environmental conditions, where contacts with whites are limited, tend to hold a negative image of non-Indians. This in itself serves to limit contacts which could lead to intermarriage. On the other hand, Indians who have grown up in the midst of the host society, where contact between whites and Indians is maintained, are more likely to develop a positive orientation, and as a consequence the probability of intermarriage between the groups increases. Thus different types of contact situations exist in areas where Indians and whites live in close proximity, and in areas where Indians find themselves isolated from the larger society. In the isolated type of situation, intermarriage is rare except when "frontier" conditions exist, in which whites marry Indian women because of a shortage of white females.

According to Roy, "the generalized White American attitude towards the American Indians has been a tangled skein of logical contradictions" (8, p. 543).

PATTERNS OF INTERMARRIAGE AMONG THE INDIANS

Culturally proscribed behavior prevents "intermarriage" by both internal and external controls. As far as marriage between Indians and non-Indians is concerned, the variety of attitudes that Indians develop in the reserve atmosphere towards non-Indians works against such unions. Because of a need for self-esteem and reduction of anxiety, when these internal controls exist, they usually prevent intermarriage which, as noted by Jerold S. Heiss, is deemed as "undesirable behavior" (4, pp. 47–55). In the atmosphere of the reserve, proscription against intermarriage is maintained, and the attitudes toward whites by and large are negative. No society, however, depends entirely on internal controls. Invariably there are external pressures helping to bring about conformity to social norms. These pressures take a variety of forms from the threat of loss of esteem to the threat of ostracism and in the most extreme cases, even death.

The attitudes of most Indians and whites lead to opposition of intermarriage. Such attitudes are a consequence of the socialization process, stereotypes prevailing in the social environments, lack of opportunities for contact, and past negative experiences. One of the main reasons against intermarriage is usually the possible disapproval by the other members of the group. This sanction is frequently exercised within traditional environments, but probably carries little, if any, weight outside of the reservation.

Having formulated a general perspective, we can offer the following hypotheses:

1. Indians born within or close to an urban environment are more likely to intermarry than those who are born and raised in a rural reserve-type environment.

2. Traditional Indian practices appear to have little or no influence on the issue of intermarriage.

3. The majority of those who intermarry are associated with the middle- and upper-income groups within American society, are not firmly attached to Indian traditions, and do not maintain ties with reservation-type environments.

Those who intermarry appear to be less bound by traditional Indian attitudes and practices. In general, they exhibit the following characteristics:

1. Nontraditional family atmosphere;
2. Nontraditional educational atmosphere;
3. Nontraditional social atmosphere (i.e., greater contact with whites);
4. Greater ambivalence concerning Indian status;
5. Greater emancipation from Indian patterns.

It is difficult, if not impossible, to note the effect of religion on the individuals who have crossed the so-called racial line, because the majority of those interviewed indicated marginal religions attachment.

Based on 19 cases examined by the author and 26 related by associates, the following pattern appears to emerge.

Marriage between Indians and non-Indians does not occur frequently. When it does occur, it takes place in three relatively distinct types of social environments and involves particular types of individuals.

1. *Intermarriage "in the city."* The prevalent pattern is that of educated young Indian males marrying educated non-Indian females with contacts usually made in educational institutions, universities, government offices, etc.

2. *Intermarriage in blue-collar environments.* This appears to be a rare occurrence and generally takes place in small settlements adjacent to areas of large Indian concentration where white men of educational level below high school frequently marry Indian women of similar educational background. In this type of social environment intermarriage seldom occurs because areas immediately adjacent to reserves are characterized by rigid caste barriers between Indians and whites.

3. *Intermarriage in frontier environments.* This usually involves white males and Indian females, and it may generally be attributed to the fact that in the frontier situation contact opportunity between white males and white females is limited as a consequence of the particular population pattern of these areas.

A number of clergy who have spent time on the reserve maintain that there is now a considerable decrease in the number of marriages between Indians and non-Indians. If this is so, and it may very well be, it can probably be explained by the fact that the smaller the proportion of minority race in the total population, the higher the rate of intermarriage. These observations appear to conflict with those of Berry who maintains that "the other color races in the United States, especially the Filipinos and the American Indians, have had considerably higher intermarriage than Negroes" (2, p. 326).

The majority of Indians interviewed (37 out of 45) expressed the desire to pass, but the remainder were proud of their Indian heritage and several of them worked in Indian organizations, clubs, and maintained traditional ties.

The most common type of marriage between Indians and non-Indians is that in which Indian males marry females of non-Indian descent. This is due to the following factors:

1. Except for the "frontier situation," Indian women have fewer opportunities for meeting men in other groups than Indian men have for meeting outside women.

2. Ethnic, racial, religious, and institutional controls exert a stronger influence on Indian women than on Indian men as far as intermarriage is concerned.

3. In Western society males have always taken the initiative in the courtship situation.

4. For a nonwhite, marrying a white woman or a woman from a minority group whose appearance and manners closely approximate those of white women is frequently viewed in North American society as a symbol of success and prestige, and as an indication of belonging to the larger community. The majority of whites who marry Indians typically are of lower socio-economic status. As Simpson and Yinger point out, "They [minorities] exchanged majority prestige for higher socio-economic standing" (10, p. 373).

In North America the pattern of marriage has been predominantly endogamous with respect to race, and also with respect to religion and ethnic group. Of the various kinds of intermarriage, racial intermarriage has usually been the least common and ethnic intermarriage the most frequent. The difficulties of assigning racial categories are insurmountable and do not call for discussion here. Suffice to say that time, place, and conditions have affected the incidence of each type of intermarriage. There is no single pattern in the trend of intermarriage incidence (1, pp. 188–189).

THE LEGAL ASPECTS OF INDIAN/NON-INDIAN INTERMARRIAGE

Earlier in this chapter we have discussed the legal implications of intermarriage as far as the Indian status is concerned. In addition to the problems we have examined, in the United States (but not in Canada), various laws have been enacted that inhibit, if they do not prevent, liaisons between people of different races. As quoted in Simpson and Yinger: ". . . [T]he legislatures of quite a number of Southern and Western states have found it expedient to enact statutes expressly punishing members of different races and sexes for living in a state of concubinage or for indulging in acts of sexual intercourse with one another, whether it be fornication or adultery. Illicit interracial sexual relationships are also punishable under ordinary statutes prohibiting unlawful cohabitation generally. Louisiana once enacted a statute which specifically penalizes cohabitation between a Negro and an Indian" (6, pp. 256–257). Typically, Indians, like other minorities, have been opposed to the anti-intermarriage acts because they limit freedom of choice in marriage, imply inferior social status, and generally leave "minority" women unprotected.

Mixed marriages can produce an emotional and/or legal bond which may prevent Indians from returning to the reservation. Aside from the legal impediments that have been discussed, Indian males who marry women of non-Indian descent may find that their spouses seldom express any desire to live within reservation confines.

Those of Indian descent who have married non-Indians are frequently "white-oriented," as pointed out by Professor Denton in his paper, "Migration from a Canadian Indian Reserve" (3). He finds that Indians establish relationships with non-Indians for a number of reasons, and in doing so they tend to break up traditional relationships. Some of the causes cited by Denton for this break-up are a limited exposure to traditional environments and, by contrast, socialization within the host environment, and the ability to establish self-sustaining economic pursuits. A combination of these conditions may contribute, together with other factors, to Indian interracial marriage. Such individuals "are operating on the cognitive assumption that they can have white friends, or Indian friends, but not both. The choice of white friends is . . . if nothing else . . . a realistic one. Given fairly widespread prejudice against Indians, an Indian who is pro-white and anti-Indian is more likely to succeed among whites" (3). Hence, most Indians who intermarry appear to pass "intentionally." This type of passing is not a flippant pattern of "passing for fun," but, rather, is a conscious behavior dictated by economic, social, psychological, political, and/or religious reasons. As Barron maintains, "for an Indian to pass socially means sociological death and rebirth." People "well established in the Indian world and older people seldom pass socially and completely. There is too much to lose and to little to be gained" (1, p. 163). On the other hand, for young Indians wishing a "piece of legitimate North American society" in terms of social, political, and economic aspirations, passing is generally considered as the means to achieve these goals. Intermarriage usually is regarded as the ultimate rite of passage for those who wish to be defined as white. Of the 45 Indians interviewed who had intermarried, 38 preferred to have their past Indian status unacknowledged.

There are a number of factors that facilitate or inhibit intermarriage. The first set of factors may be deemed demographic, and in societies where there is high spatial and social mobility, the rates of intermarriage usually increase. Higher educational attainments change recreational and travel habits, new employment opportunities, and an increase in contact situations—such as military service and exposure of individuals to contact with those of different backgrounds—generally serve to weaken the bonds of social control which formerly inhibited intermarriage.

The second set of factors are the attitudes of individuals concerned. Incidents of intermarriage increase with cultural similarities. These cultural similarities are promoted by increased conditions of contact, patterns of education, religious affiliation, and, of course, linguistic similarity.

The third set of factors that affect intermarriage rates are the "propinquous" factors. These, again, include place of residence, place of education, place of recreation, and place of work.

The social environment of a reserve has confined North American natives, and this confinement has limited their contact situations with whites. Therefore, rates of intermarriage between Indians and non-Indians have been low. These rates will probably increase as Indians are beginning to migrate in considerable numbers from reservations to urban or urban-influenced areas. Hence, as contacts increase, it is only justified to assume that the rate of intermarriage will likewise increase.

Indians are the only minority in North America who have been confined to a "legal ghetto," and in return for such confinement have obtained certain privileges which have heretofore encouraged the majority of them to maintain reserve residences. Because of increasing economic, educational, and political opportunities outside the reservations, since the 1950's there has been an ever-increasing stream of migration of Indians, especially the younger ones, to urban areas.

It must be remembered that, although Indians are frequently referred to as "racial and ethnic groups," being of different tribes, they do not possess many of the factors that unite a group from an ethnic point of view. Those living on reserves have acquired and/or developed a system of values that in many instances is at variance with those operative in the "host community."

Aside from the above factors that inhibit Indian interracial marriage, North American ideology is against contracting marital relationships with "other groups," be they ethnic, religious, or racial. Zangwill's melting-pot concept remains nonoperative because Indians, like other minorities—e.g., blacks and Jews—have tended to remain in their own "group pool" for reasons of security.

It would be inaccurate for this researcher to take the cases utilized in this study and use them for statistical purposes, since such analyses would only serve to create statistical inferences that may not have authenticity. Indians, like other minorities in North American society, tend to marry within their own social pools. Like other minorities, Indians tend to regard intermarriage unfavorably, mostly because they see it as a step that in the long run will inhibit, rather than promote, their participation as equals in North American society.

17

GEOFFREY E. FOX, M.A.

Race, Sex, and Revolution in Cuba -

Relations between the sexes in a Latin country, Mr. Fox points out, have always been strongly influenced by custom and tradition. This is just as true of Cuba, a Marxist society, as it is in the more politically traditional countries in Central and South America. The "new" Cuban society has not been able to divest itself of its traditions. This chapter is a provocative description of the conflicts that exist in Cuba between the old and the new; of the role that the revolution has played in the shaping of a new social and ethical order; and of the actual and potential changes in race relations that such a new order implies.

THE CUBAN Revolution represents a transformation not only of the political and economic order but of the moral order as well; not only of the relations between producers and production but of those between individuals in every aspect of their daily lives. The means of production have been completely socialized, but the interpersonal revolution is still in process. In the course of this process, some eight million people have discovered that not only class, but race and sex as well, are political categories and that there can be revolutionary or counterrevolutionary relations in each.

Cuba's prerevolutionary culture was a hybrid resulting from its colonial history and its uneven economic development or "underdevelopment." Popular attitudes toward sex and race combined elements of feudalism and advanced capitalism. The revolution, then, is working against not only presocialist ideas but also precapitalist ideas. As Fidel Castro observed exasperatedly, in Saul Landau's documentary film *Fidel*, underdevelopment is not just a problem of material conditions but of the condition of people's minds.

This chapter attempts to describe aspects of that prerevolutionary thinking, not out of nostalgia for the old ways, but because this is the raw metal from which a revolutionary consciousness must be forged.

Interracial marriage is not a public issue in all societies but, where it is, it is a political issue. Classification of people by "races" is a way of distinguishing those with a right to more power from those with a right to less. The terms "Negro" or "black" in the United

States tell us much less about an individual's biological ancestry than about the amount of power available to him in the society; in this sense, race is a political category, and the struggles to change attitudes toward race have everywhere become struggles for economic and political power.

Marriage too is political. Marriage is an instrument of the state for regulating not only sexual relations but other relations as well, particularly those concerning property. Laws of inheritance, respective rights of spouses, legitimacy of offspring, divorce, etc., all relate directly or indirectly to control of property. One of the most important, and usually most threatening, consequences of interracial marriages is that, when such unions take place, property and power pass from the more powerful and affluent "race" to members of the socially inferior "race." For this reason, the usual laws of succession are in some societies evaded by declaring the offspring of interracial unions "illegitimate," i.e., without rights.

Marriage is, of course, political even when race is not involved. This is obvious where the state regulates the broad division of rights and responsibilities between the sexes so that even sex becomes a political issue. This regulation is accomplished not only through marriage laws, but also through labor laws, judicial procedures, suffrage, etc. Even where the state does not intervene, the same divisions of power, which is to say political divisions, are sustained by custom. Custom means the combined authority of all those in the community who have a vested interest in the established order, or, in other words, of those who already have some measure of power.

What is eminently clear is that particular forms of relations between the sexes and between the races correspond to particular economic and political orders; therefore, changes in economic and political orders will necessarily alter these relations as well. Cuba is undergoing the most dramatic social transformation of any country in the Western hemisphere, and the consequent changes in interpersonal relations are both dramatic and traumatic.

SEX AND MARRIAGE IN CUBAN CULTURE: THE HERITAGE OF FEUDALISM

In a celebrated essay entitled "Latins Are Lousy Lovers," participant-observer Helen Lawrenson wrote:

God knows, the Cuban man spends enough time on the subject of sex. He devotes his life to it. He talks it, dreams it, reads it, sings it, dances it, eats it, sleeps it, does everything but do it. That last is of course not literally true, but it is a fact that they spend far more time in words than in action. . . . A smart American who makes an appointment to discuss business with a Cuban at a cafe always makes the Cuban sit with his back to the street; because if he does not, the Cuban will eye every woman who passes, and, like as not, at a crucial point of the business transaction, will interrupt to make anatomical comments on some pretty girl who is just going by. They telephone each other at their offices during business hours to describe in minute detail a new conquest. According to them, they always had their first affair at the age of two. This may account for their being all worn out at twenty-three. . . .

According to Cuban technique, love is a game of chess. Now it's your move; now it's mine—whoops, I caught you! . . . They are inveterate gossips and cannot make an amorous move without running off beforehand and afterward to consult with all their male friends . . . [4, pp. 27–28]

As to whether Cuban men are "all worn out at twenty-three," Miss Lawrenson would be a better judge than I. But no one acquainted with Cubans can have failed to notice the tremendous preoccupation with sexual conquest that she describes. And Lawrenson has observed something which is basic to the traditional Hispanic value system: courting in Cuba (and other Latin American societies) does not merely involve an individual man and woman, but whole social groups—his male acquaintances, her female acquaintances—whose approval is sought at every step of the highly ritualized courtship. Sexual competition is a game of honor, and honor is never secure until validated by one's community.

The culture that the Spaniards brought to Cuba was rooted in a precapitalist warrior tradition that was, as nearly as possible, the exact opposite of the values of the English and Dutch colonizers. The reason for this was that the English and Dutch Protestants had recently overcome their own feudal past, and were still in arms against all those values that Spain stubbornly held dear. The Protestants had sundered their ties with the Pope and, with them, their reverence for an antipragmatic morality; they had figuratively broken the backs, and sometimes literally chopped off the heads, of their own nobilities; and if they had not swept away their monarchies, they had at least curtailed their powers, seizing these powers for themselves to be exercised with their own prudent, practical, and businesslike counsel.

And Spain? The Spanish Crown reaffirmed its Catholic faith and strengthened its hold on Spain, even as it weakened Spain itself, by expelling Moslems and Jews in the same year it sent forth Christopher Columbus to seek Oriental treasures. There were businessmen in Spain, to be sure (although many had been expelled as infidels), but businessmen did not initiate or control the exploration and colonization of the new territories, as did the English and Dutch trading companies. Such ventures were the work of an alliance between the Crown, the lesser nobility and some of the clergy, and the Crown's self-willed creature, the colonial bureaucracy. The Spanish colonies were never run primarily as a business, but as a crusade to enlighten heathen "Indians," a treasure-hunt to enhance the royal glory, and an opportunity for quick riches for those who administered in the name of the Crown. With the colonies Spain could, she hoped, humiliate the heretics of northwestern Europe.

All through the nineteenth century, and even earlier, business-minded men strove mightily to reform Spain's colonial structure, but even though monarchs tumbled from the throne, the bourgeoisie never found the strength to govern for and by itself. Nor was it ever able to win a decisive victory in the ideological war against the ancient value system, with its status ascriptions, its appeal to the ultimate authority of God rather than to the rationality of man's senses, and, particularly relevant in this context, its code of honor concerning the relations between men and women.

According to a medieval tradition that has survived in Spain, man is the predator, woman is the mother. All of childhood is preparation for these roles. The Spanish word for mother *(madre)* suggests nurturance, and is sometimes applied to "the Mother Church," or "the Motherland," to suggest both nurturance and the strong emotional bond, even indebtedness, felt by the speaker; the word for father *(padre)*, as it is used, indicates only that the bearer of that title has a property right over a wife and children. Being a father is incidental to a man's sense of his own worth (although of course one is proud of honorable sons); being a mother is the whole purpose of a woman.

Man the predator must protect his women from other predators;

if he cannot, he demonstrates his weakness and is "dishonored." Since his daughters are learning to be nurturing, they can hardly be expected to put up effective resistance to importunate young men, so this task falls to the father and his sons. The Spaniards and Latin Americans believe that any normal woman can be aroused to great passion—frigidity has never been viewed as anything but pathological, and chastity is revered only because, like fasting, it is such an extraordinary defiance of the laws of nature—so the men of the family must always be watchful of their wives', daughters', and sisters' contacts with other men.

Their fears are well grounded. The culture does in fact urge men to make a sexual conquest of any available woman. The image of the manly *(varonil)* man is one who satisfies his urges (whether of love, rage, or gas pains) when he feels them; who can arouse and satisfy great passion in women; and who is pleased to win another man's honor—that of the father of a young woman, for example—by disgracing him. Women, of course, are to be seduced—rape is considered crude and a confession of the failure of one's sexual magnetism—so they are not thought of as victims. Men cling to the belief that all women are in fact waiting to be seduced, so that the only important question is one of technique. Also, a man need feel no remorse when he abandons a conquest, for she was obviously a wanton anyway. That women insist that these are not their feelings at all is generally dismissed by men as part of *their* (the women's) technique, designed to make them more attractive to men.

Obviously a father is relieved of a terrible burden once his daughter marries. No longer does he have to defend her maidenhead nor, which amounts to the same thing, curb her will to join the company of a young man. The wedding is normally a more joyous occasion for the bride and her father than for any of the other participants; after their long battle throughout her adolescence, father and daughter are finally joined in a common purpose. But if the girl leaves the home unmarried, or marries someone dishonorable, the father is disgraced before the whole society.

The social standing of one's marriage partner is extremely important because honor is an attribute of the family. This, of course, is another medieval survival. Dishonor taints all one's living relatives (deceased ancestors are mercifully exempt) and his progeny; although descendants of dishonored persons may gain prestige through exceptionally good conduct, the ancestral shame remains a social handicap.

Another aspect of the predator-mother dichotomy should be brought out here, one that is particularly important in modern Cuba: work outside the home validates masculinity; work inside the home is the fulfillment of femininity. This view has two important corollaries: reversal of roles, or sharing of them by both sexes, threatens the very basis of the relationship between man and woman; and, secondly, work outside the home is not merely instrumental to physical survival, but is also essential to a man's honor.

It may be useful to summarize how these values, still vital in present-day Cuba, differ from those of societies of Northwestern European culture. Briefly, in Cuba a more aggressive sexuality is presumed normal for both men and women, although men are supposed to take the initiative in sexual contacts; women are credited with much less responsibility for their own conduct; men's behavior is determined more by a desire for the esteem of others than by a desire for material "success"; and the shame of a dishonored parent or remoter ancestor is more heavily weighted against his descendant.

Now we turn to explore how racial cleavages have complicated this picture in Cuba.

RACE RELATIONS: THE HERITAGE OF SLAVERY

Slavery existed in Cuba even before the arrival of Columbus, and endured for almost four hundred years after he departed. But slavery is a word that covers many different forms of human bondage, and the system underwent at least two major transformations in those four centuries.

The first transformation occurred early, and was completed before the beginning of the nineteenth century. This was the identification of *slaves* with *black Africans*. Throughout the sixteenth century, as the colony of Cuba was being established, Europeans, North Africans, Orientals, and African Negroes were all held in slavery in the Mediterranean area. When the Spaniards arrived in Cuba, they first enslaved the Carib Indians and other people they found there. However, these indigenous people either succumbed to European diseases, or died in armed resistance, or fled to other islands, so that soon there were no more "Indians" to enslave. Black Africans then became the cheapest available labor force.

The second transformation was the result of technical advances in sugar production and changes in international market relations, which permitted the development in Cuba of a capitalistic plantation economy. Particularly important in this development was the revolution in Haiti that culminated in independence in 1804, which (1) so devastated that island's plantations that Europe's greatest sugar supplier was suddenly eliminated from the market, (2) brought to Cuba hundreds of white refugees skilled in sugar production, and (3) spurred Cubans to increase their discipline and vigilance over the slaves lest they have a similar uprising. The important technical advances included the discovery of superior varieties of cane and the development of more efficient machinery for refining sugar.

The second great transformation of the social meaning of slavery, then, was that the slave was reduced to an anonymous instrument of production, analogous to the oxen or the refining machinery of the sugar plantations. Degrading as slavery had been in the past, now the slave had lost even the last vestige of human rights. The European proletarian at least had his marriage relationship, while the Cuban plantation slave could rarely hope even to have children, or if he had them, to keep them. Slave owners no longer had any kind of personal bond with their slave field hands, who made up four-fifths of the total slave population. By the middle of the nineteenth century, most of the owners lived in the cities and left the management of the plantations and the slaves to overseers, whose only mandate was to bring in a profit. During the early decades, when slaves were cheap, the common policy was to work a slave to death; later, when the British navy reduced the flow of slaves from Africa, overseers were required to take somewhat better care of their slaves to lengthen their work lives, but all manner of cruel corporal punishment remained commonplace.

A combination of forces, including a liberal movement in Spain, the Ten Years' War in Cuba (1867–1877), the abolition of slavery in the United States, and changing manpower needs as a consequence of the introduction of steam power, all led to the abolition of slavery in Cuba in 1886. Rural blacks, uneducated, mostly unskilled, totally unorganized, suddenly became proletarians competing for wage labor against Spanish immigrants, indentured Chinese, and poor rural whites. It had become cheaper for plantation owners to hire during the six-month *zafra* (harvest) and lay off workers during the *tiempo muerto,* the "dead time," when there was no harvest and little employment, than to maintain slaves *or* employees the year round. The abundance of hungry workers kept wages low even during the active part of the year.

Many of these black workers drifted into the larger cities where, with rare exceptions, they lived a marginal existence in the severest poverty. The rare exceptions were mainly those who became successful entertainers of the white middle class. After 1920, a few of the many who had remained in the rural areas became prominent labor leaders, and many were active in the Communist Party which was organizing in the cane fields. In the ill-fated revolution of 1934, "soviets" were set up, mainly by black workers, on several sugar *centrales;* in the following decades, blacks continued to struggle for their rights through labor unions and sporadic political movements, and many participated in the revolutionary war of 1957–1959.

A great deal has been written about the differences in race relations between the colonies founded by the Spanish and Portuguese and those founded by the British and Dutch, and some quite preposterous hypotheses have been advanced to explain these differences. A popular one is the allegedly benevolent influence of the Catholic religion on Iberian culture—a benevolence that was strangely ineffective in such Catholic colonies as Haiti, Cuba, and Maryland. Even if systematic differences in race relations between Catholic and Protestant nations could be demonstrated, we would at most have isolated an epiphenomenon. Men have generally interpreted their religion according to their material interests, and a study of the history of Cuba shows that religion and the Church were of little consequence in race relations there, except perhaps to provide a rationalization for the importation of Negroes in the first place. Another, quite different, hypothesis rests on some very doubtful psychological assumptions: that because the Iberian "somatic norm image" (ideal physical type) was darker than that of northwestern Europeans, the former were more accepting of mixed bloods (3). In order to accept this explanation, we would have to accept the notion that racism is mainly a consequence of physical repugnance before an exotic human type. Yet racism can be virulent between groups whose average physical types are much closer to one another than those of Spaniard and mulatto, e.g., Cambodians and Vietnamese, or numerous groups in sub-Saharan Africa, or Jews and Arabs. And the "somatic norm image" is itself probably subject to exigencies other than esthetic; there are many "somatic norm images" in Cuba today, and they have become darker (at least some of them) to accommodate the sociological fact of the presence of mulattoes and blacks in the society.

In any case, the differences between Iberian and Northern European race relations are greatly exaggerated. Slavery in Cuba—the one Hispanic society where slavery was of enduring economic importance—was no more benign than slavery in the United States. In the post-slavery period, Cuba too had its lynchings—notably in the aftermath of the civil rights "uprising" in Oriente Province in 1912. Jim Crow did not exist in law, but it was a fact in private employment, government offices, and recreational facilities (beaches, night clubs, parks, etc.). Negro rights have been a political issue throughout this century in Cuba as in the United States. The American bard of blackness, Langston Hughes, had his counterpart and comrade in the Cuban poet Nicolás Guillén. The anti-Negro stereotypes—laziness, stupidity, irresponsibility—were similar and similarly widespread in both countries.

Cuban race relations have been more like those of the American South than of the American North, the type Pierre van den Berghe has labeled "paternalistic" in contradistinction to the "competitive" type of more highly industrialized societies. There has been little physical segregation but wide status differences between the races, and miscegenation, as van den Berghe says of this general type, has been "condoned and frequent between upper caste males and lower class females" (8, p. 32).

But in Cuba there was no sectional division between the areas of plantation economy and urban industrial-commercial economy. The one important sectional division in Cuba has been between the mountainous, sparsely populated, small-farm country of Oriente Province, and the more populous, sugar-dominated remainder of the island. In Cuba, plantation interests ruled the towns; the towns were commercial ports for marketing sugar in exchange for manufactured goods and even foodstuffs produced abroad. Underdevelopment of Cuban industry was an acceptable price for the survival of the Cuban plantation plutocracy, even if it meant that the plantations themselves fell under the control of those who controlled Cuba's foreign markets.

Plantation slavery was a unique combination of feudal and capitalistic productive relations. The moral justification for slavery was that poor ignorant blacks needed whites to look after them, and slave owners held to a paternalistic, *noblesse oblige* attitude with regard to slavery even as they pressured their overseers to increase profits and cut losses. In Cuba, for a variety of reasons including especially the island's late entry into the world sugar market, plantations were relatively efficient capitalist enterprises; nevertheless, by remaining aloof from the day-to-day operations of their plantations, the sugar élite was able to sustain a precapitalist and even anticapitalist code of honor not unlike that of the antebellum South. Moreover, this code of honor was compatible with the values held by the descendants of Spanish peasants who made up the white proletariat.

RACE AND SEX

For the blacks, whether in slavery or after emancipation, the values from Spain's past remained by and large completely alien. Nor were the blacks (except in Oriente Province) able to become peasants themselves, as had happened in the United States South, and thus become also more receptive toward these ancient values. Blacks were on the whole unimpressed by the "honor and shame" traditions of sexuality, and were imputed by whites to be sexually irresponsible and primitively uninhibited. Also, blacks in Cuba had seldom experienced work as anything but degrading and wearisome; for the Spanish peasant and his descendants, work was important in itself because it was work that distinguished a true man from lesser breeds, such as women, *sin vergüenzas,* (the "shameless") gypsies, and the like. Blacks then were seen as shiftless and lazy, not because they did not work hard (for they remained brutally exploited in the canefields), but because they did not share the particular work ethic of the whites.

Miscegenation, as common in the island as in the antebellum South, has been governed in Cuba by the Hispanic traditions, whereby there was no dishonor in seducing a woman of lower caste, but it was dishonorable to legitimize the offspring of such a union. In fact, one attraction of black women for white men has been that the former were outside the stultifying code of etiquette so that a man felt free to behave without the inhibitions imposed by such code. A related advantage of black women was that they were unlikely to have fathers or brothers who would take offense at the man's "dishonorable" intentions.

Among the small farmers and casual laborers of Oriente Province, marriages and consensual unions between black men and white women were apparently not uncommon. I have interviewed several émigré workers who were the offspring of such unions. In general, it appears that this type of union occurs when the black man is in a position to offer economic security. However, most of the white male workers interviewed considered this type of union as very degrading to the white woman.

It has been argued, by Cleaver and others, that white men in the United States fear that they may lose their women to the superior sexual competence of black men. Whatever the merits of the argument for the United States, Cuban whites do not seem to share this fear. Probably they do not have the same misgivings about their own sexuality. Their view of blacks is not that they are sexually more competent, but that they are less responsible; that is, that they do not abide by the rules of honor. Specifically, blacks are accused of indiscreet sexual display ("All they think about is clothes and fucking," said one mulatto of his darker compatriots) and of failing to live up to family responsibilities.

In point of fact, black and white workers in similar occupations share the same values to a greater extent than these stereotypes suggest. The black independent farmer, the black industrial worker, and the black agricultural laborer all show an intense concern for providing for their families. As for the claim that blacks are too ostentatiously interested in sex, this seems like a very odd thing for any Cuban to complain about, whatever his color. I suspect that what the whites are really objecting to is not the sexual display itself (the sort of thing Helen Lawrenson refers to), which they also engage in, but that a lower-status person such as a black should be behaving toward women, especially white women, as though he were the equal of the white. The same behavior takes on a different meaning when performed by persons of different status.

Cuban whites of all social classes have tended to view interracial marriage (as distinct from concubinage) as a status loss for the white party because blackness is a hereditary disgrace remindful of a slave past, and because blacks are less likely, it is thought, to observe the rules of honor and are therefore "dishonorable." The status loss may be offset if the black or mulatto spouse has wealth or prestige of another sort. However, these offsetting advantages must be very great indeed to induce a father to consent to his white daughter's marriage to a black man, because the dishonor is not hers alone but is visited upon her father with even greater force.

THE IMPACT OF THE REVOLUTION

Major concerns of the Cuban Revolution have been the liberation of workers from economic hardship, the liberation of women from passivity and subservience, and the liberation of blacks and mulattoes from discrimination. The first concern is shared by all Cuban workers, and the revolution has gained most of its adherents because of it—although not all workers, of course, are satisfied by the rate of progress toward this goal. The other concerns have aroused sharp resistance within the ranks of the working class, sometimes strong enough to turn adherents into opponents of the revolution.

The measures taken to combat racial discrimination are amply described in writings that are readily available (7, pp. 138–168; 1). Very briefly, racial discrimination in employment, schooling and use of beaches, parks, hotels, etc., was declared illegal by the Revolutionary Government almost as soon as it had taken power. Scholarships and various special education programs have been set up to overcome the disadvantages of the poor in general and the blacks in particular. In the great expansion of artistic activity which has been fostered by the revolution, particularly in cinema and television, themes of Afro-Cuban history and of the contemporary struggle against prejudice have been very prominent. The active part played by blacks in Cuba's history of struggle for national liberation and workers' rights has made this emphasis easy and natural. Also, much attention is given in the press and television to the struggles of nonwhite peoples around the world.

The old traditions of relations between the sexes are also under attack, although less directly (6, 7). For example, women are now employed in agriculture, although when this began some years ago, the government apologized on the grounds that, of course, women were not supposed to do such work, but that it was a necessary and temporary expedient. Now, however, revolutionaries are questioning whether there is in fact any reason why women should not drive tractors and plant coffee.

Also, girls and young women are now very likely to spend long periods away from their families in schools and work projects. This is very disturbing to conservative fathers, although the government takes great pains to segregate the girls from the boys. The goal—the government's, that is—is not sexual liberation so much as national development, but the result is still a profound disturbance of the moral order. Women serve in the militia (sometimes to escape parental tyranny), run schools, hold important posts in local "defense committees" (but not in the national leadership of these committees), and a few higher governmental positions. Women's liberation is likewise a popular theme of revolutionary art, as in the movie *Lucia,* for example.

Although these changes are undoubtedly welcome to a great many Cubans, and are tolerated by most of the rest, they nevertheless are causing much anxiety. Even supporters of the regime may feel uncomfortable when they need to have some request approved by an official, and the official in charge turns out to be a black man. The blacks themselves are sometimes uncomfortable in such dealings with blacks, because it seems somehow inappropriate that a black man should be in authority. Men are even more disconcerted to see women in unaccustomed roles. Cuban women complain that when their revolutionary husbands permit them to work, to serve guard duty, and to attend committee meetings, they still expect them to come home to clean house and fix dinner and wash the clothing without any assistance from them. More often the husbands expect their wives to attend to their household duties, but do not permit them to serve the revolutionary ones.

For the most part we would expect these anxieties and conservative attitudes to dissolve rapidly as people become accustomed to the new ways, and as the older people are gradually replaced by the post-revolutionary generation. But there is one deep-rooted fear that will be more difficult than any other to extirpate, although it too should disappear in time: the white fear of degradation through sexual contact with blacks.

This fear has been a principal motivator of working class white emigration from Cuba. Particularly striking was the case of an émigré who, he claimed, had fought for the revolution in the guerrilla war, but whose main concern, when I interviewed him, seemed to be to keep his daughters safe from blacks. "But I'm not prejudiced!" he insisted. An old couple told me that what was wrong with revolutionary Cuba was that the blacks no longer knew their place, that they were even in the couple's favorite dancing club! White fathers do not want their daughters to accept scholarships because they would come into contact with black youths.

Just how pervasive these fears are among the workers who remain in Cuba, I do not know. Sutherland found that they were still troublesome (7, pp. 138–168). This question, and the related one of what kinds of moral adjustments people are making to the new social order, are important enough to merit more thorough investigation by Cuban social scientists. The answers lie largely in the society that will eventually emerge in socialist Cuba.

Meanwhile Cuban blacks must still confront that racial, sexual arrogance so succinctly captured by César López:

. . . Y es que era tan bonita
que nadie la miraba, en realidad no es que nadie
la mirara, sino que nadie la miraba como ella quería que la miraran.

Así era el tiempo en la ciudad ante una negra bella, lo más
que se pensaba y se decía, a voz, a grito limpio casi,
es que estaba muy buena para *templar* con ella . . . [5]

. . .

. . . It's that she was so pretty
that nobody looked at her, really it's not that nobody
looked, but that nobody looked at her the way she wanted to be
    looked at.

And that's the way it was in the city with a beautiful Negress, the
    most
that anyone thought and that anyone said, aloud, almost shouting,
is that she was very good to *make out* with . . .

18

GEORGE K. YAMAMOTO, M.A.

Interracial Marriage in Hawaii

Hawaii has long been considered the most receptive climate for interracial unions. It is surprising that current statistics indicate a slowing down of the rate of such marriages, and Mr. Yamamoto knowledgeably documents his insights into the historical and demographic reasons for this phenomenon. His analysis provides valuable material for predicting future rates of interracial marriages and how they will be affected by the growing pride in ethnic and racial identity among the peoples of the world.

A TOTAL OF 38,120 marriages was recorded in Hawaii during the period 1965–1969. Of this total, 13,338 or 35.0 percent, were across traditional boundaries of race or ethnicity. This percentage of interracial marriage is considerably higher than the percentage for the American nation as a whole, and exceeds by far that of every other state in the Union. Whether Hawaii is indeed a "melting pot" of races is certainly debatable, but the fact that a significant proportion of new and legitimate sexual unions are "unorthodox" is indisputable.

How did this unusual situation develop in this corner of American society? Is this apparent permissiveness, if not encouragement, of mate selection across racial lines "exportable" to other corners of American society? What do these variations in preferences in interracial mate selections indicate? Are there discernible developments that suggest further ignoring of racial lines in marriage, or are there signs that indicate that a peak has been reached by the late 1960's and that there may even be a retrogression in the proportion of interracial marriages?

THE EARLY DAYS OF INTERRACIAL CONTACT

When Captain James Cook and the men of his two ships accidentally sighted Hawaii in 1778, the people of the islands, numbering perhaps about 300,000, had lived there in isolation for many centuries. Other foreigners came to Hawaiian shores in the following decades—explorers, traders, soldiers, seamen, missionaries—from England, France, the United States, Spain, and Russia.

The early contacts of the Hawaiians with the people from the more advanced nations of the West appear to have been essentially the meeting of equals, based on the exchange of goods and services. While the degree of egalitarianism between Westerners and Hawaiians in the first hundred years or so after the initial contact may have been somewhat overplayed by modern students of race relations in Hawaii, it is a fact that the kingdom of Hawaii was not militarily conquered and made a colony of an advanced power, as happened to several other peoples of the Pacific. This historical accident has probably made all the difference in the world for the subsequent relations among peoples in Hawaii and for the extent and patterns of interracial marriage. While the native Hawaiian mode of life and values was assaulted and changed, and the island was eventually annexed by the United States in 1898, the early egalitarian relations still provided a setting in which marriages between native Hawaiian women and men from far away were recognized and accepted. Of special significance was the marriage of Hawaiian women of high rank to able white men who provided valuable services to the Hawaiian king, and the appropriate high status accorded their mixed-blood children. Intermarriages of this type, taking place in the early stages of sustained interracial contact, seem to have set the direction toward the general acceptance of interracial marriage in Hawaii. This recognition and acceptance have not been seriously and effectively challenged since, despite the subsequent influence of adverse attitudes from both Westerners and cohesive immigrant groups from Asia.

The attitude of the Protestant missionaries (who first arrived in Hawaii in 1820) toward the relations between Hawaiians and Caucasians was both a challenge and an encouragement to interracial marriages. The missionaries, in fact, though questioning the desirability of miscegenation, supported the frontier-type egalitarian relations established earlier. New Englanders, these missionaries frowned on the liaisons of Caucasian seamen and traders with Hawaiian women. They also became concerned with the "corruption" of their own children's manners and morals in a social atmosphere that may have taken egalitarian relations too seriously. But the missionaries were spreading the gospel of Christian goodness and doing this with the permission of the political authorities of the kingdom who often included white men married to Hawaiian women and whose rela-

tives included persons of mixed blood. The net effect was represented by the Christian religious sanction of the marriages, interracial or otherwise, that the missionaries solemnized, however much
they were against any free and easy sexual moves between or within
the races.

ENTER NEW PEOPLES: THE PLANTATION SYSTEM

A Hawaiian kingdom census taken in 1853 showed that of a total
population of 73,000, slightly over 2,000 were foreigners—almost all
Caucasians—and nearly 1,000 were *hapa-haoles*, or "half-Cauca-
sians." But in the following 60 or 70 years, people from foreign shores
and their children increased a hundredfold, while the native Hawaiian population continued to decline (the earlier onset of this decline
was owing primarily to "foreign diseases" to which the long-isolated
Hawaiians were not immune), and the mixed-blood part Hawaiian
gradually began to outnumber the pure native stock. The number of
people living in Hawaii leaped to 154,000 in 1900, to 256,000 in
1920, and to 423,000 in 1940.

Of the 154,000 persons counted in 1900 in Hawaii, by then a
territory of the United States, native Hawaiians numbered 30,000;
another 7,200 were English-speaking Caucasians; and still another
9,800 were part-Hawaiians, the overwhelming number being Caucasian-Hawaiian mixtures. These had been the predominant ingredi-
ents of the slow blending of races and cultures that took place for
nearly a hundred years after Captain Cook and his men landed on
Hawaiian shores. But by 1900, over two-thirds of the population were
made up of peoples of newer, different backgrounds. There were
26,000 Chinese; 61,000 Japanese; and 18,000 Portuguese, who were
Europeans but non-English-speaking Catholics. By the end of the
following decade these immigrant groups were being augmented by
Koreans, Puerto Ricans, and Filipinos.

What was the significance of this change in population composi-
tion for the long-established tradition of egalitarian relations between races and for the seemingly easy accommodation of interracial
marriage as part of the acknowledged rules of the game for life in
Hawaii? The relatively sudden increment of new people, not part of
the original components that helped established what one scholar
called the "unorthodox race doctrine of Hawaii," did indeed present
a situation that was to severely test the strength of that doctrine of

Europeans meeting darker-colored peoples on an egalitarian basis. For these new tens of thousands were not only predominantly Asians —people of a quite different background from the Euro-American and emerging American-dominated Hawaiian civilization—but they were also peoples of varied tongues who had been recruited as laborers for the rapidly developing sugar and, a little later, pineapple plantations. These large-scale enterprises, financed and operated by Caucasian entrepreneurs, needed a large labor supply that could not be satisfied by the decreasing number of native Hawaiians, who in any case would not have been easily persuaded to work voluntarily under conditions of considerable regimentation.

In the late 19th and early 20th centuries, the majority of Hawaii's people were involved with the sugar and pineapple industries, either as employees or as family members of employees. The development of the plantation system of commercial agriculture in the New World and in the Pacific during the 18th and 19th centuries usually involved an occupational structure necessary for the coordination of the various economic activities. But historically the plantation also appears to have functioned as a racially stratifying institution. In nearly all instances, the entrepreneurial, managerial class was of a different racial or ethnic background from the laboring class, who in the early stages of plantation development usually found themselves unable to leave employment at will. This type of economic and power relationship tended to bring about an association of class status with race. It linked socioeconomic attributes with racial traits so that the second and subsequent generations on the plantations "inherited" certain cultural attributes and values as ancestral racial qualities.

The plantation was hardly fertile ground for fostering egalitarian relations among races. Upper and lower economic strata in the plantation communities were sharply divided on the basis of *haole* (Caucasians of northwest European descent) entrepreneurial and managerial personnel and *non-haole* laborers. The laborers themselves, coming from village communities in the old countries, tended to form ethnic communities based on their own language, customs, and taken-for-granted values amidst strangers in a strange land. Reliable statistical information concerning interracial marriage for the late 19th century is not readily available. It can be reasonably assumed, though, that with such a large proportion of the population located within the physical and social confines of the plantations, the earlier trend toward increasing interracial marriage was significantly slowed down, if it did not actually retrogress. Heterosexual social relations culminating in marriage were extremely unlikely to cross the class and color lines separating the managerial from the field hand personnel. Intimate, egalitarian social relations between *haoles* and *non-haoles* through upward occupational mobility on the part of immigrant workers or their children did not, or could not, come about. Equal status between *haoles* and *non-haoles* on the plantation through downward mobility on the part of *haoles* was also not possible. And within the laboring class itself, each immigrant group— Chinese, Portuguese, Japanese, Filipino, or others—aware of their own values and traditions, exerted social control over their members' conduct including the selection of mates from within the fold.

THE CITY AS MEETING GROUND

Even as the plantation system began to dominate the economy of Hawaii and to exert control within its borders over racial relations, the capital city of Honolulu was developing, not only as a port city as it had been for many decades, but also as the financial and management center for plantation activities and the many related economic pursuits. Just outside the city were the increasingly important military establishments of Pearl Harbor, Hickam Field, and Schofield Barracks with their thousands of unattached soldiers and sailors, far away from the social control of their mainland home communities. Immigrant plantation workers, having fulfilled their employment contracts, gravitated primarily to Honolulu to seek a living outside the more paternalistically secure but less free economic and social climate of the plantation community. The coming of many tens of thousands of immigrants, mostly of peasant stock, of non-Anglo-Saxon race and culture, did indeed provide a challenge to the continuing acceptability of informal, egalitarian social relations and marriages across racial lines.

Ironically, perhaps, the invasion of half a dozen or more of these new peoples not only provided a test of the "unorthodox racial doctrine of Hawaii" but also served as the basis for a more complex system of race and ethnic relations and for a much more varied series of pairings in marriage vows. In addition to the established Caucasian-Hawaiian marriages, other combinations of interracial and interethnic marriages began to appear on the island community scene. Chinese-Hawaiian, Caucasian-Chinese, Japanese-Hawaiian, Caucasian-Japanese, Filipino-Hawaiian, Filipino-Puerto Rican, Korean-Japanese, the Caucasian combination of *haole* and Portuguese, an occasional Negro-Hawaiian—these and many more types of mixed marriages were in time to become fairly commonplace. The ever-increasing part-Hawaiians not only married fellow part-Hawaiians (some of whom were Caucasian-Hawaiians, others Chinese-Hawaiians) but, together with their pure Hawaiian cousins, selected or were selected by members of all the other groups. Economic class linkage to race and the ethnocentrism of the various foreign-origin groups were operative on the plantations, of course. As the greater physical and social mobility afforded by the urban centers brought people of a variety of backgrounds together at school, at work, in residential neighborhoods, and at play, the proportion of marriages that crossed conventional racial or ethnic lines continued to increase. An increase, it should be noted, that was accompanied by a widely shared public consensus of the moral rightness of racial equality, however much breached privately in actual practice.

In the period 1912–1916, about 12 percent of the marriages were outmarriages. There followed a steady increase in outmarriages, both in absolute numbers and in percentage until nearly 38 percent of marriages recorded in Hawaii in the period 1960–1964 were intermarriages. The 19th century intermarriages and some of those well into the 1950's were at least in part owing to the shortage of females of marriageable age in certain groups, most conspicuously in the Caucasian and Chinese groups. If many of the men of these groups, and later other groups with similar disproportionate sex ratios, were to marry at all in Hawaii, it had to be with females from a group other than their own. This for a long while meant Hawaiian women, but with the passage of time, men of these groups took as wives women from new groups as well as from the Hawaiian group. The men from groups where males outnumber females have consistently had higher-than-average outmarriage rates. As a corollary, the women of such groups have had low outmarriage rates, indicative of their premium value as brides for the men of their group. The pattern has continued to the present; for example, for the period 1960–1969 the outmarriage rate for Negro males was 46 percent while that of Negro brides was only 13 percent. The 1970 U.S. Census Report for Hawaii discloses that for Negroes 21 years of age or over, there are 7 males for every 3 females.

A balanced sex-ratio demographic factor, therefore, plays an important role in maintaining low outmarriage rates for both males and females of the group. The Japanese, for example, with a more even distribution of the sexes than most other groups in Hawaii, had outmarriage rates of less than one percent for both males and females during the period 1912–1916, and less than 7 percent for both sexes nearly a generation later (1930–1940) when the outmarriage rate for all Hawaii was 23 percent. The numerically large size of the Japanese population helped to reinforce the effect of the even sex ratio on outmarriage rates. This larger population was better able than most other immigrant groups to maintain its ethnocultural identity through establishment and support of local community Japanese institutions like language schools, newspapers, and voluntary associations. They also maintained close informal relations among themselves in heavily concentrated sections not only of Honolulu and other urban areas but also in rural independent farming areas. Maintenance of an endogamous orientation in the face of increasing outmarriages in many other groups was thus facilitated by the demographic factors represented by relatively large size of the group and an even distribution of the two sexes.

The demographic factors of men outnumbering women and of small group size in the ethnic groups migrating to Hawaii were, then, important factors in the higher-than-average outmarriage rates. The lack of women of their own background, the weakness of group control over marriage choice, the possibly romantic, exotic nature of these interracial unions, and, of course, the willingness of women of Hawaiian and, later, of other extractions to marry them—these, one might say, started the ball rolling. The increasing number of mixed-blood children, and the children's children, were not placed under any special discriminatory handicaps, and this served to further the acceptability of interracial marriage by the larger Island community.

What is now being witnessed more and more, however, is a selection of mates across conventional ethnic lines regardless of the demographic factors we have been discussing. This latter type of intermarriage seems to indicate that young people of various ethnic origins of long residence in Hawaii are increasingly sharing a common local culture and experiences.

WHO MARRIES WHOM IN INTERRACIAL MARRIAGES IN HAWAII?

More than a third of the marriages in Hawaii in the past 20 years have been outmarriages. The major ethnic groups have differed in the percentage of outmarriages, however, from the very high percentages of Hawaiians, Koreans, and Puerto Ricans, to the medium rates of Chinese, part-Hawaiians, and Filipinos, and the lower rates of Caucasians and Japanese, with significant differences between males and females especially in the latter two groups. We have suggested that group size and sex ratio may be relevant in accounting for the differences. Other possibly relevant factors include group status in the community and length of residence in Hawaii as a group. Perhaps more interesting than the differential rates of outmarriage is the observable lack of consistency in the marriage choices on the part of those who do intermarry. For example, in 1965, the 793 Caucasian men who intermarried selected the following brides: 12 Hawaiian, 312 part-Hawaiian, 59 Chinese, 155 Filipino, 152 Japanese, 35 Puerto Rican, 20 Korean, 4 Negro, and 44 others. In the same year, the 380 Japanese women who intermarried selected the following grooms: 152 Caucasian, 1 Hawaiian, 91 part-Hawaiian, 53 Chinese, 54 Filipino, 6 Puerto Rican, 17 Korean, and 6 others. Still another example the 323 Filipino men who intermarried selected the following brides: 75 Caucasian, 4 Hawaiian, 150 part-Hawaiian, 11 Chinese, 54 Japanese, 14 Puerto Rican, 4 Korean, and 11 others.

How might these assumed preferences be accounted for? Parkman and Sawyer probably present the most sophisticated analysis of the major dimensions underlying the totality of intermarriage choices of recent decades.* The abstract of their study reads:

> Hawaii's uniquely high intermarriage permits assessing the relative distances separating the eight major ethnic groups. From these distances (based upon fifty thousand marriages), multidimensional pair analysis tests a similarity model for mate selection. . . . intermarriage between any two groups is highly predicted by the similarity of their positions on two major independent dimensions: (1) East-West (variation in race, religion, and nationality),

*This 1967 article is the only study specifically cited in the body of this chapter. The other important works consulted in writing this chapter are listed in the bibliographical references at the end of the book. I have freely used ideas and information that the authors present in their works, some of which were written by former teachers and present colleagues.

indexing the cultural traditions that the group inherits, and (2) Urbanicity (percentage of the group living in Honolulu), indexing the extent to which the group has acquired the dominant contemporary way of life . . . So in Hawaii, as elsewhere, like marries like, and these are the bases: a similarity of the past, and a similarity of the present. [10]

IS INTERRACIAL MARRIAGE IN HAWAII STILL "NO BIG THING"?

In the period 1940–1949, 29 percent of the marriages in Hawaii were outmarriages. For 1950–1959, 33 percent were outmarriages. For the 5-year period 1960–1964, it was 38 percent. But for 1965–1969, the intermarriage rate was down to 35 percent. Moreover, a year-by-year inspection of the rate of intermarriage shows that there was very little variation in the years 1960 to 1964—from a low of 36.7 percent in 1961 to a high of 38.6 percent in 1963. In the years 1965 to 1969, however, the first two years' rate of outmarriage was about 38 percent and the rate each of the last three years less than 34 percent.

Are the intermarriage rates of the last few years the beginning of a trend of leveling off, if not of a slow but continued decline? Whether the rates of recent years represent a temporary fluctuation in a long-term continuing rise in outmarriage rates or whether they are an indication of a plateau having been reached, how might this halt or decline be explained? Actually, of the numerically major groups, only the Caucasians showed a significant decline in outmarriages from 1960–1964 to 1965–1969. Outmarriage percentages remained about the same for the Filipino group, both males and females, and for part Hawaiian females. But the Japanese and Chinese outmarriage percentages rose significantly. Positive net migration rates (more coming in to Hawaii than leaving) in the past five years appear to have been greatest for the Caucasian and Filipino groups. Does this increase of newcomers in these groups have the effect of decreasing or stabilizing their outmarriage rates? Are the still rising Chinese and Japanese rates, particularly the latter, a consequence of the weakening of traditional social controls and their greater acquisition of "the dominant contemporary way of life" in Hawaii? What about the continued rise in outmarriages on the part of part-Hawaiian males and the seeming leveling off on the part-Hawaiian female side?

Speculative explanations for the slowing down of the increase in

TABLE 1

INTERRACIAL MARRIAGES AS PERCENTAGE OF ALL MARRIAGES, 1912-69

% Outmarriages

		1912–1919	1920–1930	1930–1940	1940–1949	1950–1959	1960–1964	1965–1969
Hawaiian	Grooms	19.4	33.3	55.2	66.3	78.9	85.9	85.7
	Brides	34.9	52.1	62.7	77.2	81.5	85.4	92.7
Part-Hawaiian	Grooms	52.1	38.8	41.0	36.9	41.3	47.0	56.4
	Brides	66.2	57.7	57.9	64.2	58.4	56.8	56.5
Caucasian	Grooms	17.3	24.3	22.4	33.8	37.4	35.1	24.3
	Brides	1.7	13.8	10.7	10.2	16.4	21.1	19.1
Chinese	Grooms	4.7	24.8	28.0	31.2	43.6	54.8	61.1
	Brides	5.7	15.7	28.5	38.0	45.2	56.6	65.4
Japanese	Grooms	0.5	2.7	4.3	4.3	8.7	15.7	23.0
	Brides	0.2	3.1	6.3	16.9	19.1	25.4	30.4
Korean	Grooms	25.4	17.6	23.5	49.0	70.3	77.1	73.1
	Brides	0.0	4.9	39.0	66.7	74.5	80.1	83.6
Filipino	Grooms	2.8	25.6	37.5	42.0	44.5	51.2	50.0
	Brides	2.8	1.0	4.0	21.0	35.8	47.5	48.3
Puerto Rican	Grooms	21.4	18.6	29.8	39.5	51.3	65.0	73.8
	Brides	23.4	39.7	42.8	50.3	60.5	67.2	78.0
Total		11.5	19.2	22.8	28.6	32.8	37.6	35.0

Sources: Andrew W. Lind, Hawaii: The Last of the Magic Isles, (London, Oxford University Press, 1969), Table 7, p. 14; Annual Reports, State of Hawaii Department of Health Statistical Supplements, 1960–69.

intermarriage rates, and even of a seeming reversal in trend, in the 1960's include the possibility that the people of Hawaii are finally shedding the notion that they are participants in a "melting pot" and that they are now beginning to take pride in their distinctive ethnic identities in an ethnically pluralist Island community.

Given the fact of free migration between Hawaii and continental United States, it would not be particularly reasonable to have expected or hoped for the great majority of Island residents to be of mixed blood "by the year 2000" or any date in the near future. But a stabilization of intermarriage rates or even a decline need not necessarily reflect any retrogression in the expectation of egalitarian social relations. Many "pure" mainlanders have taken up residence in the Islands in recent years, and very possibly a higher proportion of part-Hawaiians and other mixed-bloods have moved to the mainland. Of course, more generally, Caucasians as well as members of other ethnic groups migrate out as well as move into Hawaii. If so, the people of Hawaii, still with unusually high intermarriage rates compared with other sections of the United States, are becoming a more typical part of the mobile American population.

BIBLIOGRAPHICAL REFERENCES

Part I, Chapter 2   A Theory of Marital Choice

1. Berscheid, E., and Walster, E. *Interpersonal Attraction.* Reading, Mass.: Addison-Wesley, 1969.
2. Burma, J.H., Cretser, G.A., and Seacrest, T. "A comparison of the occupational status of intramarrying and intermarrying couples: a research note." *Sociology and Social Research* 54 (1970): 508–519.
3. Carter, H., and Glick, P.C. *Marriage and Divorce: A Social and Economic study.* Cambridge, Mass.: Harvard University Press, 1970.
4. Davis, K. "Intermarriage in caste societies." *American Anthropologist* 43 (1941): 376–395.
5. English, H.B., and English, A.C. *A Comprehensive Dictionary of Psychological and Psychoanalytical Terms.* New York: David McKay, 1958.
6. Fanon, F. *Black Skin, White Masks.* New York: Grove Press, 1967.
7. Heer, D.M. "Negro-white marriage in the United States." *Journal of Marriage and the Family* 28 (1966): 262–273.
8. Heiss, J.S., and Gordon, M. "Need patterns and the mutual satisfaction of dating and engaged couples." *Journal of Marriage and the Family* 26 (1964): 337–339.
9. Homans, G.C. *Social Behavior: Its Elementary Forms.* New York: Harcourt, Brace & World, 1961.
10. Merton, R.K. "Intermarriage and the social structure." *Psychiatry* 4 (1941): 361–374.
11. Murstein, B.I. "the complementary needs hypothesis in newlyweds and middle-aged married couples." *Journal of Abnormal and Social Psychology* 63 (1961): 194–197.
12. Murstein, B.I. "Empirical tests of role, complementary needs, and homogamy theories of marital choice." *Journal of Marriage and the Family* 29 (1967): 689–696.

13. Murstein, B.I. "Stimulus-value-role: a theory of marital choice." *Journal of Marriage and the Family* 32 (1970): 465–481.

14. Murstein, B.I. "What makes people sexually appealing?" *Sexual Behavior* 1 (1971): 75.

15. Murstein, B.I. "A theory of marital choice and its applicability to marriage adjustment and friendship." In B.I. Murstein (ed.), *Theories of Love and of Attraction.* New York: Springer, 1971.

16. Murstein, B.I. "Who will marry whom? Studies in marital choice." *Unpublished manuscript,* Connecticut College, 1972.

17. Osmundsen, J.A. "Doctor discusses 'mixed' marriage." *New York Times,* November 7, 1965, 73.

18. Parrott, G., and Coleman, G. "Sexual appeal: in black and white." Paper presented at American Psychological Association Convention, September, 1971.

19. Schellenberg, J.S., and Bee, L.S. "A re-examination of the theory of complementary needs in mate selection." *Marriage and Family Living* 22 (1960): 227–232.

20. Thibaut, J.W., and Kelley, H.H. *The Social Psychology of Groups.* New York: John Wiley & Sons, 1959.

21. Udry, J.R., Bauman, K.E., and Chase, C. "Skin color, status, and mate selection." *American Journal of Sociology* 76 (1971): 722–733.

22. Washington, J.R., Jr. *Marriage in Black and White.* Boston: Beacon Press, 1970.

23. Winch, R.F. *Mate Selection: a Study of Complementary Needs.* New York: Harper, 1958.

24. Wirth, L., and Goldhamer, H. "The hybrid and the problems of miscegenation." In O. Klineberg (ed.), *Characteristics of the American Negro,* New York: Harper, 1944.

Part I, Chapter 3   Potential Role Conflicts in Black–White Marriages

1. Anderson, James Carl. "Interracial dating and marriage." *Unpublished paper,* University of Minnesota,

2. Cleaver, Eldridge, *Soul on Ice.* New York: McGraw-Hill, 1967.

3. *Ebony* 24 (September, 1969).

4. *Ebony* 25 (January, 1970).

5. Furlong, William Barry. "Interracial marriage is a sometime thing," *New York Times Magazine,* June 9, 1968.

6. Gordon, Albert I. *Intermarriage,* Boston: Beacon Press, 1964.

7. Grier, William H., and Cobbs, Price M. *Black Rage.* New York: Basic Books, 1968.

8. Kenkel, William F. "Influence differentiation in family decision-making." In Jerold Heiss (ed.), *Family Roles and Interaction,* Chicago: Rand-McNally, 1968.

9. Kirkpatrick, Clifford. *The Family as Process and Institution.* 2nd ed. New York: Ronald Press, 1963.

10. Mogey, J.M. "A century of declining paternal authority," in John N. Edwards (ed.), *Perspectives in Marriage and the Family.* Boston: Allyn and Bacon, 1969.

11. Myrdal, Gunnar, with the assistance of Richard Sterner and Arnold Rose. *An American Dilemma.* New York: Harper and Row, 1944.

12. Peters, William. "Are there boundary lines in love? Five true stories," *Ebony* 45 (June, 1968).

13. U. S. Bureau of the Census, *Current Population Reports, Population Characteristics, Population of the United States by Metropolitan-Non-Metropolitan Residence,* 1969 and 1960. Series P-20, No. 197, March 6, 1970, P-1.

14. U.S. Bureau of the Census, *Current Population Reports, Population Characteristics, Selected Characteristics of Persons and Families,* Series P-20, No. 204, July 13, 1970, P-2.

Part I, Chapter 4   Children of Interracial Marriages

1. Goodman, Mary E. *Race Awareness in Young Children.* New York: MacMillan, 1964.

2. Spiegel, John D. "The resolution of role conflict within the family." *Psychiatry* 20, (1957): 1–16.

3. Teicher, Joseph D. "Some observations in identity problems in children of Negro-white marriages." *Journal of Nervous and Mental Diseases* 146, (1968): 249–256.

Part I, Chapter 6   Race and Family Power Structure

1. Aldous, J. "Wives' employment status and lower-class men as husband-fathers: support for the Moynihan thesis." *Journal of Marriage and the Family* 31, (1969): 469–476.

2. Almond, G., and Verba, S. *The Civic Culture.* Princeton, N.J.: Princeton University Press, 1963.

3. Bakke, E.W. *Citizens without Work.* New Haven: Yale University Press, 1940.

4. Bernard, J. *Marriage and Family among Negroes.* Englewood Cliffs, N.J.: Prentice-Hall, 1966.

5. Blood, R.O., and Wolfe, D.M. *Husbands and Wives.* New York: Free Press, 1960.

6. Burgess, E.W., and Locke, H.J. *The Family.* New York: American Book Company, 1953.

7. Frazier, E.F. *The Negro Family in the United States.* New York: Citadel Press, 1948.

8. Frazier, E.F. *Black Bourgeoisie.* New York: Free Press, 1957.

9. Geismar, L.L., and Gerhard, U.C. "Social class, ethnicity, and family

functioning: exploring some issues raised by the Moynihan Report." *Journal of Marriage and the Family* 30 (1968): 480–487.

10. Hamel, H.R. *Job Tenure of Workers, January 1966.* Washington, D.C.: U.S. Dept. of Labor, Special Labor Force Report No. 77, 1967.

11. Herbst, P.G. "Family living: patterns of interaction." In O.A. Oeser and S.B. Hammond (eds.), *Social Structure and Personality in a City.* London: Routledge and Kegan Paul, 1954.

12. Herzog, E. *About the Poor.* Washington, D.C.: U.S. Dept. of HEW, Children's Bureau Publ. 451, 1968.

13. Hyman, H., and Reed, J.S. "Black matriarchy reconsidered: evidence from secondary analysis of sample surveys." *Public Opinion Quarterly* 33 (1969): 346–354.

14. Laurence, J. "White socialization: black reality." *Psychiatry* 33 (1970): 174–194.

15. Moynihan, D.P. *The Negro family: the case for national action* (the Moynihan Report). Washington, D.C.: U.S. Dept. of Labor, Office of Policy Planning and Research, 1965.

16. Moynihan, D.P. "Employment, income, and the ordeal of the Negro family." In T. Parsons and K.B. Clark (eds.) *The Negro American.* New York: Houghton Mifflin, 1966.

17. Pakter, J., *et al.* "Out of wedlock births in New York City: I — sociological aspects." *American Journal of Public Health* 51 (1961): 846–865.

18. Parker, S., and Kleiner, R.J. "Social and psychological dimensions of family role performance of the Negro male." *Journal of Marriage and the Family* 31 (1969): 500–506.

19. Parsons, T., and Bales, R.F. *Family, Socialization and Interaction Process.* New York: Free Press, 1955.

20. Rainwater, L. "Crucible of identity: the Negro lower-class family." *Daedalus* 95 (1966): 172–216.

21. Straus, M.A. "Conjugal power structure and adolescent personality." *Marriage and Family Living* 24 (1962): 17–25.

22. TenHouten, W.D. "Scale gradient analysis: a statistical method for constructing and evaluating Guttman scales." *Sociometry* 32 (1969): 80–99.

23. TenHouten, W.D. "The black family: myth and reality." *Psychiatry* 33 (1970): 145–173.

24. TenHouten, W.D., and TenHouten, D. "Profiles of black and white youth." Los Angeles: Report for OEO Contract B99–4891, 1970.

25. Valentine, C.A. *Culture and Poverty.* Chicago: University of Chicago Press, 1968.

26. Ventura, S.J. "Recent trends in differentials in illegitimacy." *Journal of Marriage and the Family* 31 (1969): 446–450.

27. Whelpton, P.K., Campbell, A.A., and Patterson, J.E. *Fertility and Family Planning in the United States.* Princeton, N.J.: Princeton University Press, 1966.

Part I, Chapter 8   Interracial Dating

1. Bernard, Jessie. *Marriage and Family Among Negroes.* Englewood Cliffs: Prentice-Hall, 1966.
2. "Black/White Dating." *Life,* May 28, 1971, 56–68.
3. "Black and White Dating." *Time,* July 19, 1968, 48–49.
4. Frazier, E. Franklin. *Black Bourgeoisie.* New York: Crowell-Collier, 1962.
5. Gordon, Albert I. *Intermarriage.* Boston: Beacon Press, 1964.
6. Harré, John. *Maori and Pakeha: A Study of Mixed Marriages in New Zealand.* New York: Frederick A. Praeger, 1966.
7. Lester, Julius. "White Woman-Black Man." *Evergreen,* September 1969, 21–23, 73–78.
8. Mehlinger, Kermit. "That Black Man-White Woman Thing." *Ebony,* August, 1970, 130–133.
9. Petroni, Frank A. "Teen-age Interracial Dating." *Trans-action* 8, (September, 1971): 54–59.
10. Petroni, Frank A. "Uncle Toms: White Stereotypes in the Black Movement," *Human Organization* 29 (Winter, 1970): 260–265.
11. Petroni, Frank A. "Adolescent Liberalism the Myth of a Generation Gap," *Adolescence* (in press).
12. Petroni, Frank A., Hirsch, Ernest A., and Petroni, C. Lillian. *2, 4, 6, 8, When You Gonna Integrate?* New York: Behavioral Publications, 1970.
13. Personal communication from Mr. Walter Warfield, former director of State Civil Rights Commission, Minneapolis, Minnesota.

Part I, Chapter 9   Black–White Marriages in the United States

1. Annella, M., "Interracial marriages in Washington, D.C.," *Journal of Negro Education* 36 (1967): 428–433.
2. Baber, Ray E., "A study of 325 mixed marriages." *American Sociological Review* 2 (1937): 705–716.
3. Baker, Ray S., *Following the Color Line,* New York: Doubleday, Page and Co., 1908.
4. Barnett, Larry D., "Interracial marriage in California." *Marriage and Family Living* 25 (1963): 424–427.
5. Barron, Milton L., *People Who Intermarry,* Syracuse: Syracuse University Press, 1948.
6. Burma, J.H., "Interethnic marriages in Los Angeles, 1948–1959." *Social Forces* 42 (1963): 156–164.
7. DePorte, J.V., "Marriages in the state of New York with special reference to nativity." *Human Biology* 3 (1931): 376–396.
8. Drachsler, J., *Intermarriage in New York City: A Statistical Study of the Amalgamation of European Peoples,* New York, 1921, 49–50, 100.
9. Drake, St. Clair, and Cayton, Horace R., *Black Metropolis,* New York: Harcourt, Brace and Co., 1945.
10. Golden, Joseph, "Characteristics of the Negro-white intermarried in

Philadelphia." *American Sociological Review* 18 (1953): 177–183.

11. Gordon, Albert I., *Intermarriage*, Boston: Beacon Press, 1964.

12. Heer, David, "Negro-white marriages in the U.S." *Journal of Marriage and the Family* 28 (1966): 262–273.

13. Herbert, Leona Anne, "A study of ten cases of Negro-white marriages in the District of Columbia." *Unpublished Master's thesis*, Catholic University, Washington, D.C., 1939.

14. Hoffman, Frederick L., "Race Traits and Tendencies of the American Negro." *Publications of the American Economic Association* 11 (1896): 1–329.

15. Jacobson, Paul H., *American Marriage and Divorce*, New York: Rinehart and Co., 1959.

16. Lynn, Sister Annella, *Interracial Marriages in Washington, D.C. 1940–47*. Published dissertation, The Catholic University of America Press, Washington, D.C., 1953.

17. Merton, Robert K., "Intermarriage and the social structure: fact and theory." *Psychiatry* 4 (1941): 361–374.

18. Panunzio, Constantino, "Intermarriage in Los Angeles, 1924–33." *American Journal of Sociology* 47 (1942): 690–701.

19. Pavela, Todd H., "An exploratory study of Negro-white intermarriage in Indiana." *Marriage and the Family* 26 (1964): 209–211.

20. Reuter, Edward B., *Race Mixture: Studies in Intermarriage and Miscegenation*, New York: McGraw-Hill, 1931.

21. Roberts, Robert, E.T., "Negro-white intermarriage: a study of social control." *Unpublished Master's thesis*, University of Chicago, 1940.

22. Schuyler, George S., *Racial Intermarriage in the United States*, Girard, Kansas: Haldeman-Julius, 1929.

23. Smith, Charles Edward, "Negro-white intermarriage in metropolitan New York." *Unpublished doctoral thesis*, Teachers College, Columbia University, December, 1960.

24. Stephenson, Gilbert T., *Race Distinctions in American Law*, New York: D. Appleton and Co., 1910.

25. Stone, A.H., *Studies in the American Race Problem*, New York, 1908.

26. U.S. Bureau of the Census. *U.S. Census of Population: 1960. Subject Reports Marital Status;* Final Report PC (2)-4E, U.S. Government Printing Office, Washington, D.C., 1966, Table 10.

27. Wirth, Louis and Goldhamer, Herbert, "The hybrid and the problem of miscegenation." *Characteristics of the American Negro* by Otto Klineberg (ed.) New York: Harper, 1944.

28. Wright, Richard R., *The Negro in Pennsylvania: A Study in Economic History*, Philadelphia: A.M.E. Book Concern Printers, 1912.

Part II, Chapter 12   "Interracial Marriage" Among Puerto Ricans

1. Berry, Brewton, *Race and Ethnic Relations*. Boston: Houghton Mifflin, 1958.

2. Fitzpatrick, Joseph, "Attitudes of Puerto Ricans Toward Color." *The American Catholic Sociological Review* 20, 3, (1959).
3. Fitzpatrick, Joseph, "Intermarriage of Puerto Ricans in New York City." *The American Journal of Sociology* 71, 4 (1966).
4. Garn, Stanley (ed.) *Readings on Race.* Springfield: Charles C. Thomas, 1960.
5. Gordon, Milton, *Assimilation in American Life.* New York: Oxford University Press, 1964.
6. Harrison, G.A., *et al. Human Biology.* New York: Oxford University Press, 1964.
7. LaRuffa, Anthony, "The Puerto Rican in Two Societies: A Comparative Study of Assimilation." Paper presented at the *39th International Congress of Americanists*, Lima, Peru (August 6, 1970). To be published in the Proceedings.
8. Rogler, Charles, "The Morality of Race Mixing in Puerto Rico." *Social Forces* 25, 1 (1946).
9. Sereno, Renzo, "Cryptomelanism, A Study of Color Relations and Personal Insecurity in Puerto Rico." *Psychiatry* 10, 3, (1947).
10. Steward, Julian, *et al. The People of Puerto Rico.* Urbana: University of Illinois Press, 1956.
11. Thomas, Piri, *Down These Mean Streets.* New York: Alfred A. Knopf, 1967.

Part II, Chapter 13 Interracial Marriage in Brazil

1. Furtado, Celso. *Formacao Economica do Brasil.* Editora Universidade de Brasilia, 1963.
2. Harris, Marvin. *Patterns of Races in the Americas.* New York: Walker and Company, 1964.
3. Kersner, Marylink, and Lowndes, Vilma. "O preconceito quanto a raca e ao status socio-economico." *Unpublished term paper*, Catholic University of Rio de Janeiro, 1970.
4. Lamounier, Bolivar. "Race and class in Brazilian politics," *Unpublished term paper*, UCLA, 1966.
5. Moog, C. Vianna. *Bandeirantes and Pioneers.* New York: George Braziller, 1964.

Part II, Chapter 14 Some Problems of Interracial Marriage for the Japanese

1. Ariyoshi, Sawako. *Hishoku* (Not Color). Tokyo: Chuo Koron Sha, 1964.
2. Berger, Michael. Personal communication.
3. DeVos, George, *et al.* "Personality Patterns and Problems of Adjustment in American-Japanese Intercultural Marriages." *Unpublished report*, School of Social Work, University of California, Berkeley, 1959.

4. Endo, Shusaku. "Eden Made" (Up to Aden). *Shin Nippon Bungaku Zenshu* (Collection of Contemporary Literary Works), 9. Tokyo: Chikuma Shobo, 1964.
5. Fujisaki, Sumi, "Senso Hanayome no Higeki wa Ima mo nao" (Still continuing tragedy of war-brides). *Fujin Koron* (September, 1970): 218–224.
6. Wagatsuma, Hiroshi. "The social perception of skin color in Japan." *Daedalus* 96, 2 (Spring, 1967): 407–443.
7. Yamazaki, Ryuko. "Me naki uo" (Fish without eyes). *Bungei Shunju* (August, 1966): 230–275.

Part II, Chapter 15   Interracial Marriage—Trinidad, W.I.

1. Braithwaite, L. Social Stratification in the West Indies. *Social and Economic Studies* 11; 2, 3.
2. Klass, Morton. *East Indians in Trinidad: A Study of Cultural Persistence.* New York: Columbia University Press, 1961.
3. Neihoff, A.J. *East Indians in the West Indies.* Milwaukee University Press, Publications in Anthropology, No. 6.
4. Rodman, Hyman (ed.). *Marriage, Family and Society.* New York: Random House, 1967.
5. World Council of Churches. "Report of the Seminar on Christian Family Life," in *Sex, Love and Marriage in the Caribbean.* Geneva, Switzerland, 1964.

Part II, Chapter 16   North American Indians and Intermarriage

1. Barron, Milton L. *People Who Intermarry.* Syracuse University Press, 1948.
2. Berry, Brewton. *Almost White.* New York: Macmillan Company, 1963.
3. Denton, Trevor. "Migration from a Canadian Indian Reserve." *Unpublished paper,* Brock University, January, 1971.
4. Heiss, Jerold. "Premarital Characteristics of the Religiously Intermarried in an Urban Area," *American Sociological Review* (February, 1960): 47–55.
5. Jacoby, Harold S. "A Half Century Appraisal of the East Indians in the U.S." Stockton, California: 6th Annual College of the Pacific Faculty Research Lecture, May, 1956.
6. Mangum, C.S. *The Legal Status of the Negro.* University of North Carolina Press, 1940.
7. Nagler, Mark. *Indians in the City.* Ottawa: Canadian Research Centre for Anthropology, Saint Paul University, 1970.
8. Roy, Prodipto. "The Measurement of Assimilation: The Spokane Indians," *American Journal of Sociology* 47, 5 (1962).
9. Silcox, C.E. and Fisher. *Catholic, Jews & Protestant.* New York: Harper and Row, 1934.

10. Simpson, George and Yinger, Milton. *Racial and Cultural Minorities,* third edition. New York: Harper and Row, 1953.
11. Steward, Julian. "The Changing American Indian." Linton, Ralph. *The Science of Man in the World Crisis.* New York: Columbia University Press, 1945.

Part II, Chapter 17   Race, Sex, and Revolution in Cuba

1. Fox, Geoffrey E., "Cuban Workers in Exile." *TransAction* 8, 11 (September, 1971): 20–31.
2. Frank, Andre Gunder, *Capitalism and Underdevelopment in Latin America.*
3. Hoetink, Harry. *Caribbean Race Relations: A Study of Two Variants.* London: Oxford University Press, 1967.
4. Lawrenson, Helen. "Latins Are Lousy Lovers," pp. 23–32 in Lawrenson, *Latins Are STILL Lousy Lovers.* New York: Hawthorn Books, Inc., 1968. (This article was originally published in *Esquire,* October 1936. Cf., in same volume, two later pieces: "The Sexiest City in the World —Havana 1, 1955," and "The Other Revolution—Havana 2, 1961.")
5. López, César, "Qué le ocurrió," pp. 6–12 in *Cuba Sí! Poesie Cubaine —Poesía Cubana.* Montreal: Réédition-Québec, 1970.
6. Purcell, Susan Kaufman, "Modernizing Women for a Modern Society: The Cuban Case." Meeting of the Latin American Studies Association, Austin, Texas, December 3–4, 1971. (Dittoed)
7. Sutherland, Elizabeth, *The Youngest Revolution: A Personal Report on Cuba.* New York: The Dial Press, 1969.
8. Van den Berghe, Pierre L. *Race and Racism: A Comparative Perspective.* New York: John Wiley and Sons, 1967.

Part II, Chapter 18   Interracial Marriage in Hawaii

1. Adams, Romanzo. "The unorthodox race doctrine of Hawaii." In E.B. Reuter (ed.). *Race and Culture Contacts.* New York: McGraw-Hill, 1934.
2. Adams, Romanzo. *Interracial Marriage in Hawaii.* New York: Macmillan, 1937.
3. Arkoff, Abe, Meredith, Gerald, and Dong, Janice. "Attitudes of Japanese-American and Caucasian-American students toward marriage roles." *Journal of Social Psychology* 59 (1963): 11–15.
4. Broom, Leonard. "Intermarriage and mobility in Hawaii." *Transactions of the Third World Congress of Sociology,* 1956, 277–282.
5. Cheng, C.K., and Yamamura, Douglas S. "Interracial marriage and divorce in Hawaii." *Social Forces* 36 (1957): 77–84.
6. Freeman, Linton. "Homogamy in interethnic mate selection." *Sociology and Social Research* 39 (1955): 369–376.

7. Glick, C.E. "Interracial marriage and admixture in Hawaii." *Social Biology* 17 (1972): 278–291.
8. Hormann, B.L. "Racial complexion of Hawaii's future population." *Social Forces* 27 (1948): 68–72.
9. Lee, L.L. "A brief analysis of the role and status of the negro in the Hawaiian community." *American Sociological Review* 13 (1948): 419–437.
10. Lind, Andrew W. *Hawaii's People.* Honolulu: University of Hawaii Press, 1967.
11. Lind, Andrew W. *Hawaii, The Last of the Magic Isles.* London: Oxford University Press, 1969.
12. Parkman, Margaret A., and Sawyer, Jack. "Dimensions of ethnic intermarriage in Hawaii." *American Sociological Review* 32 (1967): 593–607.
13. Petersen, William. "The classification of subnations in Hawaii: an essay in the sociology of knowledge." *American Sociological Review* 34 (1969): 863–877.
14. Schmitt, Robert C. "Demographic correlates of interracial marriage in Hawaii." *Demography* 2 (1965): 463–473.
15. Taeuber, Irene B. Hawaii. *Population Index* 28 (1962): 97–125.
16. Wittermans, Elizabeth. *Inter-ethnic Relations in a Plural Society.* Groningen: Wolters, 1964.
17. Yamamoto, George K. "Some patterns of mate selection among Naichi and Okinawans on Oahu." *Social Process* 21 (1957): 42–49.

Index